CULTURE**SHOCK!**

A Survival Guide to Customs and Etiquette

COSTA RICA

Claire Wallerstein

Marshall Cavendish
Editions

This edition published in 2006, reprinted 2008, by:
Marshall Cavendish Corporation
99 White Plains Road
Tarrytown, NY 10591-9001
www.marshallcavendish.us

Other Marshall Cavendish Offices:
Marshall Cavendish International (Asia) Private Limited. 1 New Industrial Road,
Singapore 536196 ■ Marshall Cavendish Ltd. 5th Floor, 32–38 Saffron Hill,
London EC1N 8FH, UK ■ Marshall Cavendish International (Thailand) Co Ltd.
253 Asoke, 12th Flr, Sukhumvit 21 Road, Klongtoey Nua, Wattana, Bangkok
10110, Thailand ■ Marshall Cavendish (Malaysia) Sdn Bhd, Times Subang,
Lot 46, Subang Hi-Tech Industrial Park, Batu Tiga, 40000 Shah Alam, Selangor
Darul Ehsan, Malaysia

Marshall Cavendish is a trademark of Times Publishing Limited

ISBN 10: 0-7614-2492-X
ISBN 13: 978-0-7614-2492-5

Please contact the publisher for the Library of Congress catalog number

Printed in China by Everbest Printing Co Ltd

Photo Credits:
All photos by or from the author except page 233 (age fotostock/ALVARO
LEIVA); pages 4, 122 (age fotostock/DOUG SCOTT); pages 77 (alt.TYPE/
REUTERS); pages 34, 68, 103, 138, 141, 146, 154, 179, 188 (Frans Baas);
pages 11, 18, 38, 52, 58, 185 (Instituto Costarricense de Turismo).
■ Cover photo: Photolibrary

All illustrations by TRIGG

ABOUT THE SERIES

Culture shock is a state of disorientation that can come over anyone who has been thrust into unknown surroundings, away from one's comfort zone. *CultureShock!* is a series of trusted and reputed guides which has, for decades, been helping expatriates and long-term visitors to cushion the impact of culture shock whenever they move to a new country.

Written by people who have lived in the country and experienced culture shock themselves, the authors share all the information necessary for anyone to cope with these feelings of disorientation more effectively. The guides are written in a style that is easy to read and covers a range of topics that will arm readers with enough advice, hints and tips to make their lives as normal as possible again.

Each book is structured in the same manner. It begins with the first impressions that visitors will have of that city or country. To understand a culture, one must first understand the people—where they came from, who they are, the values and traditions they live by, as well as their customs and etiquette. This is covered in the first half of the book.

Then on with the practical aspects—how to settle in with the greatest of ease. Authors walk readers through topics such as how to find accommodation, get the utilities and telecommunications up and running, enrol the children in school and keep in the pink of health. But that's not all. Once the essentials are out of the way, venture out and try the food, enjoy more of the culture and travel to other areas. Then be immersed in the language of the country before discovering more about the business side of things.

To round off, snippets of basic information are offered before readers are 'tested' on customs and etiquette of the country. Useful words and phrases, a comprehensive resource guide and list of books for further research are also included for easy reference.

CONTENTS

Introduction vi

Acknowledgements x

Dedication xi

Map of Costa Rica xii

Chapter 1
First Impressions 1

Chapter 2
Overview of the Land and History 8

History 9

Modern Politics 25

Dismantling a Nanny State 31

Education and Literacy 33

The Country 37

Farming and Land Distribution 40

Provinces and Towns 42

Protected Areas 47

The Environment 56

Chapter 3
The People 64

Black Costa Rica 68

Indigenous Peoples 72

Nicaraguans 82

Gringos 84

Quakers 86

Religion and Witchcraft 87

Values and Attitudes 92

Women 103

Homosexuality 104

Chapter 4
Social Customs and Attitudes 107

To 'Quedar Bien' 108

Gestures 110

Conversation Topics 112

Insults 113

Bribing and Bargaining 113

Flirting and Romance 113

Gossip 115

Piropos 116

Names and Surnames 118

Nicknames 119

The Pulpería 121

Dress Style and Body Image 121

Chapter 5
Survival Skills 124

Getting There 125

What to Bring from Home 127

Accommodation 127

Telecommunications 131

Where the Streets Have No Name... 134

Getting Around 137

Buying a Car or Bringing Your Car to Costa Rica 142

Health 143

Banking and Money 151

Shopping 153

Crime 156

Newspapers and the Media 159

Chapter 6
Food and Entertaining 161

Basic Tico Fare 162

Sweet Stands 168

Fruits and Vegetables 168

Afro-Caribbean Food 171

Coffee 171

Dining and Entertainment Etiquette 175

Chapter 7
Enjoying Costa Rica 177

Cultural Background 178

Guanacasteco Culture 184

Sports	187
Free Time	193
Activities, Hobbies and Sports to Pick Up	194
Fiestas	202
Calendar of Events/Fiestas	203

Chapter 8
Learning the Language
208

Voseo	214
Vos or *Usted*	215
Tiquismos	216
Afro-Caribbean English	220

Chapter 9
Business Practice and Customs
221

What Kind of Business?	224
Red Tape for Foreign Workers in Costa Rica	226

Types of Companies	228
Rules for Employers	230
Business Customs	231
The Business Environment	232

Chapter 10
Fast Facts
244

Heroes and Villains	247
Acronyms and Abbreviations	257
Places of Interest	258

Culture Quiz	262
Do's and Don'ts	269
Glossary	274
Resource Guide	282
Further Reading	290
About the Author	296
Index	297

INTRODUCTION

Costa Rica was the first country in the Americas, by a few hours at any rate, to declare war on Nazi Germany and Japan after the bombing of Pearl Harbour. Hitler failed to retaliate, however, because—according to a Costa Rican joke—he couldn't find the country on his world map. It was totally obscured by a squashed fly.

The joke may be corny, but it doesn't exaggerate the Lilliputian size of Costa Rica. At 51,000 sq km (19,730 sq miles), it is about half the size of Ireland, and yet is one of the most visited destinations in Latin America.

Unsurprisingly, scores of travel guides have already been written about the place. Aside from a handful of outdated or Spanish anthropological texts, however, most books limit themselves to either glossy photographs of the country's national parks and wildlife or bus timetables and restaurant reviews. The Ticos (as the Costa Ricans call themselves) are a proud people, and often complain that visitors don't really understand them.

A Costa Rican tour guide told me he regularly has to answer questions such as: "So, how far are we from San Juan?" (the capital of Puerto Rico, a different place entirely), "How big is this island?" and "Have you got any cannibals here?". "They've seen all the Discovery Channel documentaries about our wildlife and endangered species," he complained. "But what about the human species?"

The lack of information for visitors wanting more than a cursory cultural overview could have a lot to do with the fact that Costa Rican culture can seem so bland at first sight. It is almost as if the country only began to carve its own identity with the civil war in 1948, and then gave up soon afterwards when North American cable television and package tourists arrived.

The country was an impoverished backwater during the Spanish Empire and didn't have an advanced pre-Colombian civilisation, such as the Mayas or Aztecs, to leave behind any awe-inspiring archaeology or any sense of a shared ancient past. The only place where any real folkloric traditions remain in Costa Rica is the northern province of Guanacaste—which until 1824 was part of Nicaragua. Costa Rica also did not fight the kind of bloody independence battle with Spain that left an indelible stamp on its neighbours. Most of the country today bristles with fast-food restaurants, *gringo* fashions, soap operas and pop music imported from other Latin American countries.

Scratch the surface, however, and you will find that Costa Rica is actually rather unique precisely because of its special history. Travellers arriving from neighbouring countries will immediately notice the physical and social differences from flashy, brash, outgoing Panama and underdeveloped Nicaragua, plagued by inequality and corruption.

One of Costa Rica's unique characteristics is, well, its lack of large extremes. Historically poor, rural, and lacking in mineral riches, it has a tradition of self-reliance and individualism, an enormous middle class (ostentatious displays of wealth are frowned upon) and a hatred of violence: the army was abolished in 1948, former president Oscar Arias Sánchez won the Nobel Peace Prize in 1987, and the country is the seat of the United Nations' University for Peace.

Costa Rica is also a country of paradoxes. It is socialist yet fiercely anti-Communist, it is a 'green idyll' yet with one of the region's highest rates of deforestation, it is urbanised but with a rural mindset. Paul Theroux, in *The Old Patagonian Express: By Train Through the Americas*, noted how Costa Ricans 'go to bed early and rise at dawn; everyone—student, labourer, businessman, estate manager, politician—keeps farmer's hours',

Ticos—who earned their nickname because of their habit of turning words into cute diminutives (making, for example, a momento a *momentico* for example)—are also almost unnervingly friendly and polite. Yet they are more reserved and less spontaneous than most other Latinos, and are expert fence sitters who avoid firm stances and confrontation. Theroux—in fact quite a fan of the Ticos—thought they were 'the most predictable people in Latin America'.

Costa Ricans are hugely proud of everything that makes them different. They traditionally view everything in terms of *nuestra idiosincracia*, painting themselves as the peaceful and cultured 'Swiss of Latin America.' The idiosyncrasy they boast of includes a deeply ingrained sense of equality, a belief in education and an aversion to parvenus and snobs. Increasingly, however, realistic Ticos admit they are kidding themselves with such blanket self-congratulation and harsher critics would describe them as boring and smug.

Whatever your view, it's clear that major cracks are appearing in the *idiosincracia*—especially since the catastrophic corruptions scandals of 2004—and that Costa Rica is starting to suffer something of a crisis of both culture and identity.

This crisis has various causes. Firstly, the massive inflow of aid money, especially from the United States, once anxious to cultivate a bastion of non-Communism in Central America, has all but dried up since the 1980, when the region's civil wars came to an end.

No longer the proud oasis of stability among war-torn neighbours, Costa Rica finds itself in an embarrassing struggle to prop up its rambling social security system amid spiralling debts and a declining quality of life.

Like a miniature United States, Costa Rica has historically received refugees with open arms. Large-scale immigration in recent decades, particularly of Nicaraguans (who are now estimated to constitute up to 20 per cent of the population), however, has created competition for jobs and access to the country's overburdened free education and health care system. To most outsiders, this country is still about as threatening as the Little House on the Prairie, but intolerance and serious crime—until recently almost unheard of—are on the rise.

As a small country, Costa Rica cannot remain untouched by globalisation, and the coming of CAFTA (the Central American Free Trade Agreement) seems now to be unavoidable. Ticos are intrinsically conservative and many of them—not just grandparents eulogising the good old days but very often young adults as well—lament what they see as 'infection' from the outside, and their country's loss of innocence. Newspaper opinion articles almost daily reflect this feeling of assault on traditional values and identity.

One Tico woman told me, "It's as though we've been the guardians of a beautiful treasure which we always took for granted. Suddenly, we can see that the treasure is on the verge of falling from its altar and smashing to the floor but we're helpless to stop it."

Such doom and gloom can seem a little excessive. It's true that Costa Rica is changing rapidly from a coffee and banana republic into an urbanised modern state dependent on high-tech industries and tourism. The winds of change are sweeping in here faster than in many of its neighbours and yet there is only a nebulous divide between town and country, past and present.

Not far outside the Meseta Central, you will still find working cowboys, indigenous communities and Afro-Caribbeans speaking an antiquated English dialect. Even within the urban areas, beneath their increasingly slick outer shell, Ticos still live in a world of herbal remedies, magic and rural traditions. Many city dwellers still grow vegetables on a small plot of land and almost everyone aims for nothing more than to retire to a small house in the country with some coffee plants and chickens.

For me, being in Costa Rica is like constant time travel. One minute you're never too far from the veneer of modernity, another you feel you've slipped back to a more innocent age, when people had time for politeness, generosity and hanging out in rocking chairs watching the world go by. In my entire time in Costa Rica, the only people who were ever rude to me were other foreigners.

I hope this book will help to shed some light on this occasionally contradictory Costa Rican reality, help you understand how the Ticos see their world, and give you some useful tips on how to live, work and have fun here.

ACKNOWLEDGEMENTS

I would particularly like to thank Tía Julieta, María Fernanda and Tina la Perrita Salchicha for giving me a home in Escazú and, for friendship, wine and help (in varying degrees), John McCuen, Aisling Mahon, Darren Mora, the staff of the British Embassy in San José, Sergio Chávez and the anthropology students of the Universidad de Costa Rica, Randall Ortega (despite everything) and literally hundreds of other people whose humour, hospitality and tips helped my months in Costa Rica to be so much fun.

For the wonderful pictures, I would especially like to thank Frans Baas and the Instituto Costarricense de Turismo.

To Lou and Betty, my parents,
whose tales of far-flung lands first gave me a taste for travel.

MAP OF COSTA RICA

LAGO DE
NICARAGUA

NICARAGUA

CARIBBEAN SEA

SAN JOSÉ
●
COSTA RICA

GULF OF
NICOYA

NORTH
PACIFIC OCEAN

PANAMA

GULF
OF DULCE

FIRST IMPRESSIONS

'One of the first impressions of Costa Rica is how Western
it is... However, pretty quickly you notice the roads and
pavements really are something else. In the rural areas
it's not unknown for whole sections of hillside to slide
away taking the road with them. Even main roads seem to
spring large, unexpected and spectacularly deep potholes.
How anyone drives safely at night, I really don't know.'
—UK tourist Marilyn Dixon,
who passed through Costa Rica as part of a world tour.

When you touch down in San José, it can be hard to believe you're in a capital city. Like just about everything else in Costa Rica, it is small scale—nearly all the buildings are low rise and if you look down the length of some of the city centre's long, straight avenues you can see rolling green hills at the end.

Greenery is, in fact, one of the most immediate impressions the country makes on you. Costa Rica puts some of the world's other famously wet spots to shame. Coming from England, I don't get over-excited by green fields and trees—but in Costa Rica, it is sometimes hard to even see the trees, so totally covered are they in mosses, orchids, ferns, creepers and bromeliads. All this vegetation is of course, thanks to the humidity and rain. Some parts of the country get a whopping 7.6 m (25 ft) of rain per year!

Given the wall-to-wall greenery and Costa Rica's world famous reputation for eco-tourism, I wasn't expecting to find pollution, especially in the cities. While efforts are clearly made to conserve the special areas that provide the focus for so much of the country's massive tourist industry, little more than a cursory nod seems to have been given to other areas of environmental protection. Trucks—many of them loaded down with timber (yes, deforestation is a major issue in this green idyll)—belch out plumes of thick black diesel smoke, while recycling is virtually non-existent and littering seems to be a national sport.

I didn't expect all the Ticos (Costa Ricans) I met to be tree huggers going around barefoot and wearing organic hemp T-shirts, but with the country so internationally synonymous with environmental conservation, I was shocked at how few of them I met had ever even visited a national park. Many people seemed to feel very proud of their country's reputation, but that visiting the rainforest was just 'something foreign tourists do'.

Another surprise in San José and the main Central Valley is that it's not as hot as you might expect, given that you've arrived in a tropical country. At around 1,000 m (3,280.8 ft), the temperature here always hovers around a spring-like 23°C (73.4°F). Travel up north to dusty Guanacaste, or down to the coasts, and you will be really scorching. In fact, you don't even need to go that far. With its jagged topography, the country has many distinct microclimates. Two places that are just 15 minutes apart can have quite different weather—unbelievable until you experience it!

It's not only in terms of the weather (San José's at least) that you might feel you are in fact somewhere closer to home. It's immediately clear—especially if you're arriving here from Guatemala or Nicaragua—that Costa Rica is not as culturally colourful as these countries. Neither is it as poor. Poverty definitely exists (18 per cent of the population was classed as 'poor' in 2004) but this is generally a country of the middle class, and it's often said to be the most Americanised country in Latin America.

Like most trite descriptions, of course, this isn't entirely fair—when you scratch the surface you will realise that Costa Rica does have a very particular character that is all of its own. But during my first days in the capital, I was certainly overwhelmed by the huge numbers of American stores and fast food outlets (there are more than 20 malls and 30 places to eat sushi in the Central Valley alone) and the fact that the people, in general, were also so much whiter than in neighbouring Central American countries. Immediately obvious in the cities and resorts is the almost total absence of indigenous faces, and the large number of expats—especially

The laid-back lifestyle along Costa Rica's coasts makes the city's stresses seem a million miles away.

late middle-aged Americans and Europeans—who come to this comparatively safe, manageable country of educated, often English-speaking people either on holiday or to retire. With a population of only four million, the country receives a massive 1.3 million foreign visitors each year.

San José's chaotic pot-holed streets and crazy traffic are constant reminders to any visitor, however, that you are definitely not in the First World. Drivers seem to be permanently pumped up on testosterone (this isn't just a first impression, but a lasting one!). I personally had numerous white-knuckle moments when I tried to cross a busy city road or when I prayed that the driver of the bus which I had stupidly boarded would not crash while overtaking around hairpin mountain bends. In a 2005 survey by the University of Costa Rica, 58.8 per cent of Ticos felt they were risking their lives every day by crossing the road on the way to work.

In general, however, the capital and surrounding towns are pretty low-key, easy to get around, and you soon feel comfortable here. In fact, San José has more the feel of a big village, especially as you seem to bump into the same people again and again.

Things can seem a little muted at first. Though there are some good bars and clubs in San José, Ticos are not huge party fiends like some other Latino nations. Having spent a lot of time before travelling to Costa Rica in Spain (where people often only sit down to eat at 11:00 pm and routinely stay out partying until dawn), I had to adjust my body clock in a big way. Many restaurants in Costa Rica close at 10:00 pm or 10:30 pm. In their homes, Ticos are often tucked up in bed by 10:00 pm—or even 8:30 pm in rural areas, unless there's something like a really great fiesta or soap opera that can't be missed (Ticos LOVE television) to keep them up.

If you're used to the rest of Latin America, you will probably find the Ticos more shy and serious than many other Latinos, especially those from more effusive Caribbean countries. However, they make up for this by being genuinely helpful, polite and friendly. One of the first things you will notice is people's constant use of the phrase *Pura Vida*. Literally this means 'Pure Life', but it's generally used to mean 'cool', 'great', 'OK' or can even be used as a greeting. For example, if asked, 'How are you?', a Tico would probably reply: '*Pura vida*'; or 'Do you fancy going to the cinema? '*Pura vida*'. This entirely Tico linguistic invention is a sign of the fresh and optimistic outlook that Ticos have on life.

Costa Rica's extremely rugged terrain historically meant many communities spent centuries in almost complete isolation from each other—leading to the evolution of hundreds of other amazing and unique words and phrases. If you're a Spanish speaker, you'll start hearing these almost straight away!

This terrain has had a big effect on transport links too, and this continues today. The infuriatingly truck-clogged, bendy, pot-holed, often mist-shrouded or soaking wet, single-lane roads mean you can only expect to average 50 kmph (30 mph) even on main roads.

Feeling at Home

Time, preferably combined with a sense of humour and a decent level of Spanish, will help you to really get under the country's skin, and to realise just how much less bland and predictable Costa Rica is than some guidebooks suggest. However, despite the amazing wildlife, you will rarely ever feel that you're in a truly foreign or exotic place. Some see Costa Rica's understated culture and relative lack of 'difference' as a drawback, but I don't. With the Ticos' quiet helpfulness, friendliness and sense of humour, it simply means that it takes hardly any time at all to feel really at home.

Considering the close vicinity of the fiery fare of Mexico, Tico cuisine (like most Central American food) is much more simple and hearty. If you like rice and beans, you'll be in your element! I found it odd at first to eat rice and beans with breakfast, lunch and dinner, and was thankful for the large number of international restaurants in San José when I was desperate for variety. But almost without realising it, this simple staple became second nature. I even missed it after I'd left, and it certainly gave me the slow-release energy to keep going on long jungle treks. What the Costa Rican food menu lacks is certainly compensated for by the huge variety of delicious, fresh juices and shakes—a much better way to re-balance your vitamin levels than a soul-destroying detox diet.

After the high tech Central Valley (the friendly investment climate is turning Costa Rica into a 'Silicon Valley of the South', with Acer, Microsoft, GE, Abbot Laboratories, Continental Airways and Intel all in operation), it's amazing to discover just how near by the country's famous wild places really are. When you find yourself wading, waist-deep, through a river mouth bubbling with small sharks, or have just narrowly avoided grabbing hold of a snake that you mistook for a liana, it's hard to believe that you're still in the same, tiny country. As the entire country is so small, the areas of wilderness are necessarily small too. But while this certainly isn't the Himalayas or Papua New Guinea, you do sometimes have to pinch yourself to believe it!

OVERVIEW OF THE LAND AND HISTORY

'Of all the Spanish colonies,
Costa Rica enjoyed the least influence as a colony.
It was initially a tough and unpopular place to settle,
with few valuable or easily exploited resources.'
—*Geographical World Travel Guide*

HISTORY

Costa Rica has been inhabited for at least the past 11,000 years, but its early history remains something of a mystery. Few sites have been excavated, and the records kept by the Spanish *conquistadores* are far from reliable.

The Ticos' comparative 'whiteness' in relation to other Central Americans—combined with the fact that today there are only around 150,000 indigenous people living in the country—led academics to believe, until quite recently, that only around 27,000 people were living in the country when Columbus arrived.

Recent archaeological digs, however, have revealed structures, burial sites, and artefacts of a complexity and scale too great to have been made by a population of anything less than 500,000 people.

Perhaps the Indian population was almost totally annihilated as a result of warfare, European diseases such as smallpox and flu, to which they had no resistance, and by the mass transportation of slaves to other parts of the Empire—such as the notorious gold mines of Peru, from which few emerged alive. The country's total population would not recover to its pre-Conquest levels until 1930.

Prior to the arrival of the Spaniards, the country seems to have acted as both a bridge and a filter for cultures from north and south, as well as an important trade route. Linguistic research has bolstered the theory that the Chorotegas who settled in the north of the country had moved down from Mesoamerica (today Mexico), while other groups migrated up from South America.

The Chorotegas (the word comes from Choltec which means 'people who fled') are thought to have arrived around 800 CE to escape civil strife in their northern homeland. Like the Aztecs, who arose later in Mexico, they worshipped similar anthropomorphic deities, farmed corn, and lived in towns with central plazas—a living arrangement which made them particularly vulnerable to round-ups by the Spaniards. Their sculptures, polychrome ceramics, elaborate three-legged *metate* corn-grinding tables, calendar, paintings and games also resembled those of the Aztecs to the north. Skilled craftsmen are also still found in the town of Guaitíl.

The groups influenced by the south were nomadic hunters and slash-and-burn farmers who grew root crops, slept in hammocks, chewed coca leaves and built elaborate irrigation systems. They spoke languages from the Chibcha language group and their most important god was Sibö.

Although there is hardly any gold and no jade in Costa Rica, sophisticated jade and gold working developed using raw materials which came from either war or trade with other cultures.

Gold working reached its peak in the Diquis Delta in the south-western part of the country, with recurring themes such as frogs (a symbol of fertility), circular breast plates representing the sun, jaguars, crocodiles and stylised, hook-beaked birds (copies of which are still seen hanging round many male Tico necks on chunky gold chains). The birds are thought to have represented vultures, related to the god of creation and death—Spanish chroniclers noted how the Indians let vultures feed on the bodies of the dead after battle.

Many pre-Colombian people practised human sacrifice, and tombs show evidence that slaves were sacrificed to accompany their masters into the afterworld. Warrior cults and fertility rites were also important, all of which made the Spanish feel perfectly justified in their 'soul-saving' campaigns, enforced baptisms and sword-point conversions to Christianity.

The most intriguing remains of this period are hundreds of stone spheres, also from the Diquis Delta. The near perfect spheres, ranging from the size of a grapefruit to more than

An archaeologist examines one of the mysterious pre-Columbian stone spheres found in the Diquis Delta.

2 m (6.5 feet) in diameter, have not been found anywhere else in the world. Made mostly from sandstone, some of these stones have even been found more than 20 km (12.5 miles) from the quarries where they were carved between the years 500 and 1500 CE. It has been suggested the spheres were used as grave markers, navigation tools, or ancient star charts—but just like Stonehenge and the stone heads of Easter Island, their real purpose remains unknown.

Columbus

Christopher Columbus landed in Costa Rica on his fourth and final voyage to the New World in his quest to find a sea passage to Asia. On 18 September 1502, he dropped anchor at Isla Uvita, just off the shores of Puerto Limón, to repair his storm-damaged fleet.

The area became known as Costa Rica or Rich Coast, allegedly because of the gold gifts given to the Italian explorer and his crew by the locals. The name really could not have been less appropriate as there was actually very little naturally occurring gold in the country.

The Caribbean coast's extreme heat and rainfall, impenetrable jungle and punishing terrain made inland exploration almost impossible. The real conquest of the country would not come for another 20 years when Gil González reached Nicoya after marching up the Pacific coast from Panama.

Roman Catholic Spain, newly freed from six centuries of control by the Muslim Moors, saw the conquest largely in terms of religious zealotry. González claimed to have 'saved' 32,000 pagan souls in the name of the King of Spain.

After a slow start, the following decades of conquest in Costa Rica would be bloody, typified by fierce indigenous resistance, massacres, and in-fighting among the Spaniards.

By 1562, Juan Vásquez de Coronado, using the successful tactics of Hernán Cortés' earlier campaign in Mexico, finally managed to dominate the fertile Meseta Central (the central highlands where most of the population still lives today) and the Pacific coast by exploiting rivalries between indigenous groups.

As settlement began in earnest, King Philip II granted colonists the right to divide up the indigenous inhabitants under the *encomienda* system, in which families either had to work as slaves for two generations, or pay food tributes to their new masters.

Vásquez de Coronado set up his capital in Cartago. For now, the inaccessible Caribbean coast—swampy, disease-ridden and the lair of British pirates—remained largely ignored. The pirates, however, also raided the Pacific coast, with Sir Francis Drake himself landing in 1579 on what is now called Bahía Drake, near Golfito.

The English 'privateers', as they called themselves, were first sent to plunder Spanish possessions by Queen Elizabeth I, and became a thorn in the side of the Spanish Empire in the Caribbean for centuries. They also developed a self-serving alliance with the coastal Miskito Indians of Honduras and Nicaragua, who repeatedly raided Costa Rica's Caribbean cacao plantations, resulting in Costa Rica paying a kind of 'protection money' to the Indians between 1779 and 1841.

Colonial Times

Costa Rica was the poor relation of all the Spanish colonies, isolated at the southernmost point of the Captaincy General of Guatemala.

The country did not have any gold and little by way of a labour force. Most of the surviving Indians were holed up in the forests, making it impossible to support a plantation economy. Great disease epidemics led to the indigenous population falling to just 999 in 1714, while intermarriage (the original settlers were nearly all male) diluted the indigenous blood line still further, meaning that colonists ended up having to work their own farms.

The settlers soon found that, far from discovering their fortune in the New World, they were facing a struggle just to survive. All but abandoned by Spain, by the early 18th century they were using cacao beans as currency (as the Chorotegas had traditionally done) and fashioning clothes out of goat hair and tree bark.

These humble beginnings would have major repercussions in Costa Rica, which is still famous for its tranquil and largely egalitarian society. In sharp contrast, the *hacienda* economies of Mexico and Guatemala would result in the much larger indigenous populations being left destitute, landless and indebted to their masters—leading to massive class distinctions and civil wars in the 20th century.

The poverty-stricken population, living in isolated *caseríos* (hamlets) among the broken terrain became self-reliant and individualistic, a characteristic still very evident among Ticos today. Sociologist Constantino Láscaris in his book *El Costarricense* said the national character was also shaped by the fact that early settlers came from the Canary Islands, Catalunya and Galicia. He said that such people were traditionally more reserved and distrustful than the outgoing Andalucians who populated neighbouring Nicaragua—and where the people today still have a very different personality.

A scattered population also meant taxes were hard to collect. The Bishop of León in Nicaragua also became horrified by both low attendance at masses among his Costa Rican flock and the number of couples—often close relatives—living in sin. In 1711, he commanded that churches be constructed and towns built around them.

The typical Tico trait of rebelliousness in the face of authority was also well established by this stage, and settlements were slow in growing. Cubujuquí (today Heredia) came into being in 1706, Villa Nueva de la Boca del Monte (San José)—largely settled by smugglers exiled from Cartago—was not founded until 1737, and Villa Hermosa (Alajuela) did not exist until 1782. When the capital, Cartago, was destroyed by the eruption of the Irazú volcano in 1723, it consisted of only 70 adobe and thatch houses, two churches and two chapels.

Many Costa Rican historians are apt to paint the country's colonial era as a kind of wholesome bucolic idyll. Carlos Monge Alfaro, for example, described life thus: 'Each farm was a small world in which the family was born and raised far from other farms. Their simple life, without ambitions or desires, gave the inhabitants a rude, mistrustful and very individualistic character. They were without exception peasants who toiled the soil for their food; as a result Costa Rica became a rural democracy. Unlike other Spanish colonies, the country had no social classes or castes, no despotic civil servants who looked down on others, no powerful creoles owning land and slaves and hating the Spaniards and no oppressed mestizo (people of mixed indigenous and European blood) class resentful of the maltreatment and scorn of the creoles.'

While it is clear that everyone was pretty much poor, however, such rose-tinted analysis ignores the fact that there was racial segregation and social distinctions, based on the Spanish class system.

Each Spanish colony was settled by *hidalgos* (noblemen) and *plebeyos* (commoners). There was a hierarchy of *hidalgos*, with the crème de la crème getting the first stab at the most lucrative colonies, such as Peru. Only provincial nobles went to Costa Rica.

Only *hidalgos* had the right to positions of power, and their sons stepped into their shoes when they died. Around a dozen families (several of which are still potent forces in the country today) intermarried between 1821 and 1970 to consolidate their power. Three out of four congressmen came from this original dynasty and 75 per cent of Costa Rican presidents were descended from just three families.

With only those with Spanish blood having access to resources, social advancement came to be based on skin colour. People tried to marry their children off to whiter-skinned suitors, even if they were poorer, and neighbourhoods were segregated along colour lines. Spaniards were at the top of the hierarchy, working down through *mestizos*, Indians, and mulattoes to the bottom of the pile—blacks.

By the end of the colonial period, most of the racial distinctions had gone and everyone had some level of mixed blood. The power of the original noble family names, however, persisted.

Independence

By October 1821, Costa Rica's population had swollen to around 65,000 inhabitants. Most of them were surprised when a messenger bearing the news of Central America's independence from Spain arrived after a three-week journey by mule from Nicaragua.

Unlike the other countries of the Spanish Empire, which fought fiercely for their independence, isolated Costa Rica, long forgotten by Spain, was never involved. Today, it is the only country in the continent whose town plazas do not give pride of place to the busts of independence heroes.

On hearing the news, the four largest Meseta towns—Cartago, San José, Heredia and Alajuela—agreed to remain neutral to each other, displaying the kind of Tico aversion to confrontation and decision-making that stay ingrained in the national psyche to this day.

As Nicaragua, Mexico and Guatemala each sought to control Costa Rica, the four cities started to squabble over which should be the capital. The biggest rift was between the wealthier aristocrats of Heredia and Cartago, who favoured joining the new Mexican empire and the more liberal republicans of San José and Alajuela. After a typically small-scale Tico battle that left just 20 dead, the republicans won and the capital was moved to San José. Further disputes arose in 1824 with Nicaragua, after the inhabitants of Guanacaste narrowly voted to leave the civil war-torn northern neighbour and become part of Costa Rica.

Costa Rica's first president was a schoolteacher, Juan Mora Fernández, and during his term the country was part of the short-lived federal republic of the five Central American states.

The Coming of Coffee

In the early 1830s, the dictator Braulio Carrillo took the step that would define Costa Rica's identity right up until the present day—the introduction of coffee. The young nation desperately needed a cash crop to sustain it and coffee, the fashionable new drink in Europe, seemed the ideal choice. Plants were handed out to the poor and tax breaks and free land offered to anyone who would grow the crop. Coffee-growing spread rapidly in the Meseta Central, which offered the perfect combination of altitude, climate and fertile volcanic soil.

Things didn't fully take off until an English merchant, William Le Lacheur, docked his empty ship in the Pacific port of Puntarenas in 1843 looking for cargo to take home. Although Le Lacheur couldn't pay up front, some producers entrusted him with their crop on credit. London loved the coffee, Le Lacheur returned in 1845 with the proceeds, and in that year alone 29 ships transported Costa Rican beans to Europe.

As a Spanish colony, Costa Rica had been forbidden to trade with the British, Spain's sworn enemy. Now independent, there was no restriction and Britain, the world's economic power then, would be for decades the biggest purchaser of the country's *grano de oro*, or 'golden bean'.

Roads and bridges were built to transport the lucrative crop, carried by ox carts to the port of Puntarenas—a journey of up to six days—before being laden onto ships for the lengthy journey south around Cape Horn at the southern tip of South America. This journey was considered easier than

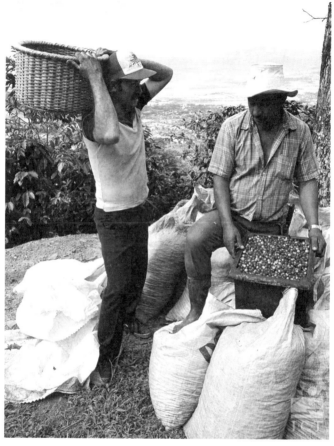

Local workers loading up ripe red coffee 'cherries' which are still a mainstay of the country's economy.

hacking a route through the steep ravines and impenetrable forests to the Caribbean coast.

Costa Rican coffee (at this time only Arabica was grown) was of very high quality, and the country soon became the richest in the region. With numerous small towns, this wealth was quite evenly spread around and a large middle class developed, still very much evident today. The coffee elite consisted of those—often foreigners—who had the cash and foresight to invest in transport and processing equipment.

Thanks to trading links with Europe, the rich were soon sleeping on Manchester linen and sending their sons to school in England and France. Meanwhile, the old adobe structures were torn down as San José started to sprout coffee-funded, neo-Baroque, European-style buildings, (most importantly the Teatro Nacional—*see* Chapter Seven: Enjoying Costa Rica. *page 178*).

Coffee, however, was also responsible for under-development. This crop was virtually the country's only export from 1840 to 1890, and with all available land being turned over to this monoculture, production of basic food stuffs fell. The country became dependent on imports, leaving it vulnerable to price shocks in the future.

William Walker

Everything was pottering along nicely until the mid-1880s, when invaders from the north brought a major threat to Costa Rica's very survival—a war which still makes Ticos swell with pride today.

The invader was William Walker, a Tennessee gold miner, adventurer and journalist, who intended to turn Central America into a confederacy of southern American states where slavery would be institutionalised. Supported by a group of US slave owners and industrialists, Walker arrived in Nicaragua in 1855, where he planned to force slaves to dig a canal from the Pacific to the Atlantic.

By March 1856, Walker and his 300 men had invaded Guanacaste in northern Costa Rica. President Juan Rafael Mora quickly called up an army of 9,000 civilians to oust the foreign troops, who were holed up in a large ranch house, La Casona, located in what is today the Santa Rosa National Park. (Unfortunately, illegal loggers burnt down La Casona, a much-prized piece of Tico heritage, in 2001 to protest forest protection measures.)

Walker's troops were forced back to Rivas, in Nicaragua, where Costa Rican drummer boy Juan Santamaría set fire to the wooden building where they were taking cover. The invaders fled after shooting Santamaría, who became Costa Rica's national hero.

Walker continued to threaten the isthmus until 1860, when he was captured and executed by firing squad in Honduras.

Coincidentally, President Mora was executed the same year. Mora had lost favour because of a cholera epidemic brought back by his troops. He was deposed in 1859, and killed after staging a failed coup in 1860.

Without having fought for their independence, the Walker crisis, although comparatively small scale, united Ticos with a sense of national pride and identity they had never experienced before. Patriotism is still extremely strong in Costa Rica today. Even before the army was abolished in 1948, the standing army was small because, Ticos boasted, it would never be difficult to call up a force big enough to protect their country.

Railways and Plantations

In 1871, President Tomás Guardia ordered the construction of a 'jungle railway', through thick forests and plunging ravines, to the Caribbean coast. This railway was both a means of speeding up coffee exports (it would cut three months off the journey to Europe) and a symbol of national progress and achievement.

Under American-born engineer Minor Keith, the railway started to take shape. The Chinese and Italians hired workers rapidly succumbed to diseases such as malaria, dysentery and yellow fever, that thrived in the hot, swampy conditions. Finally, 11,000 black labourers from Jamaica—who were more accustomed to the climate and genetically resistant to malaria—were contracted. Nevertheless, the 150-km (93-mile) long railway was not completed until 1890, and took more than 5,000 lives to build.

Keith was paid in part paid with a 99-year lease on 320,000 hectares (470,720 acres) of land in the area—a move that was to have an unimaginable impact on the country. The enterprising engineer planted bananas on the land, and set up the United Fruit Company in 1899. Exports spiralled from 100,000 stems in 1883 to one million in 1890 and 11 million by 1913. Costa Rica was, for many years, the world's biggest banana producer. Today it is second only to Ecuador.

Most of the Jamaican railway builders, waiting to be paid for their labour, ended up working in the plantations—where they often rose to higher positions than the Ticos because they spoke English. Growing union activity and banana diseases led to plantations moving to the Pacific coast in the early 1930s, where the government stipulated that preference be given to native 'white' workers.

The blacks, prohibited from leaving the Caribbean coast until 1948 when they were finally recognised as citizens, went from being relatively well-off to having to eke out a living growing cacao or fishing.

Social Reform and Civil War

Although dictatorial presidents, electoral fraud and monopoly by the elite, which had hitherto been commonplace, did not disappear, things started to change after Guardia's death in 1882. Political life became increasingly secular—civil weddings and divorces were legalised and the death penalty abolished. The Jesuits were expelled, and the country's only university, the Universidad de Santo Tomás was closed down because it was dominated by clerics.

As a result, the sons of rich coffee barons had to be sent to Europe or South America for higher education. This boosted the reform movement further as they came home suffused with ideas of democracy.

Voting at this time was still restricted to literate, male landowners. From 1889 onwards, every president but one was legitimately elected. A crunch came with World War I as a result of a sharp fall in coffee demand and a rise in debt. The politically powerful coffee elite had deliberately kept taxes indirect and regressive, as they still are today—despite having a sprawling welfare state to sustain. The highest level of personal income tax in Costa Rica is still only 15 per cent, while taxes on goods and services are sky high.

In 1914, President Alfredo González Flores proposed tax reforms that proved even more unpopular than he could have imagined.

González Flores was driven from power by minister of war Federico Tinoco. The latter, who ruled with an iron fist, filled the jails with political prisoners and gagged the press.

Costa Ricans were horrified at the removal of liberties they had come to expect. Schoolteachers and children marched through the streets, setting fire to a pro-Tinoco newspaper plant. When the government sent troops against them, public outrage grew still further. By August 1918, General Jorge Volio Jiménez, a former Catholic priest, led a coup uprising and Tinoco fled into exile in Europe.

In 1923, Jorge Volio set up the Reformist Party, which espoused extensive agrarian and social reforms. He should have known that his repeated attacks on the ruling elite would be dangerous. Jorge Volio ended up confined in a Belgian psychiatric asylum. However, his ideas did not disappear with him. By the time of the 1930s depression, social discontent and poverty were growing—exacerbated by a population increase of almost a third between 1930 and 1949. Banana workers on the foreign-owned plantations suffered particularly brutal exploitation (as documented by Carlos Luis Fallas in his novel *Mamita Yunai: El Infierno de las Bananeras*) and led the country's first major strike in 1934. Troops were sent in to restore order.

With both fascist and communist ideas taking hold in the country, President Rafael Angel Calderón Guardia, a devout Catholic elected in 1940, sought to maintain moderation. He introduced health insurance for urban workers, a Labour Code (reinstating the right to strike—outlawed in 1924) and social guarantees, as well as legislation to allow landless peasants to acquire land titles by cultivating unused plots.

Landowners and businessmen were unsurprisingly wary of Calderón however, and by 1942, he had no choice but to team up with the communist Vanguardia Popular, the party of Jorge Volio's intellectual heir, Manuel Mora. This move meant the unfortunate Calderón lost the support of the country's farmers, who saw communism as a fundamental threat to their way of life, while his Catholic sympathies aroused the suspicions of intellectuals.

As a result, an opposition candidate, newspaper publisher Otilio Ulate, won the 1944 elections. The *calderonista* Congress, however, voted to annul the result, installing a Calderón puppet Teodoro Picado instead. Presidents were constitutionally barred from immediate re-election, but Calderón hoped to make a comeback in 1948.

What Calderón had not bargained for, however, was a group of disaffected young middle-class men, who formed the Social Democratic Party, led by an extraordinary coffee farmer called José 'Don Pepe' Figueres Ferrer. Figueres had gained notoriety as the first political exile since the Tinoco years, after he had attacked Calderón on a radio programme in 1942. Other political groups—from oligarchs to idealists—joined Figueres' party in the single hope of toppling Calderón, and the by now staunchly anti-communist United States lent its support.

One of Figueres' main gripes with communism, according to political scientist Olivier Dabene quoted by the Biesanz family in The Ticos, is that it was a 'subversive, imported ideology', that couldn't meet the needs of the Tico *idiosincracia*. While Figueres' aims might not have seemed so very different from those of Calderón's, Ticos have always been wary of foreign ideas and influences that don't take Costa Rica's unique characteristics into account.

Figueres and his band of followers declared war on the government, leading to the only large-scale bloody uprising in the entire history of this peace-loving country in 1947. As with the repulsion of William Walker, the sides in the civil war were not exactly evenly matched. Figueres' troops were well armed, partially by the CIA, while Picado had to call in machete-wielding banana workers to help him out.

The fighting lasted six weeks and claimed 2,000 lives before a peace treaty and amnesty were signed. Figueres ruled for 18 months—enough time for him to issue more than 800 decrees which would drastically alter the very fabric of the country, before handing the reins of power back to the legitimately-elected Otilio Ulate. Figueres won a second term in 1951, as well as a third in 1970, during which he would oversee the country's so-called cultural revolution.

Figueres abolished the army, allowing comparatively huge amounts to be spent on health and education. It was also hoped that banning the army would prevent the political instability and coup attempts that had brought many other Latin American countries to their knees.

Since 1948, Costa Rica has relied (for protection) on the 1947 Rio Reciprocal Assistance Treaty, in which all American countries agree to support any member under attack. The country also banks on the strength of its vulnerability, which it hopes would lead to a massive international outcry if any aggressor tried to invade.

Some of Tinoco's simpler projects, such as getting shoes for all Ticos had huge effects too. At the time, at least half of all adults went barefoot. Today, the country has a First

World life expectancy (up from 40 years in 1927 to 77 years in 2005) and literacy rate.

Other reforms included the barring of former presidents from power for eight years after the end of their term; from the 1970s presidents were limited to just a single term—a law revoked in 2004. Banks were nationalised, women and illiterates given the right to vote, and black Costa Ricans born in the country were finally acknowledged as citizens. A system of autonomous institutions was also set up to manage basic services such as banking and public utilities.

Calderón, who had fled to Nicaragua, attempted two unsuccessful invasions and coups, backed by his friend the Nicaraguan dictator Anastasio Somoza García. Calderón later returned to Costa Rica, where he died after a final failed attempt to win the presidency in 1970.

Post-1948

While the civil war changed structures in the country, power remained pretty much in the hands of the same, small coffee elite. However, peace has been the tradition of the past half century. In fact, in 1994, Figueres' son, José María Figueres Olsen took over as president from Calderón's son Rafael Angel Calderón Fournier without a hint of rancor.

Ticos were hugely proud of their status as an oasis of democracy and anti-communism in the civil war-ridden Central America of the 1970s and 1980s. Costa Rica also became—despite its size—an important player on the international stage.

Prosperity boomed and large amounts of international aid flowed in, particularly from the United States after Costa Rica switched its quiet support for the Soviet-funded Sandinista regime in Nicaragua to the US-backed Contras. The northern part of the country was even used as a Contra training ground, in direct violation of its supposed neutrality. At one point, US funds made up more than one-third of the Costa Rican government's operating expenditure, and only Israel received more aid from the United States per capita.

Government bureaucracy grew exponentially until the early 1980s, by which time 20 per cent of all workers were employed by the state and the public sector accounted for more than a quarter of the gross national product.

With nearly all growth financed by international lending, the world economic crisis of the early 1980s hit Costa Rica especially hard. Coffee and banana prices slumped, inflation rocketed, and in 1981, the country became the first Third World country to default on its debt payments.

In 1986, the liberal Oscar Arias Sánchez was elected as president. A former political scientist, he started to mediate with his neighbours in the civil wars of Nicaragua, El Salvador, Guatemala and Honduras, that had between them left 200,000 people dead and two million displaced. Within 18 months, Sánchez came up with a peace plan that called for a ceasefire, the cessation of military aid to the Contras, amnesties for political prisoners and guerrillas and inter-governmental negotiations for free and fair elections. Although the plan was not fully implemented, the five presidents approved an accord in August 1987 based on his plan. Arias was awarded the Nobel Peace Prize in 1987.

Although national pride was running high, the Arias-brokered peace plan carried a high price for Costa Rica. By 2005, the country's external debt had reached US$ 6 billion—one of the highest per capita in the world and with Central America now at peace, US aid dried up. Creditors refused further help unless Costa Rica slimmed down its overweight bureaucracy through privatisation and by encouraging foreign investment and competition.

University of Costa Rica anthropologist Sergio Chávez explained that Ticos have failed to fully accept their decline since the 1980s: 'We are a tiny nation, and so we are proud of what we have achieved and all the times when we have been centre stage in world affairs. Unfortunately, times have changed, but we still tend to live in the past. We simply don't want to face up to our current mediocrity.'

MODERN POLITICS

Power in Costa Rica has traditionally swung between the two main political parties. Figueres' Partido de Liberación Nacional (PLN), formed in 1951, and the opposition coalition, the Partido Unidad Social Cristiana (PUSC), formed in 1990. Minority parties haven't done well at the top level because 40 per cent of the vote is needed to win the presidency— although this could change drastically in the 2006 elections following the massive corruption scandals of 2004 (see below). Meanwhile, the party in power rarely wins an election—partly, it seems, because of Ticos' deep-seated distrust of authority. In polls, the Legislative Assembly is repeatedly voted the least trusted of all public institutions.

The constitution of 1949, designed to prevent the emergence of dictatorships or overly-strong legislatures that weakens the power of both the president and the parliament, provides for weakened powers for both the president and the parliament. While this avoids alienating anyone, it also hampers decision-making.

The PLN, in favour of state intervention, has traditionally had a slight edge in the popularity stakes, although in today's times of belt-tightening, the rather more frugal PUSC has been gaining favour. Like the Republicans and Democrats in the United States, there really isn't a great deal to choose between the two, and personality is often more important than policies on polling day.

No president would ever win, however, unless he was suitably *humilde* (humble), a favourite Tico trait. Oscar Arias, during his presidential campaign in 1986, was even sent to a special image clinic in New York, as his advisers were worried about his overly proud manner. Presidents tend to dress simply, and can often be seen out strolling in the street or shopping like regular citizens without any bodyguards. In the early 1980s, president Luis Alberto Monge even had his pocket picked in downtown San José.

Ticos are also proud of the fact that their elections are some of the cleanest and most peaceful in the world. An electoral tribunal, manned by unpaid volunteers, takes over all election-related police and government functions in the run-up to the poll. Election days are rarely marred by violence as travel writer Paul Theroux noted in *The Old Patagonian Express*: 'In the rest of Central America, an election could be a harrowing piece of criminality; in Costa Rica the election had been fair and something of a fiesta. "You should have been here for the election," a woman told me in San José, as if I had missed a party.'

German sociologist Ilse Leitinger, who has worked in the country for more than half a century, said, "Costa Rica must be the only place on the planet where you can see cars leaving polling stations on election day full of smiling people waving the flags of opposing parties out of each window."

The single, four-year term limits imposed until recently by the constitution in order to prevent dictatorship seem to lead to exactly the kind of corruption and favour-currying they were originally designed to prevent—which exploded in the most dramatic way in 2004. Government ministers are not elected but appointed by the president, while term limits (only recently abolished) meant expertise gained slowly over the period was effectively useless at the end of each administration.

"Politicians don't need to care about their performance or re-election, so they just concentrate on earning enough *chorizos* (literally 'sausages' but meaning kickbacks or bribes) to line their own pockets and those of their friends," one commentator told me.

Another problem is that, while Costa Rica passes a huge number of often very forward-looking and innovative laws, the framework is rarely in place to actually enforce them. Even if enacted, they are often swathed in labyrinthine regulations that breed their own corruption—and add more fuel to the Ticos' characteristic lack of respect for authority.

The Biesanzes in *The Ticos: Culture and Social Change in Costa Rica* provide an example. Unlicensed *piratas* (unlicensed cab drivers) operate entirely illegally, yet have so little concern for legal repercussions that they have openly set up an Association of Pirates.

Similarly, while people keep their own homes spotlessly clean, to the extent of placing their rubbish in special dog-proof cages on posts to avoid dirtying the road outside their houses, it's a different story on public land. People not only chuck waste willy-nilly out of car windows, but seem to aim it right at the signs warning of a 100,000 colón (Costa Rican currency) fine for littering. The most successful means of keeping Ticos tidy seems to be to resort to shaming them with signs saying: 'If you throw litter, you are a person of very little culture.'

Many voters are clearly disillusioned with both the political system and the law, with rural *campesinos* (peasants) particularly disenfranchised. Abstention in the 2002 elections, particularly among first-time voters, was 31 per cent. While this may not be high for the US or UK, it was by far the highest level in Costa Rica in more than four decades.

As authority-suspicious people living in a paternalistic country, Ticos do have a few means of making the state more accountable. The Ombudsman's Office, set up in 1993, received 20,000 complaints in 1995, mostly from the poor alleging neglect or mistreatment by public employees or corporations.

They also have the constitutional court, or the Sala Cuarta of the Supreme Court. Challenges against legislation on constitutional grounds in this court are common and often successful, such as the repealing of the seat belt law (*see 'Getting Around' in* Chapter 5: Survival Skills *on page 136*), although the backlog of cases is massive.

The Democratic Dream Implodes

In the February 2002 elections, no candidate managed to win 40 per cent of the popular vote, leading to a run-off election (for the first time ever), which was won by Abel Pacheco of the PUSC. A psychiatrist, television presenter, songwriter and owner of San José trouser store, Pacheco vowed to govern with austerity and to create 'at least 40,000 jobs a year'.

However, without a majority in the government, the promises to tackle poverty never really took off, while his privatisation and tax reform plans were dogged by opposition, with huge strikes and demonstrations against both the proposed liberalisation of government monopolies in 2003 and CAFTA (the Central American Free Trade Agreement).

But much worse was to come. In 2004, Costa Rica's pride in its (relatively) corruption-free political system was to implode in the most spectacular fashion. An initially low-key corruption investigation led to two former presidents being jailed, a third being wanted for questioning, and President Pacheco—the self-styled 'Mr Clean' himself—also under the spotlight for corruption, which he had once declared to be a 'cancer' of society.

It all started when top officials of two of the biggest state monopolies, the Costa Rican Social Security Fund (CCSS) and the Costa Rican Institute of Electricity (ICE), were investigated for embezzlement, bribe-taking and other sins—and started to sing like canaries.

They first pointed the finger at former president Rafael Angel Calderón (PUSC, 1990–1994) who was said to have received a US$ 9.2 million kickback to ensure a big contract for a Finnish pharmaceutical company. This money was part of a loan from Finland supposed to go towards helping development work for the country's poor.

Then it emerged that former president Miguel Angel Rodríguez (1998–2002, PUSC) had apparently received part of a US$ 2.4 million kickback from French telecommunications company Alcatel (one of the biggest cable companies operating in Costa Rica) for the award of ICE contracts for 400,000 cell phone lines.

Curiously enough, this all took place at the same time as the watchdog group Transparency International released its annual corruption perception index, showing Costa Rica was felt to be the third least corrupt country in Latin America!

Then a third former president, José María Figueres Olsen (PLN, 1994–1998) admitted to receiving US$ 900,000, also from Alcatel, over a three-year period. However, he insisted the funds were for professional consulting services. Despite requests from the Legislative Assembly, Figueres has not returned to face investigation from Switzerland, where he lives. As of November 2005, he had not been charged, and continues to issue letters to the Costa Rican government claiming the charges were trumped up by his political enemies.

In June 2005, the rumbling investigations almost inevitably turned to President Pacheco, with a parliamentary inquiry looking into the funding of his 2002 presidential campaign, travel records and business contacts.

According to Costa Rican law, donations to political campaigns cannot exceed US$ 28,000, and there can be no foreign donations. Pacheco's campaign received and acknowledged contributions of US$ 100,000 from Alcatel and US$ 500,000 from various Taiwanese businessmen. In addition, the Costa Rican government partially paid for two trips he took to Seville to meet Spanish businessman Bernardo Martín Moreno—who later just happened to win the state-controlled right to develop Costa Rica's Papagayo area for tourism. Pacheco also appointed Moreno as honorary consul for Costa Rica.

President Pacheco strenuously maintained his innocence but his credibility was at rock bottom in late 2005. Rodríguez had been acquitted and Calderón was awaiting trial.

Unsurprisingly, Costa Rica has suffered greatly from this string of scandals. The much-vaunted 'Switzerland of Latin America' label has become increasingly hard to justify, with many foreign investors now writing the country off as just another banana republic that has basked smugly for too long in the achievements of decades past.

More embarrassment came as Figueres was forced to resign as chief executive officer of the World Economic Forum, and Rodríguez from the coveted post of Secretary General of the Organisation of American States—after only two weeks in the post.

"This is the end of Costa Rica being exceptional," Luis Guillermo Solís, a political analyst with the University of Costa Rica (UCR) commented sadly in the national press.

The scandals have taken a heavy toll on civic pride too, as could be seen from the probably unsurprising results of a 2004 University of Costa Rica poll on perceptions of corruption. Nearly half (48.6 per cent) of Costa Ricans said they did not trust the justice system, up from just 28.7 per cent in 1988, and more than half (53.3 per cent) said the Legislative Assembly was 'useless', up from 28.2 per cent. More than three-quarters (75.6 per cent) felt the country's municipal governments were rotten with corruption, and

78 per cent said 'anything was possible' in Costa Rica if you have enough money.

On another level, many analysts believe the scandals are also likely to drastically change Costa Rica's traditional two-party political map—at least in the short term.

The two main parties have become increasingly factionalised, while several smaller parties, which would never have stood much chance before, have emerged—such as the Citizen Action Party, Libertarian Movement, and Union for Change. These could stand to gain greatly in the 2006 elections.

However, they will have to contend with the political heavyweight and Nobel Peace Prize winner Oscar Arias, who has returned from years away from the limelight to throw his hat into the ring. (The constitution was changed in 2004 to allow the same candidate to stand for a second stab at power.) It remains to be seen whether Arias—who many Ticos talk of in reverential tones almost as though he were the Messiah—will himself be able to escape the general feeling of disgust with traditional party politics. Many analysts believe the public will now simply be more inclined to paint all politicians with the same brush, believing them all to be corrupt, and leading to a sharp spike in already rising rates of political disaffection and electoral abstention. While most polls indicate that Arias will win, he will probably lack a majority in Congress—like Pacheco before him—and therefore the authority to enforce his (pro-free market) plans.

DISMANTLING A NANNY STATE

Costa Rica still has an enormous government (public employees constitute more than 15 per cent of the work force), and a large number of autonomous institutions with their fingers in innumerable pies. More than half of these institutions have been disbanded or privatised as part of the economic structural adjustment pacts of the 1980s, but at one point there were more than 200 of them, many staggeringly inefficient.

The reforms demanded by international lenders have spurred economic growth by forcing a diversification of the economy. The education and welfare spending cutbacks, however, have unsurprisingly brought about a much wider distinction between rich and poor in a country which traditionally liked to bill itself a 'classless democracy'.

Such social changes in this previously relatively egalitarian state are likely to increase much, much more with the advent of CAFTA (the Central American Free Trade Agreement). While some sectors will apparently be shielded from outright privatisation, they will at least have to allow competition. There has been much opposition to the agreement, which many people believe will increase poverty and destroy agriculture in the country as it will be flooded with cheaper imports. However, there is now a growing sense of uneasy acceptance as people realise that Costa Rica really has little choice and cannot really stop the process. If it rejects CAFTA, it will simply find itself all alone and at a trading disadvantage in a sea of other CAFTA states.

For the meantime, however, the remaining autonomous institutions—such as the state banks, the CCSS (Caja Costarricense de Seguros Sociales or Social Security Fund) and the ICE (Instituto Costarricense de Electricidad; responsible for both electricity and telecommunications—are still massive, and account for a majority of public sector funds. Supporting them has led to a cycle of increasing internal debt, which has only been moved from one place to another by the central government 'borrowing' from them (by forcing them to buy bonds).

A major headache for the government has been the fact that many Ticos see the autonomous institutions as their 'heritage' and birthright. With so many Ticos employed by them, breaking these institutions up has been almost impossible. The whole country ground to a halt for a week during riots in 2000 (and again in 2003) when the government announced plans to privatise the ICE. Tyre-burning students, union members, environmentalists and angry citizens blocked streets around the capital, claiming that selling off the ICE, despite its problems, would result in job losses and higher costs for consumers, with corrupt politicians pocketing the profits.

Their reasoning? Despite its bungling over the purchase of cell phone lines and its notoriously slow service as the country's only Internet provider, the ICE's service is incredibly cheap as almost 80 per cent of electricity is from hydroelectric sources. The company also has the widest distribution network in the region. The ICE is continually providing new connection to unprofitable rural areas, which would otherwise be left in the dark under privatisation.

The violence of the ICE riots is particularly important given that, unlike many other Latinos, the Ticos have always been very passive and slow to protest. Don Pepe himself once lambasted his countrymen for being as 'docile as sheep'. Even in the 1947–1948 civil war, only a small minority of people took an active part.

Another polemic issue in Costa Rica is tax. Everybody wants to live in the protective shelter of their big government, but no one wants to pay the taxes to fund it. Personal taxes are low but according to a former minister of the economy quoted by the Biesanzes: 'Costa Ricans seem to have created a culture in which cheating the tax collector is an act to be celebrated.'

He added that 90 per cent of income taxes and 65 per cent of sales taxes go unpaid—mostly by big businesses. This sum, in 1994, was more than double the fiscal debt. Recent legal changes have introduced punishments such as imprisonment for tax evasion for the first time, and impending revisions are likely to see personal and corporate rates (for rich individuals and large companies) increase to stem the financial haemorrhage.

EDUCATION AND LITERACY

Even in the days when they had a military, Ticos used to boast that they had more schoolteachers than soldiers.

In what used to be a poverty-stricken rural backwater, it is understandable that the country's high standards of schooling are a source of enormous national pride. With foregone military budgets funding the massive education system, the only armies these days are hordes of neatly-uniformed

Education is a prized asset and children use all means to get to school.

schoolchildren on their way to and from school—one of the most ubiquitous images of Costa Rica.

Ticos have a 96 per cent literacy rate, almost the highest among Latin American countries. Many people sport *anillos de graduación*, or high school graduation rings, bearing chunky jewels and flowery inscriptions, given by proud parents.

The country's first president was a teacher, and believing that education can ensure democracy, Costa Rica was one of the world's first nations to introduce free, obligatory education in 1869.

Education is seen as the means to income (salaries are determined by academic level) and status—everyone wants to be *culto* ('cultured'). As nearly every job, however menial, requires a high-school education, many adults study at evening classes or through distance learning, choosing from the huge array of courses available.

However, the school system is in decline. Although Ticos are legally supposed to complete six years in school until age 14, many do not finish their education, and the average school career is shorter than in other countries such as Panama, Colombia and Cuba. Traditionally, many children missed weeks of school each year to help with the coffee harvest. Today, many drop out altogether through their family's need for them to work. Figures from the Ministry of Economy show that by 1998, more than 15 per cent of children aged between 5–17 were already working, 39 per cent of them for 57 hours a week (21 hours more than the legal maximum). Those aged 5–11 received on average only 11.6 per cent of the minimum wage.

Despite efforts to provide a standard level of nationwide education, many rural schools are poorly equipped. Most teachers would rather work in the cities than far-flung rural backwaters, increasing still further the gulf between education standards in urban and rural areas. The curriculum (like much else in Costa Rica) is centrally controlled, meaning little provision is made for the different history, culture, and circumstances of indigenous and Afro-Caribbean children.

According to the Biesanzes in *The Ticos*, per capita funding for education fell by 35 per cent in the 1980s alone and a 1994 United Nations survey revealed the country now actually invests less money per capita in education than most other Latin American countries. The average class size in public schools is 40 children.

As a result of these factors, around 20 per cent of children now attend private schools. Public school teachers are badly paid, so the best ones end up in the private schools. As most politicians send their own children to private schools, education has become less and less important in the national budget.

While the level of education in Costa Rica is clearly high for the region, and one of the reasons why the country is so popular with foreign business investors, it seems that a good education is increasingly becoming an issue of wealth.

Reluctant Literacy

So, despite the much-trumpeted statistics, it is not a shock to learn that Ticos are not big readers. Real literacy levels may actually not be as high as the figures suggest, as the tests measure little more than the ability to write your own name. In fact, many people from the lower classes clearly have trouble writing. Although Spanish is a phonetic language—meaning spelling mistakes should theoretically be all but impossible—misspellings are common everywhere. It is common, for example, to see welcome signs saying *bienbenido* (instead of *bienvenido*), vendors selling *copoz* (instead of *copos*), and no-smoking notices saying *grasias por no fumar* (instead of *gracias por no fumar*).

Shop assistants use calculators to do the simplest of sums and, according to the Biesanzes, directory inquiries staff waste large amounts of time dealing with people too flummoxed by alphabetical order to use telephone directories.

Nearly every time I have seen a Tico reading a book, it has been the Bible. While reading novels in public, I have even been told by well-meaning strangers that I could ruin my eyesight or make myself sick.

The government is clearly concerned. Newspapers and advertising hoardings carry messages from role models such as football trainers urging young people to read, but apparently to little avail.

Bookshop owner Darren Mora said, "People don't get into the habit of reading because books are too expensive for many people. In any case, most bookshops only stock text books and literary classics."

Libraries are not exactly user-friendly either. You can't just browse among the books, but have to fiddle through old-fashioned card files, fill in a form for each book and ask the librarian—who will probably demand your *cédula* (identity card) or passport—to bring the books to you. You may not remove the books from the library and can only use them for a few hours.

"How are you going to read a novel in an environment like that?" asked Mora. "My nephew, who's in university, has never read a non-academic book in his life, and I know there are many others like him."

Although most Ticos say they're too busy to read, many people—especially women—spend hours watching the huge variety of addictive Mexican or Venezuelan *telenovelas* (soap operas), which they freely admit is a bad habit. Most houses have several televisions, and flickering screens can be seen even in the tiniest shack in a San José *tugurio* (shanty town).

Higher Education

Following the closure of the University of Santo Tomás in 1888, the country didn't have another university until the University of Costa Rica was established in 1940. The number of universities, however, has mushroomed out of control since then. With the higher status and better job prospects associated with having a degree, demand for university education is massive. Now, there are four state universities and almost 40 private ones that together churn out tens of thousands of graduates each year. Many of these private institutions offer only specialised courses and standards are often low.

This rapid growth in the number of graduates, combined with the decline in public sector jobs (traditionally a huge source of graduate employment) since the crisis-hit 1980s, means the number of graduates now outstrips the number of professional jobs available.

UCR student Tomás Fernández said, "This is a small country, so opportunities are limited. Soon we're going to be in a situation like Cuba, with lawyers and doctors driving taxis. Already most of us are looking for work abroad as it's really the only way forward."

THE COUNTRY

For its size, Costa Rica is one of the most physically diverse countries imaginable. Local newspaper advertisements announce houses for sale just 15 minutes outside San José and boast of their 'great climate'. It's not a joke, as within the space of just a few miles, the topography, vegetation and temperature can go from being strongly reminiscent of rolling Devon hills to something more like *Out of Africa*.

One of the country's most distinctive features is its volcanoes. Seven of them are active and straddle the meeting place of two tectonic plates along the Pacific Rim of Fire. These also give rise to frequent earth tremors, occasional quakes and have helped build the three mountain ranges that run through the country. Costa Rica's spine is the continental divide, rising to 3,820 m (12,533 ft) at Mount Chirripó in the Talamanca range, the second highest peak in Central America.

On mountaintops, vegetation is limited to elfin cloud forest and stunted *páramo* (Alpine moor-land) shrubs. The temperature can drop to freezing, and hot water bottles are recommended for a comfortable night's sleep in the highest villages.

At the other extreme, in the north-western province of Guanacaste, the land is arid and the climate oppressively hot, with temperatures rising above 35°C (95°F). Guanacaste's desiccated and deforested, though beautiful, plains are home to huge cattle ranches, and are dotted with shady Guanacaste trees, shaped like giant mushrooms. The remaining natural forest is deciduous, the trees losing their leaves in the unbearable summer heat.

Cattle on the Guanacaste plains—the archetypal scene of the north.

In between the two extremes lies the Meseta Central, the central highland plateau which is now home to well over half the country's population in the urban sprawl of San José and its surrounding towns. This is the traditional coffee-growing area, and the climate is mild thanks to the altitude—San José stands 1,150 m (3,773 ft) above sea level—and temperatures rarely exceed 25°C (77°F).

Both coasts are hot, and are home to steamy banana and African palm plantations (excluding the Guanacaste part of the Pacific coast). While the Pacific side has a distinct dry season, the Caribbean coast is rainy all year round, and blanketed in a profusion of wild greenery.

There's no escaping the fact that Costa Rica (again, except Guanacaste) is a very wet country. During the rainy season (May to November), one can expect at most an hour or so of rain each day in neighbouring Nicaragua, but in Costa Rica it sometimes seems the clouds will never lift again, and parts of the country receive 7.5 m (25 ft) of rain a year. "Costa Rica has two seasons," Ticos joke, "the rainy season and the even rainier season."

Like Eskimos with their 57 words for snow, Ticos have up to a dozen terms for rain—from drizzly *pelo de gato* (literally 'cat's fur') to a *baldazo* or *aguacero* (downpour), and a *temporal* (heavy rain falling without let-up over several days during the rainy season). Thanks to the large amount of rain, Costa Rica also has more rivers and a higher volume of water for a country its size than any other nation in the world except New Zealand.

Costa Rica's variety of terrain and climate has given rise to mind-boggling biodiversity. Although it only covers 0.03 per cent of the planet's surface, Costa Rica is thought to contain around 5 per cent of the world's plant and animal species—more per square kilometre than any other country in the world. Corcovado National Park, in the south-west corner of the country, has been called by *National Geographic* magazine 'the most biologically intense place on Earth'.

The country is home to 1,500 types of trees, 6,000 species of flowering plants (including more than 1,000 orchids), 10 per cent of the world's butterfly species and more bird varieties (850) than in the United States and Canada combined.

The country contains 12 'life zones' based on forest type, altitude and precipitation, which may each contain an even larger range of habitats. Despite everything the tourist literature may say, however, none of these zones is actually a rainforest. Although you will, undoubtedly, get incredibly wet in Costa Rican forests, true rainforests only exist in Asia, Africa and South America, where enormous forests create their own rain, which falls every day.

The Instituto Nacional de Biodiversidad (INBio) has an excellent website providing details and news stories about Costa Rica's species and environment. The address is http://www.inbio.ac.cr.

FARMING AND LAND DISTRIBUTION

The entire history of Costa Rica has been based on agriculture. Ticos' roots with the land remain strong. The city centres are almost 100 per cent commercial with city dwellers preferring to live on the outskirts, where many still rear chickens or at least have a small vegetable or maize patch. The names of barrios in the capital also reveal their recent rural history, for example, Hatillo (little ranch) and Dos Pinos (two pines). But with more than half of the people now living in urban areas, the face of agriculture has changed drastically.

Today, according to the Biesanzes in *The Ticos*, more than half of all Costa Rican landowners own less than 10 hectares (14.7 acres), which adds up to about 5 per cent of the total farming land. Of these, 37 per cent have *minifundios* of less than 2 hectares (3 acres), which are too small to satisfy the basic needs of a family. In the 1990s, just 2.8 per cent of landowners owned large *latifundios* (usually cattle ranches), which made up 47 per cent of the country's farmland.

In contrast with the past, there are now thousands of *campesinos* with no land, and with no choice but to work as day labourers for larger landowners. Despite ongoing but under-funded government land distribution programmes, the numbers of such *campesinos* and the scale of rural poverty are growing all the time. This is a result of both population growth and the fact that nearly all land is now privately owned or in state-protected parks. As a result, many desperate people are flooding to the cities, where their lot rarely improves.

Perhaps most importantly, the role of coffee in the country has changed dramatically. Carolyn Hall said in *El Café y el Desarrollo Histórico-Geográfico de Costa Rica*: 'Fifty years ago, to talk of alternatives to coffee was considered heresy or an affront to the fatherland; the 'golden bean' was so venerated in Costa Rica that tearing out a coffee field virtually constituted national agony.'

When coffee prices rose after World War II, dozens of countries rushed to plant coffee, the world's second biggest dollar commodity after oil. Supply soon outstripped demand and prices went into a free fall from which they have never really recovered.

Many farmers complain that the cost of producing coffee is more than what they earn from it. Hundreds of fields have been ripped out and today, the crop only covers 2 per cent of the land, while San José's rapid growth has permanently cemented over what were once some of the country's most fertile coffee lands.

The crop accounted for only 16 per cent of export earnings in 1995. With ongoing attempts to diversify the economy, many former coffee fields have been planted with higher-earning ornamental plants and ferns.

Bananas are the other major source of income from the land, and now bring in twice as much money as coffee. Costa Rica is the second biggest banana producer in the world after Ecuador.

The difference is that, where the coffee economy was traditionally one of small entrepreneurial family farmers, banana farming requires a lot more land to be profitable. This has led to domination by big, often foreign-owned, firms with local workers (the majority of whom are Nicaraguans) being exploited as *peons*. Increasingly, many plantations have closed down due to disease, and have been given over to other crops, such as African palm.

The other main farming activity is cattle ranching, which increased to such a point that by 1975, there were as many cattle in the country as people. The clearing of land for cattle farming has drastically changed the landscape. Despite declining beef sales, more than two-thirds of all the country's agricultural land was pasture by 1994.

PROVINCES AND TOWNS

Costa Rica is divided into seven provinces: San José, Heredia, Alajuela, Cartago, Puntarenas, Guanacaste and Puerto Limón (generally just known as Limón). Almost three-quarters of the population live in the Meseta Central provinces of San José, Heredia, Alajuela and Cartago, while Limón is the most sparsely populated province. Few of the towns are big, but listed below are some of the most interesting.

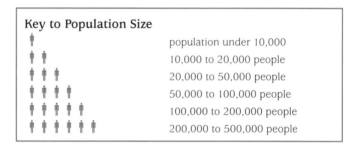

Key to Population Size

population under 10,000
10,000 to 20,000 people
20,000 to 50,000 people
50,000 to 100,000 people
100,000 to 200,000 people
200,000 to 500,000 people

Alajuela

Located 18 km (11.2 miles) north-west of San José, Alajuela is slightly warmer than the capital. Home to the international airport and birthplace of the national hero Juan Santamaría, Alajuela is a little less dirty and bustling than San José, but otherwise fairly similar. The Ojo de Agua Springs Complex is a popular weekend spot with Ticos. Alajuela is also a good base from which to explore the butterfly farm at La Guácima, the craft village of Sarchí, and the Poás Volcano.

San José

The capital city is infuriating and charming at the same time, with congested narrow streets, crowded markets, hustlers and beggars, excellent museums, galleries and theatres, fast food outlets and cosmopolitan restaurants. Located on the Meseta Central, the city has a cool, pleasant climate. There's only a small amount of colonial architecture, which survives in Barrios Amón and Otoya, but the lavish Teatro Nacional and pre-Colombian gold and jade museums are must-sees. The economic and cultural centre of the country, it's almost impossible to go from one point in the country to another without passing through chaotic Chepe as the locals call San José.

Cartago 🕴 🕴 🕴 🕴 🕴

In the shadow of Volcán Irazú, the old capital of Cartago is most famous for the Byzantine-style Basílica de Nuestra Señora de Los Angeles, the cathedral that is home to the nation's patron saint, La Negrita. Up to a million pilgrims make a trip here on 2 August. Cartago also boasts the ruins of the Iglesia de la Parroquia Church, which collapsed during the earthquake of 1910. The city is also near beautiful Orosí, Lankaster Gardens (famous for its orchids) and the rarely visited Parque Nacional Tapantí.

Heredia 🕴 🕴 🕴 🕴 🕴

Located 11 km (6.8 miles) north of San José in the heart of coffee-growing country, Heredia is a student town with the most traditional feel of all the big Meseta Central capitals. Heredia has interesting architectural sites, such as the cathedral, built in a squat, earthquake-proof style, and El Fortín, a small fortress just off the Parque Central. Nearby is the colonial town of Barva and the excellent *finca* of Café Britt (Costa Rica's most popular coffee) which runs a fascinating tour about the history of coffee in the country.

Puerto Limón 🕴 🕴 🕴 🕴

The capital of Limón province, this city has a large black population plus a Chinese community (the legacy of the railway construction years). Isla Uvita, where Christopher Columbus first set foot on Costa Rican soil, is just offshore. 'Was there a dingier backwater in the whole world?' asked Paul Theroux in *The Old Patagonian Express*, going on to say that Limón smelt of 'dead barnacles and damp sand, flooded sewers, brine, oil, cockroaches, and tropical vegetation which, when soaked, gives off the hot moldy vapor you associate with compost heaps in summer'. Limón's reputation as dirty and rough is rather unfair, but no one can deny it has been somewhat neglected since the banana boats shifted to the nearby, deeper natural harbour at Moín. Limón is famous for its big street carnival celebrating Columbus' arrival in the New World held on 12 October.

Puntarenas

The capital of Puntarenas province was Costa Rica's biggest port before the railway was built to Limón. Goods were brought here by ox cart and then shipped around Cape Horn to Europe—a journey of several months. Ferries run from here to the southern tip of the Nicoya Peninsula, home to popular surfing beach villages such as Montezuma and Malpaís. Puntarenas, built along a tongue of sand in the Gulf of Nicoya, is popular with Tico holidaymakers, though the seawater here is polluted.

Ciudad Quesada (San Carlos)

An important farming and ranching centre, with a huge cattle fair and auction held each April. Ciudad Quesada is situated on the north-western slopes of the Cordillera Central and is famous for its beautifully tooled leather saddlery.

Guápiles

The transport centre for the Río Frío banana-growing region, Guápiles is just over 60 km (37 miles) north-east of San José. Guápiles is a good base from which to visit the Rainforest Aerial Tram in the Braulio Carrillo National Park.

Liberia

The capital of Guanacaste, Liberia is a hot, dusty town in the heart of cattle country with many whitewashed colonial houses. Many houses still have *puertas de sol*—an ingenious corner door, which lets light in but keeps heat out. Life centres around the shady Parque Central, although the town gets very busy during the late-August festival celebrating Guanacaste's annexation to Costa Rica. Liberia is a good base for visiting Pacific coast beaches, the traditional pottery-making village of Guaitíl, and the Rincón de la Vieja, Palo Verde, Guanacaste and Santa Rosa national parks.

Nicoya � ♦ ♦

The biggest town in the Península de Nicoya, it has a pleasant central park and a white colonial church. Nicoya is a big cattle centre located close to beaches, Santa Cruz (Costa Rica's folklore capital) and the traditional pottery-making town of Guaitíl.

Turrialba ♦ ♦ ♦

The town is a base for white-water rafting on the Río Reventazón River and trips to the Guayabo archaeological site. Also fascinating is the nearby tropical agronomy research centre. Centro Agronómico Tropical de Investigación y Enseñanza (CATIE) is one of the top five tropical research centres in the world.

Golfito ♦ ♦

Situated on the Golfo Dulce, one of the world's few tropical fjords, Golfito is the most important port in the south. It was the headquarters of United Fruit Company from 1938 to 1985 (when the company finally pulled out of Costa Rica because of banana disease, rising costs and labour agitation). In the northern part of the town, you can still see the old company houses with their airy verandahs and lush gardens. Surrounded by thickly forested hills, Golfito was used as the setting for *Chico Mendes*, a film about a real life Brazilian rubber trapper working to save the rain forest. Golfito is pretty run-down these days, but it is still popular with Ticos for its duty-free shopping.

Quepos ♦ ♦

This is a small, ugly town which made its fortune from bananas and then African palm. Today, tourism is the biggest earner, as Quepos, 'the Benidorm of Costa Rica', is located very close to the Parque Nacional Manuel Antonio. Quepos is a gay-friendly town and is also big on sport fishing.

Cahuita ♦
A laid-back Caribbean beach village located 40 km (25 miles) south of Limón and adjoining the beautiful marine park: Parque Nacional Cahuita. Like nearby Puerto Viejo, Cahuita is a quiet place, where Rasta colours are out in force, and horses snooze on the beach or wander the streets snatching flowers from gardens. You can snorkel, dive, surf and fish here.

Fortuna ♦
The base for trips to the active Arenal Volcano, as well as white-water rafting and windsurfing on the Lago de Arenal reservoir. Fortuna is a clean, tranquil country town with a nearby waterfall, caves, wildlife refuge and hot springs.

Jacó ♦
This is a busy central Pacific coast surfing town filled with bars, clubs and nightlife. Jacó is also a good base from which to visit Parque Nacional Carara. The long beach at Jacó has some of the most consistent waves and rip tides in the country.

Puerto Jiménez ♦
Known as Puerto Hellmenez by local expatriates because of its stifling climate, Jiménez grew largely as a result of logging and gold mining, which gives the place a decidedly dusty, frontier feel. It is also the base for heading into the wilderness of the Osa Peninsula's remote Corcovado National Park.

Puerto Viejo ♦
This town in the banana-growing lands of the north-east has a steamy jungle feel. Historically, goods were shipped down the Sarapiquí River to the San Juan River on the Nicaraguan border, and from there to the Caribbean. Several jungle lodges

and the La Selva biological research station take advantage of the proximity of the tropical wet forest of the Parque Nacional Braulio Carrillo.

San Ramón 👤

Located halfway between San José and Puntarenas, San Ramón is known as the 'city of presidents and poets', as many Ticos in these two occupations were born or lived here. It is a friendly town with a big Saturday farmers' market.

Santa Elena/Monteverde 👤

A straggling community spread out along the unpaved road to the world-famous Monteverde cloud forest reserve. Monteverde has a sizeable community of American dairy-farming Quakers, foreign and local artists, a cheese factory making real Cheddar, and the Monteverde Institute, which carries out research into sustainable tourism, agriculture, etc.

Zarcero 👤

At around 1,700 m (5,577 ft) in the mountains of the Cordillera Central north of San José and near San Ramón, the Zarcero area has an almost Alpine feel. The town is most famous for its bizarre Dalí-esque topiary in front of the church. Local artist Evangelisto Blanco has sculpted dozens of trees into various human and animal shapes, and surreal arches. Look out also for regional food specialities such as *palmito* cheese and peach preserves.

PROTECTED AREAS

Forest cover declined rapidly from 75 per cent in 1950 to around 47 per cent in 2005. However, the country's very broken terrain and (until recently) relatively sparse population has left many pockets of primary, virgin forest (in 2005 adding up to 7.5 per cent of total forest cover). More than a quarter of the territory is now protected in some form or another by Costa Rica's pioneering system of parks, refuges and reserves set up since 1969. There are about 136 protected areas in Costa Rica.

Tourism is now the country's biggest foreign income earner, and as most tourists come specifically to visit the parks, environmentalists hope official protection, currently often only patchy, will be strengthened. The protected areas are broken down into:

- **National Parks (Parques Nacionales)**
  Twenty-three national parks are equipped for tourism and most frequently visited, surrounded by 'green' buffer zones in which limited farming and hunting is allowed.

- **Biological Reserves (Reservas Biológicas)**
  Nineteen areas of special ecological interest, often conserved for scientific research.

- **National Wildlife Refuges (Refugios Nacionales de Vida (or Fauna) Silvestre**
  Twenty areas preserving special habitats for wildlife.

- **Private Reserves (Reservas Privadas)**
  Six biological reserves and one national wildlife refuge are privately run reserves. These include Monteverde/Santa Elena and the Cabo Blanco on the Nicoya Peninsula. Other smaller reserves, often owned by foreigners, are also being set up.

There are also about 30 protected areas, 13 indigenous people's reserves and four wetlands.

Remember that despite the huge number of tourists, some parks are surprisingly remote and are very definitely not theme parks. Always take plenty of sunscreen, water, a hat and insect repellent. Keep your eyes peeled for snakes and peccaries. If peccaries attack, your best option is to climb a tree. On beaches, look out for jellyfish, sharks and rip tides. Several people drown on Costa Rican beaches each year—usually because they panic. Instead of fighting against the water, wait until the current becomes weaker then swim back to the beach at a 45 degree angle. Swimming back in directly will just lead you straight back into the current. Another warning: don't swim on beaches where turtles nest as these are usually patrolled by sharks waiting to gobble up hatchlings.

These are some of the most popular or important protected areas:

- **Parque Nacional Rincón de la Vieja**
  In a landscape of dry and deciduous forest, the main volcano rises to a height of 1,916 m (6,285 ft). One of Costa Rica's active volcanoes, its last big eruption was in 1992, and the 14,084-hectare (20,717-acre) park offers good hiking and opportunities to see 'glooping' mud pots, steam vents, and sulphurous springs. The park's also famous for the purple guaria morada orchid, Costa Rica's national flower.

- **Parque Nacional Palo Verde**
  Seasonal wetland that is a major attraction for birders, as many rare water bird species live or migrate here from September to March. The 16,804-hectare (24,718-acre) park, however, is under threat from wide-scale rice farming on its outskirts, which requires the use of large amounts of pesticide.

- **Parque Nacional Guanacaste**
  This 32,512-hectare (47,825-acre) park, adjacent to Parque Nacional Santa Rosa, was created out of cattle ranching land in 1989. It provides an added range of life zones to help local wildlife survive year-round in the sometimes severe conditions of dry forest.

- **Parque Nacional Santa Rosa**
  This 37,117-hectare (54,599-acre) park, the oldest in the country, is famous for La Casona—the colonial hacienda where the infamous William Walker was hounded out of Costa Rica by the army of President Mora in 1856. The park is also important as it contains the largest remaining area of tropical dry forest in Central America, and beautiful, unspoilt beaches.

- **Reserva Biológica Carara**
  Five life zones are found within this 4,700-hectare (6,913-acre) park north of Jacó. This transition zone between the dry environment further north and the Pacific wet forests of the south has abundant wildlife, and this is, aside from Corcovado, Costa Rica's most important refuge for the scarlet macaw.

- **Parque Nacional Corcovado/ Piedras Blancas**
  This 55,000-hectare (80,905-acre) park of lowland Pacific tropical forest bristles with tapirs, herds of peccaries, four species of monkeys and the largest population of scarlet macaws in Central America. If you're very lucky you may see jaguars fishing on the shore. It's still almost pristine, thanks to the fact that getting in and out requires a commando-style 20 km (12.5 mile) trek along beach, through jungle, and across rivers. Watch out as some rivers contain crocodiles and, at high tide, sharks. The park, however, has problems with illegal logging, gold mining and poaching.

- **Volcán Poás**
  North-east of San Ramón is one of the world's biggest volcanoes, topped by a stunning 1,500-m (4,921-ft) wide crater, with a sulphurous cauldron filled with steaming turquoise water. Its last major eruption was in 1910. This is Costa Rica's most-visited park and, at just over 5,000 hectares (7,355 acres), one of the smallest and easiest to reach—a road runs right to the top. A second extinct crater holds a lagoon and a system of paths runs through dwarf cloud-forest at the summit.

- **Parque Nacional Manuel Antonio**
  Over-visited and very small, this 683-hectare (1,005-acre) park on the central Pacific coast near Quepos was the setting for Ridley Scott's Columbus movie *1492: Conquest of Paradise.* White sand tropical beaches, steep forested hills, good trails, beautiful Pacific views—and one of the last haunts of the tiny squirrel monkey.

- **Parque Nacional Tortuguero**
  The 'Amazon' of Costa Rica on the north Caribbean coast is criss-crossed by waterways and lagoons, and the only means of travel through this strip of luxuriantly wet tropical forest is by boat. Wildlife, such as monkeys and crocodiles, is abundant, and the park's beaches protect the most important nesting grounds of the green turtle in the whole Caribbean, as well as those of the

hawksbill turtle. The park, however, is being steadily encroached upon by banana plantations, which are also causing pollution through the vast amounts of pesticides used.

- **Parque Nacional Cahuita**
  This 1,067-hectare (1,570-acre) Caribbean coastal park includes some of Costa Rica's remaining living coral reef.

- **Parque Nacional Braulio Carrillo**
  The closest national park to San José, and visible from the steep road that passes through it down to the Caribbean coast. It was made a national park in 1978 as a 'pay-off' compromise for the construction of this road through virgin forest, and includes 45,899 hectares (67,517 acres) of land from just around sea level up to 2,906 m (9,534 ft) at the top of Volcán Barva. This thick premontane tropical wet forest contains the world-famous Aerial Tram—an ingenious way of viewing the forest canopy.

- **Parque Nacional Volcán Irazú**
  The highest active volcano in Costa Rica at 3,432 m (11,260 ft), last erupted on 19 March 1963, coinciding with the visit of US president John F Kennedy. The summit is a lunar landscape of ash, pyroclastic material and four craters. Both the Pacific and Atlantic oceans are visible from the summit on clear days.

- **Monumento Nacional Guayabo**
  About 85 km (53 miles) from San José, this is Costa Rica's national monument and top archaeological site. Originally inhabited around 300 CE and constructed with stones brought from some distance away, Guayabo was 'discovered' in the late 19th century. The area has still not been fully excavated, but cobbled streets, aqueducts and petroglyphs have been found. Guayabo, like some other Central American indigenous sites, was mysteriously abandoned around 1400.

- **Parque Nacional Tapantí**
  A small park measuring 6,080 hectares (8,944 acres) on the northern slopes of the Cordillera de Talamanca.

The nightly spectacular at Volcán Arenal.

It's also very wet as it contains around 150 rivers and receives up to 7 m (almost 23 ft) of rain per year. The largest moth in North and South America can be found here—Thysania agripina.

- **Parque Nacional Volcán Arenal**
  A relatively new national park, it contains one of the western hemisphere's most active volcanoes as well as vast biodiversity, being home to about half of all the species of vertebrates in Costa Rica. Arenal, dormant from around 1500, erupted on 29 July 1968, with lava flows killing between 80 to 90 people and 45,000 cattle. Since then the volcano has spewed out ash and lava on an almost daily basis. Near Fortuna, you can relax at night in steaming hot springs with a cocktail, watching the volcano explode above you.

- **Reservas Monteverde and Santa Elena**
  The country's second most-visited tourist spot, this world-famous, epiphyte-laden cloud forest is made up of various private reserves, and is home to birds such as the quetzal and the three-wattled bellbird—as well as dozens of species of orchids. The endemic golden toad is sadly extinct (*refer to 'The Environment' in this chapter on page 56*). There are also plenty of adrenalin-

pumping opportunities on various canopy rides, where you whiz through the treetops harnessed onto zip cords. For the less adventurous, there are networks of canopy bridges and night tours to spot nocturnal fauna, such as tarantulas, porcupines and sloths.

- **Reserva Biológica Lomas Barbudal**
  Close to the Palo Verde park, this 2,279-hectare (3,352-acre) reserve of tropical dry forest protects many species of endangered trees, such as mahogany and rosewood. It also contains many insect species, including 250 types of bee—about a quarter of all the bees in the world—including the Africanised 'killer' bee.

- **Parque Nacional Marino las Baulas**
  Most of the terrestrial areas of this park contain all six species of mangroves in the country, as well as plenty of crocodiles and water birds. The stars of the show are the huge leatherback turtles (called *baulas*), some up to 5 m (16 ft) long, which nest here between October and March.

- **Refugio Nacional de Fauna Silvestre Ostional**
  Midway between Sámara and Paraíso, this is an important nesting area for the olive ridley sea turtle (from July to November). The park was set up to protect the nests and turtles from over-poaching by locals. Limited egg harvesting is still allowed—the eggs are popular drinking snacks (*bocas*) in Tico bars.

- **Parque Nacional Barra Honda**
  A park which protects more than 40 spectacular subterranean caverns, some over 200 m (656 ft) deep. The caves, in limestone hills on the Nicoya Peninsula, contain a variety of bizarre rock formations and specially-evolved animals.

- **Parque Nacional Marino las Ballenas**
  A 4,500-hectare (6,620-acre) marine park protecting Isla Uvita (an island about 20 minutes by boat from Limón), with its nesting colonies of frigate birds, blue-footed boobies, and other seabirds. The area is excellent for snorkelling and diving, and humpback whales migrate

through the area from December to March. Dolphins and turtles are also seen.

- **Reserva Biológica Isla del Caño**
  Located 20 km (12 miles) west of Bahía Drake, off the northern part of the Nicoya Peninsula, this reserve includes the 300-hectare (441-acre) island plus 5,800 hectares (6,531 acres) of ocean in south-western Costa Rica, and is excellent for snorkelling and diving. Some of the pre-Colombian stone spheres have also been found on the island, which is thought to have been a Diquis Indian burial ground. Bizarrely, it also has the distinction of being the place most frequently hit by lightning in the entire region.

- **Refugio Nacional de Fauna Silvestre Golfito**
  Originally protected to save the Golfito watershed, this 1,309-hectare (1,925-acre) park also protects rare and ancient plants, such as orchids, tree ferns and cycads (ancient palm-like trees with leathery leaves).

- **Parque Internacional La Amistad**
  The park straddles Costa Rica and Panama. Declared a UNESCO World Heritage Site in 1983, this is the largest protected area in Costa Rica at 250,000 hectares (367,750 acres) with 340,000 hectares (500,140 acres) of buffer zones, and a further 440,000 hectares (647,240 acres) in Panama. This reserve is an important biological bridge in the isthmus, protecting rare species and diverse environments (nine of the country's 12 life zones are found here), as well as indigenous reserves. More than 500 species of bird have been spotted here, of which 49 are endemic.

- **Parque Nacional Chirripó**
  Costa Rica's highest mountain, Cerro Chirripó, stands at 3,820 m (12,533 ft), and is located in this fairly large park measuring just over 50,000 hectares (73,550 acres). Climbing Chirripó is fascinating for the varied vegetation zones you pass through, as well as the glacial valleys. On clear days you can see both the Pacific and Caribbean oceans from the summit, although the temperature may be around freezing. In

the dry season, accommodation in mountain huts is limited and advance booking of up to three months is recommended.

- **Reserva Biológica Hitoy-Cerere**
  The wettest reserve in the parks system is very remote and seldom visited, with dense vegetation, thick mud and broken terrain that make for hard hiking.
- **Refugio Nacional de Vida Silvestre Gandoca-Manzanillo**
  This reserve contains one of Costa Rica's only two living coral reefs, beautiful beaches and many unusual bird species. Even the giant and extremely rare Harpy eagle (thought to be extinct in the country), was reportedly spotted here recently.
- **Refugio Nacional de Vida Silvestre Caño Negro**
  This remote wetland reserve contains a huge variety of waterbirds, including the largest population of olivaceous cormorants in the country.
- **Refugio Nacional de Fauna Silvestre Barra del Colorado y Tortuguero**
  This large reserve adjoins Tortuguero. It's harder to get to than Tortuguero, and is most popular with sports fishermen. The area borders Nicaragua, which made it virtually off-limits during the Sandinista-Contra war. This isolation has kept wildlife better protected than in Tortuguero, although illegal logging is rife.
- **Parque Nacional Isla del Coco**
  The inspiration for Robert Louis Stevenson's *Treasure Island* and the setting for the opening aerial shots in Steven Spielberg's *Jurassic Park*, this remote Pacific island lies about 532 km (339 miles) south-west of Cabo Blanco. Early sailors, pirates and whalers used to stock up on fresh water here, and it is also reputedly the site of numerous stashes of buried treasure. The world's largest uninhabited island, it has a unique ecosystem, with around 140 species of endemic plants and animals. Diving here is among the best in the world, with schools of hammerhead sharks seen in their hundreds. It is also a UNESCO World Heritage Site. However, wild pigs—left behind by would-be settlers who abandoned the island

in the early 20th century—are rapidly destroying the environment, along with introduced rats, cats and goats. Trips to the island are extraordinarily expensive.

THE ENVIRONMENT

With well over a million visitors each year, tourism—in large part eco-tourism—competes with the manufacture of micro-processors to be Costa Rica's major source of foreign exchange. Thanks to its dazzling biodiversity, visitors flock here to see birds and animals already rare or extinct elsewhere in the region, such as tapirs, squirrel monkeys, manatees and sea turtles.

Costa Rica is determined to exploit tourist income still further in the future, so one might imagine that vigorous steps are being taken to preserve its 'golden goose'. However, this country, which paints itself in tourist literature as an ecological paradise, looks very different when you see the piles of garbage along roadsides, trucks spewing plumes of pure soot and the broken trunks of newly felled trees.

Costa Rica has done much more to protect its wild areas than any of its neighbours and the parks are, for now, still utterly beautiful. It's important to know, however, that there are numerous and growing threats to the very resource base upon which the country's future economy hopes to depend. This is the side of the environmental story you will not read about in the tourist literature.

The Green Dream Under Threat

At the time the national parks system was being set up in the 1970s (thanks to visionary leadership within the conservation community), Costa Rica had one of the world's highest rates of deforestation. This destruction still continues at a rate of about 60,000 hectares (88,260 acres) per year, six times the size of the showcase Monteverde cloud-forest reserve, to provide new land for cattle farming and banana plantations. Such rapid deforestation, combined with heavy rains and steep mountainsides, is a serious problem. In the 1980s, Costa Rica lost two billion tons of topsoil. Today, about half the country is affected by erosion.

By the 1990s, it was realised that the national parks were increasingly ending up as islands of greenery with development encroaching on all sides, and suffering from problems around their fringes such as pesticide poisoning, logging, over-fishing, sugar cane-burning and dredging, so a system of 11 'buffer zones' was set up.

This seemed like a good solution. In reality, however, the government has only bought about 44 per cent of all the supposedly 'protected' land. With an internal debt of around US$ 600 million, this situation is unlikely to change anytime soon. In any case, even with buffer zones, many of the protected areas are simply too small to maintain species such as jaguars, which need vast territories.

Such habitat fragmentation has already contributed to the extinction of several species such as the Harpy eagle and giant anteater. In fact, 26 animal species and 456 plant species were on the endangered list in 1996. The famous golden toad of Monteverde, found only in a few rain pools in the reserve's elfin cloud forest and nowhere else in the world, was extinct by 1989—probably as a result of climate change, but possibly also through removal of too many animals by over-enthusiastic scientists.

Meanwhile, widely roaming species, although protected in Costa Rica, are often in danger in the absence of international protection. Sea turtles, largely protected (despite egg theft) by conservation projects in Costa Rica, are butchered by fishermen from neighbouring Nicaragua as they return to the country to lay their eggs. Jewellery made from their shells ends up being sold illegally, but openly, to tourists on Costa Rican beaches.

Of Costa Rica's territory, more than half is actually ocean as it extends to include Isla del Coco, located 500 km (311 miles) offshore. There are only about ten areas to protect marine environments. There are only two surviving coral reefs in the country thanks to earthquakes and the clogging effects of erosion run-off, while over-fishing has seen shrimp stocks collapse by more than 50 per cent since the late 1980s. In the Gulf of Nicoya, I found three dead turtles and a dead

Its eggs laid, a turtle returns to sea—but will its offspring hatch successfully or be collected as *boca* drinking snacks for a Tico bar?

dolphin along a stretch of beach—the victims of encounters with huge drag nets or boat propellers.

To add insult to injury, some protected areas are now no longer protected at all. The government has lifted restrictions on building in some such areas in the Meseta Central, for example, claiming this will allow poor people to build houses. Conservationists are cynical, pointing out that land in the increasingly crowded environs of San José is now at a premium, and potentially worth millions of dollars.

It's not all doom and gloom, as the rapid decline in the country's forests (from 75 per cent in 1950 to just 30 per cent in 1990) seems to have been stemmed recently thanks to a major tree-planting programme run by the National Fund for Forest Financing and paid for by a 3.5 per cent tax levied on fossil fuels. From 2000 to 2005, the country gained 15,000 hectares (37,065.8 acres) of tree cover, bringing the total up to 46.8 per cent in 2005.

However, many other innovative projects to help protect the environment, much trumpeted upon inception, have foundered through lack of official resources. One example was a programme to give tax breaks to landowners who set aside forested land, which the hugely overburdened state has been unable to fully fund.

Lack of funds for the national parks system means there are insufficient wardens. Corcovado National Park has only around ten wardens, which works out to about one warden to every 5,500 hectares (8,091 acres). Poachers capture rare species, such as the park's famous scarlet macaws, and visitors can even hear hunters' gunshots. Illegal gold mining also goes on in the park.

Paulino Valverde, a Tico scientist who works at the Sirena biological research station in the park, said, "It's just impossible. I've been here ten years and the funding has become less and less every year. I don't understand how the government wants eco-tourism to be our future source of income if it's not prepared to put in the money to protect what the tourists are coming to see."

Bruce Moffat, of the Nature Conservancy Council in San José, said that corruption is also a problem. "Government staff are paid a pittance and rich landowners can easily entice them into turning a blind eye to activities like illegal logging."

The reality is that not many Ticos have much interest in their environment. Few locals visit the national parks, even though the entry fee is a quarter of the US$ 6 that foreigners pay. All attempts at recycling rubbish have collapsed through lack of interest, and many reasonably well-off Ticos still see hunting and tree-felling as their 'right'—even though the environment can no longer take the strain.

"Unfortunately many Ticos still do not appreciate what we have here," said Ovely Quirós Ríos of the Ministry of the Environment. "A lot of the parks aren't particularly accessible, but that's not really the problem. Most people, if they're going on holiday, would just prefer to go to Miami. We hope to slowly raise awareness through education."

Air and Water Pollution

Pollution is another unpleasant surprise for many visitors, and is a particular problem in San José. The country has a very innovative legal framework to tackle pollution—but apparently lacks the resources or willpower to enforce it. Although all vehicles have had to be fitted with a catalytic converter since 1995, and must sport an *'Ecomarchamo'* sticker certifying that emissions are within certain limits, the clouds of black smoke coming out of many vehicles are testimony to the fact that the rules are flagrantly broken.

The *Ecomarchamo* programme has been riddled by technical problems and corruption, while the import tax on vehicles (more than 50 per cent of the car's cost) means old, polluting vehicles stay on the roads for longer.

Official figures from the government-funded Estado de la Nación report in 2000 show that 75 per cent of air pollution is caused by traffic pollution, which despite the efforts to bring it into check remains more than double the World Health Organisation's established safe maximum levels.

Bruce Moffat said, "Recent studies have shown that air pollution could be reduced by 50 per cent if the tariffs on bringing new cars into the country were reduced by 25 per cent. Unfortunately this is unlikely, as the tax is a huge source of income for the government."

What about the water? While Costa Rica prides itself on its hundreds of gushing rivers, the shocking truth is that pollution and mismanaged or unplanned development could leave the country with serious supply problems within just five years. More than 50 per cent of the country's sewage flows untreated into the Gulf of Nicoya, while the waterways running through the capital are so full of detergent that they look more like torrents of whipped cream. The rivers running off the flanks of the Poás Volcano near Alajuela are completely dead, thanks to the extensive farms growing ornamental plants and ferns, which require large amounts of pesticides.

Banana plantations also use large amounts of pesticides and fertilisers, and the blue plastic bags put over the fruit to speed ripening invariably end up in rivers and waterways. Pesticides used in rice fields in the north are having a serious impact on the nearby Palo Verde National Park, a regionally important site for migrating water birds.

According to the Estado de la Nación report, only 20 per cent of solid rubbish is managed acceptably, while 47 per cent of municipalities simply dump waste in open-air sites. The unresolved issue of dealing with waste is becoming more and more of a headache as cities grow uncontrolled—San José alone grew 80 per cent from 1990 to 2001.

From the Frying Pan into the Fire?

In the north, cattle ranching is the major environmental culprit. It has led to wholesale forest cutting since the 1960s to make way for pasture—in turn increasing drought and the degradation of compacted, cattle-trodden soil. Combined with the fact that the industry is non-labour intensive, ranching has directly caused poverty and massive migration away from the area.

In recent years, cattle ranching has declined with the shrinking of international markets, and the region is now setting its sights on sun'n'surf tourism, with huge complexes being built by Mexican and Spanish consortia. The very antithesis of eco-tourism, such developments are already causing social discontent by sucking up precious water to irrigate golf courses and threatening to turn the north-western coast into a new Cancún, as Bruce Moffat explains.

"This kind of development could lose the country its distinctive eco-tourism niche, and have long-term economic consequences. I think the government is basically shooting itself in the foot by promoting these get-rich-quick developments," he said.

Various other plans the government has on the drawing board include opening up some of the national parks for hydroelectric exploitation, in order to boost sales of electricity to neighbouring countries such as Nicaragua. One such project under consideration, to build one of the tallest dams in the world, would flood the valley of the Río Grande de Térraba in the south of the country and displace an indigenous population. Indigenous people feel particularly helpless because, while they have surface rights to the land in their reserves, they do not own underground resources. This means the government could theoretically grant licences for mining under their feet.

Meanwhile, inhabitants of the Caribbean coast were outraged by permission given by the government to a US firm to explore the whole coastline for oil—including the national park of Cahuita, which contains one of the country's only two surviving coral reefs (the permit was revoked in 2002 due, in part, to enormous local opposition, though the company still has the right to appeal this decision).

More recently, Costa Rica has come under the international spotlight as a centre for the incredibly wasteful shark-finning industry. Millions of sharks are killed worldwide each year for their fins, which are much prized for Asian cuisine and medicine. The sharks often have their fins hacked off and are chucked back into the sea alive, to bleed to death. Sharks, which are slow to reproduce, and therefore easily decimated, are crucial to the health of marine ecosystems, as they eliminate sick and dying fish.

Following the presentation of a petition signed by 70,000 Costa Ricans, including 10,000 schoolchildren, scientists and shark experts, a new law was introduced in 2003 to ban shark finning (though not shark fishing, where the fins are still attached to the body), as well as the fishing of whales, dolphins and turtles.

However, President Pacheco—who came to power declaring his administration would 'make peace with nature'—came under fire for not doing enough to enforce the law. It was found that Taiwanese fishing fleets were exploiting a loophole to unload fins at private docks—which do not fall under Customs law. For example, the *Tico Times* reported that in a single night, one fishing vessel landed approximately three truckloads, or 30 tons, of shark fins without the carcasses attached.

President Pacheco insisted he was doing everything he could to stop shark finning—although some doubted this, given the large sums of campaign funding he apparently received from Taiwanese businessmen.

Bruce Moffat said, "Most Ticos are quite aware of the environmental issues facing the country—but they also have no faith in the government to act honourably. Unfortunately, electoral single term limits here mean that politicians often dedicate their time in office to lining their pockets as comprehensively as possible, with no need to worry about serving their constituents—because they're not going to be re-elected anyway. In this situation, and with up to 25 per cent of the population living in poverty, it is very easy to understand why so many people feel justified in getting involved in relatively high-earning activities like illegal fishing or poaching."

THE PEOPLE

'I believe the government, if the will existed, would be fully capable of attending to and resolving the high-priority necessities of indigenous people, who are still unacceptably marginalised in Costa Rica. What sector of the nation's people could be more 'Tico' than the indigenous peoples, and yet they do not receive basic and vital assistance.'
—Yorleni Leiva, teacher on an indigenous reserve

Like all Latin American people, Costa Ricans are a mixture of many things. Among the ethnic groups which remain distinct today are the indigenous population, Afro-Caribbeans and Chinese (originally brought in to build the jungle railway), North American retirees, and an ever-growing number of Nicaraguans. The population has also been swollen over the years by people fleeing persecution and hardship from all over the world—such as Argentineans, Chileans, Colombians, Russians, Salvadorians and Cubans. You only need to see the number of cars driving through San José waving a particular country's flag after a football match to realise how many communities there are.

Many immigrant groups, such as Italians, Jews and Arabs, have long since been assimilated into the dominant culture. Author Samuel Rovinski said that this is a sign of how easily outsiders are accepted into Tico society.

This, however, has not always been the case with everyone. An entry in an 1875 official gazette seeking to limit Chinese immigration to the country claimed: 'Their abuse of opium and decided inclination to suicide leads them to have a disrespect for life, which makes them a danger, especially in domestic service.' Even today, despite some mixed marriages, the Chinese community still remains quite culturally cohesive and separate.

While all Costa Ricans are Ticos, some are clearly less Tico than others, and in many senses the term only really applies to the huge Spanish *mestizo* majority of the Meseta Central.

The country's population in 2005 stood at four million, up from just 400,000 in 1930. This growth was largely due to the fact that—despite its declining birth rate—Costa Rica has the lowest infant mortality rate (9.95 deaths per 1,000 live births in 2005) in Latin America after Cuba, and a First World life expectancy of 77 years. This can also be attributed to the high level of literacy (96 per cent in 2003), widespread use of contraceptives and family planning, and its high standard of health care.

The population is very young, with 30 per cent of Ticos under the age of 14, and only 5.6 per cent over 65. Ticos have also become, in recent decades, a very urban people (even though they retain many rural habits). Around half of the population lives in the greater San José area alone, and more than two-thirds in the urban sprawl of the Meseta Central.

'White Ticos' and Ideas of Colour

It has only been a few decades since Costa Rican tourist literature trumpeted the 'whiteness' of the people as an attraction. In his 1943 *Nueva Geografía de Costa Rica*, author Jorge León said the country was 'effectively the white state of the Caribbean... in Heredia, 96.6 per cent of the population are direct descendants from Europe—a little more than in New York'.

Compared with other Central Americans, the Ticos really do look quite different—particularly when you see the children streaming out of some of San José's more expensive private schools. Blond hair and blue eyes— owing, perhaps, to original Catalan settlers or German forefathers—are not so unusual. After all, between 1870 and 1920 immigration accounted for up to 25 per cent of population growth.

The 'whiteness' is, however, a myth. The original Spanish settlers were nearly all men, and took Indian women as wives. Mathematically, this makes virtually all Ticos *mestizos*, or of mixed blood.

The country is dominated politically, culturally, and in every other way by the 'white' Ticos of the Meseta Central. Ethnic minorities exist largely only in far-flung pockets, and even the road network is arranged so that to get from one part of the country to another, you have to go through San José.

With transport historically so difficult (the highway to Limón was only built in the 1970s), it is easy to see why areas outside the coffee-growing highlands seemed foreign for so long. Guanacaste has traditionally been little more than a place to go on trips to the beach, and few people have visited the Caribbean coast.

Now, however, with more and more people abandoning the *campo* in search of work or higher education in the cities, cultural assimilation is increasing, although colour is still an issue in Costa Rica. "It's only recently that San José has started to get so cosmopolitan, with the influx of refugees, people from the countryside and the Caribbean, and Nicaraguans," said Darren Mora, a Tico whose complexion could not be described as anything darker than café au lait. "When I was young, people here used to call me *negro*."

Although colonial society was more egalitarian here than in many other corners of the Empire, it was still organised around the Spanish class system. Only those with Spanish heritage could get into positions of influence, and everybody thus wanted to marry their children off to paler-skinned people, even if they were poorer, in order to climb the social ladder.

University of Costa Rica anthropologist Sergio Chávez said, "It is as if the people who run Costa Rica, sitting up here on the Meseta Central, have always tried to make the country's black and indigenous people invisible, and perpetuate this myth that we are all white, or at least lighter-skinned than other Latin Americans.

"Thankfully, society is more dynamic now, and colour is no longer such an impediment to advancement. But you still hear some pretty ignorant remarks, and we still don't really accept our multi-ethnic and cultural nature. We are alienated from our own culture, feel superior to our Central American neighbours, and relate instead to the United States and the paradise of Miami."

BLACK COSTA RICA

Black people in Costa Rica today make up only 3 per cent of the country's population, but despite the poverty and problems they continue to face, they are one of the most vibrant and interesting sections of the country's population.

Most black Costa Ricans arrived as slaves with the Spanish conquistadors in the 16th and 17th centuries to work on large cattle haciendas and cacao farms in the north. While they have long since been assimilated into the population at large, traces of their heritage can still be seen in the features of people from Guanacaste province.

Musical instruments still used in the country, such as the *marimba* (a giant xylophone with gourd resonators) and the *quijongo* (a basic one-stringed double bass) are of African origin. The slaves also left behind some words in Costa Rican Spanish such as *angú* (mashed plantain), *candanga* (the devil), *lapa* (macaw), *mandinga* (coward), *panga* (type of boat) and *timba* (belly).

Today, by far the biggest black population of Costa Rica lives along the Caribbean coast—which in itself forms part of a much bigger, virtually continuous belt of black, English-

In northern Costa Rica, you're rarely far from the haunting sounds of the *marimba*—originally an African musical invention but now 100 per cent Central American.

speaking people stretching all the way from Belize down to Panama.

These immigrants first arrived from Colombia, Nicaragua and Panama, as migrant turtle hunters fishing up and down the coast in the late 18th century. Later, some settled as farmers, planting the coconut groves which today line the coast. They lived almost totally isolated for nearly a century—hunting, trading with the local Talamanca Indians, and supplementing their income by making coconut oil, yucca starch for linen and salt from sea water.

Things changed in the 1870s when the population was swollen by thousands of workers from Jamaica brought in to complete construction of Minor Keith's (the North American banana magnate) railway from San José to the Caribbean. After the railway was built, many Jamaicans—waiting months for back pay—worked in Keith's new United Fruit Company banana plantations. The Jamaican communities steadily grew, hiring English-speaking teachers from their homeland, putting on Shakespeare recitals, dancing the *quadrille* (a 19th century European parlour dance still practised today), and holding Sunday Schools.

However, there was plenty of hostility between the blacks and the locals who were looking for work. The blacks, still intending to save some money and return to Jamaica, felt superior to the Costa Ricans, dubbing them *pañas* (Spaniards). It was held that the *pañas* were dirty, drunk, had lice and spat on the floors of their own houses. Children were even warned that if they were bad, the *pañas* would chop them up with a machete.

The discrimination was two-way. Although no legislation was actually passed controlling their movement, the blacks were, in effect, prevented from leaving the Caribbean area. In the late 1930s, President León Cortés even tried to introduce a colour bar in Limón.

Unfortunately, the prejudices only served the interests of the all-powerful United Fruit Company, known as Mamita Yunai (Mummy United), preventing the formation of cohesive labour unions to fight for decent conditions.

The situation was therefore ripe for the arrival of Marcus Garvey (*see 'Heroes and Villains' in* Chapter Ten: Fast Facts *on page 247*), who preached racial segregation, and formulated a 'Back to Africa' movement after witnessing the exploitation and misery of black workers in the banana plantations.

Garvey's plans were doomed to failure, however, and when the plantations were largely transferred to the Pacific Coast in the 1930s due to union activity and crop disease, the black workers found themselves trapped and increasingly destitute. Many took to cacao farming, although this would later become unsustainable as a result of pest infestations.

The official discrimination against blacks did not end until after the civil war in 1948, when José Figueres Ferrer, president of Costa Rica (from 1948–1949, 1953–1958, and 1970–1974) granted full citizenship to the blacks and gave women the right to vote.

Citizenship, however, has not stopped the communities along the coast from remaining plagued by poverty. The government still invests very little in the province of Limón. For example, while Costa Rica as a whole focused massively on improving health care following the civil war, the communities of the Talamanca coast—despite numerous requests—didn't receive their first doctor until 1977.

For many, the downside of citizenship has been cultural assimilation. Black children, taught by Costa Rican teachers from the Meseta Central, have often been ridiculed for talking in their English dialect, and many youngsters in Caribbean communities now see English as old-fashioned. I have seen older people trying to reason with children chattering away in Spanish, saying, "You should be proud to speak English, it's the language of the world"—and getting nothing but blank looks or giggles.

The old Jamaican places names have also gone—Old Harbour is now Puerto Viejo and Monkey Point is Punta Mona, while English-language Calypso music (developed by slaves as a means of transmitting messages under the noses of their masters) is giving way to salsa. Many people have left the area altogether to look for better opportunities in San José or even abroad.

Little is heard these days of once common African traditions, such as the devil cult *pocomía*. However, the *obi*-men—men with supernatural powers used to cure illnesses or work spells against, or provide protection from, enemies—still exist. Black writer Quince Duncan said that many people have died from easily-curable illnesses because of their firm belief in the *obeah*.

The Jamaican influence is obvious in many other ways. Sitting outside the brightly coloured houses on stilts (which protect against animals and flooding), adults play dominoes. Children carry school books African-style, on their heads, and some of the older men still get together for cricket matches on the beach. Festivals involve the traditional English May Pole Dance, and local cuisine is much more Kingston than San José (*see* Chapter Six: Food and Drink *on page 161*).

On Sundays, as elsewhere in Costa Rica, people get dressed up for church—although in the Caribbean it's more likely to be Baptist, Adventist or Jehovah's Witness (although some people have converted to Catholicism to make life easier). The variety of groups, according to Quince Duncan, is a relic from the old days of slavery, and was encouraged by the British to prevent social cohesion among the slaves.

Many other old traditions still persist, such as Set Up and Nine Nights. When someone dies, the body is prepared, or 'set up' for viewing. Friends and family are summoned, and stay up all night drinking, talking and playing dominoes and cards. After burial the following day, people return every night for nine nights to show respect for the dead and keep the mourning family company. The demands of modern life—such as getting to work on time—make such traditions harder to keep, but they still exist.

People also tell stories of Anansi the spider, passed down by oral tradition and almost identical to those still told to children in West Africa today. Slightly tailored to fit modern times, they are like an African version of Aesop's Fables, where the morally ambiguous spider pits his quick wits against brute force.

While there are plenty of people wandering around sporting dreadlocks, listening to reggae, and smoking ganja, Rastafarianism—unlike in Jamaica—is little more than a fashion statement, and you definitely won't find people who follow true Rastafarian religious principles such as washing with the *akee* fruit instead of soap and never eating a fish more than 30 cm (12 inches) long.

A Different Story

Not everything is reggae and sunshine though. Outspoken Puerto Viejo resident Edwin Patterson said, "We are still suffering. Limón is the poorest province in the land, despite the fact that it brings in more wealth for the state than pretty much anywhere else. We pay taxes to the government, but for them, it's as if we don't exist."

Patterson supports controversial black academic Rigoberto Stewart, who has called for autonomy for the province, and helped found the separatist Partido Auténtico Limonense. The party has long since disappeared as it couldn't win a seat in government, but in the 1980s, the province buzzed with revolutionary talk of armed uprising.

"We should be independent of Costa Rica," said Patterson. "I certainly don't feel Costa Rican, and nor do many others—I'm an African. Unfortunately, the problem is that our black population is disenfranchised and divided."

Opportunities for black people are limited. While a few have risen to fairly prominent political positions under the umbrella of one of the two big parties, many members of their community see them as sell-outs, who have agreed to toe the party line and so cannot possibly represent them.

Growing unemployment and drug problems—Patterson says around 90 per cent of the young black population uses or deals drugs either to earn a living or through sheer disillusionment—are creating pressure that he feels will only be released by violence.

Not everyone is as extreme as Patterson, however. Many mixed race couples can be seen strolling through the centre of Limón, and the pace of life in the Caribbean coastal villages is so relaxed it's very hard to imagine anyone having the energy to riot.

INDIGENOUS PEOPLES

One of the most intriguing and unique archaeological aspects of the country is its profusion of almost perfect rock spheres carved by indigenous Costa Ricans hundreds of years ago and scattered across the Diquis Delta. No one has any idea as to their purpose, and now it seems unlikely that we ever will—because nearly every sphere has been uprooted and hauled off to decorate government buildings and private gardens the length and breadth of the country, sometimes even painted in gaudy colours.

This plundering is indicative of the country's attitude to its indigenous past—and the general lack of understanding or interest in the Indians who inhabit it today. This is perhaps best illustrated by former President Rafael Angel Calderón (since disgraced in the 2004 corruption scandal), who on a state visit to Spain in 1992, explained that Costa Rica had 'no Indians'.

Katya Cordero, a mother-of-two in her mid-30s, recalled her primary schoolteacher's reaction to an essay in which she had written that Columbus had not 'discovered' the Americas. "I remember how upset I was," she said. "All I wrote was that Columbus could not have discovered the place as there were already people living here. The essay came back with a red line through it and a failing mark."

Although the Indian population today numbers just 60,000—a little over 1 per cent of the population—there were probably up to 500,000 people living in the country when Columbus arrived.

Cindy, a university student, added, "It's obvious from looking at any Tico's skin that we all have indigenous blood— but in school, there is much more focus on our Spanish than our indigenous heritage.

"A lot of people speak about the *indios* as if they were a different species. It makes me sick the way we patronise them as *nuestros indígenas* (our indigenous people), and have put them in *reservas* as if they were museum pieces or animals in a zoo. In Panama and Nicaragua, the indigenous people at least live in autonomous areas and can make their own decisions."

Until 1991, the Guaymí and Cabécar peoples did not even have *cédulas* (the identity cards which each citizen needs to do anything from opening a bank account or writing a letter to a newspaper to leaving the country). They were only given the documents— and thus officially recognised as Costa Rican citizens—after taking over roads in San José and occupying the capital's cathedral.

Within the past few decades, however, much greater official efforts have been made to recognise indigenous people's needs. A National Commission on Indigenous

Affairs (CONAI) was set up in 1973, and an Indigenous Law passed in 1977. Since 1976, 21 indigenous reserves have been created.

This, however, may have been too little too late. While communities such as the Bribris and Guaymíes remain relatively culturally intact, their distance from San José means they are often 'out of sight, out of mind'. They score very low on health and literacy indices relative to the national average.

In 1995, the 124 schools in the country's indigenous reserves met only two-thirds of demand, with 40 per cent of teachers not even graduates. Despite the government's promises of bilingual education, nearly all material used in schools is in Spanish and Meseta Central-focused.

Few Indians actually own any land now, having been tricked or cheated into selling it, or driven off by poachers and settlers. One reserve, China Kicha, even ceased to exist after being over-run by white settlers.

In the north and centre of the country particularly, reserves are so small they are like pinpricks on the map. The Huetar Indians, once fierce warriors who dominated the whole of the Meseta Central, are now confined to less than 5,000 people living in two small reserves.

The incursions have had a major impact on the indigenous people's physical and cultural survival. They have been unable to fight back against hunters, miners and bigger interests, such as the United Fruit Company (suspected to have orchestrated the poisoning of the last Bribri *cacique* (chief) Antonio Saldaña, who in the 1930s fought against the conversion of his lands into banana plantations).

Meanwhile, deforestation means that in many areas, indigenous people are now unable to hunt for food, find medicinal plants or build traditional houses. They are left with no option but to work for a pittance on Tico farms or as drug traffickers. Many are on the verge of genetic extinction through intermarriage. Languages, art, religions and cultural practices have almost disappeared.

As elsewhere in the continent, evangelical churches have sprung up all over the indigenous reserves, encouraging indigenous people to renounce their pagan traditions. By 1905, the Bible Society had even published the Gospel of Saint John translated into Bribri.

Carlos Pérez, a Huetar Indian from the Quitirrisí reserve near San José, said, "We have lost our own religion, but we deal with this now by trying to think of Jesus in our terms. To us, he was like an indigenous healer—he healed with his hands, mud and saliva, just as our ancestors did."

Unlike the Huetares, the Bribris retain their religion, and a creation myth that describes how they were made by the god Sibö from ears of corn. White people, however, came from Plékeköl, the king of the leaf-cutter ants.

In *Taking Care of Sibö's Gifts*, Gloria Mayorga explained: 'Just look at the leaf-cutter ants, how they all work together cleaning and clearing all land around their nests. Where the leaf-cutter ants live, all the vegetation is gone, because they cut every last leaf to take them back to their big nests. That's how the white man is. He works very hard, but he destroys nature. He chops down all the trees to make his big cities, and where he lives all the vegetation is gone, there are no trees, no rivers, no animals. There is nothing there... he destroys everything in his path.'

With so much lost, many indigenous people are now determined that what remains of their culture must survive. Projects such as iguana farms, organic fruit farming, traditional craft workshops and eco-tour guiding have been set up to help ensure an income. Indigenous people are also becoming more self-confident in denouncing hunters and loggers, are running their own reforestation programmes and making efforts to document and recover their culture.

Carlos Pérez said, "The birth rate among Ticos is low now, but we Indians still have six or seven children. I really hope that in 20 years or so, our population will have grown to a size where we will finally have a political voice in our own country."

Unfortunately, however, many indigenous communities are very divided and greedy community leaders have misappropriated a lot of foreign aid money. The budget for CONAI, which actually achieves very little, is also in continual decline.

Alcoholism has also wrought havoc among people who traditionally drank *chicha* (a fermented drink of corn or other crops) only on ceremonial occasions. Carlos Pérez's grandfather, like many others, became hooked on drink and gave a Tico a large tract of land—later turned into a profitable coffee *finca*—in exchange for a bottle of rum and a kilo of meat. While it is illegal to sell alcohol anywhere within an indigenous reserve, it is easily available at the *pulperías* (small stores) which have sprung up all around the reserves.

Oscar Mena, 74, the only remaining Quitirrisí Huetar with knowledge of traditional healing, said, "The younger people especially are fascinated by outside cultures. Many leave the reserve and are almost ashamed to acknowledge their heritage.

"We need more work opportunities here so that people don't leave and become corrupted. But I think that by the time people come to really appreciate what we had, I will be dead, and all my knowledge will be gone with me."

The Bribris
The Bribris live on both sides of the Talamanca mountains. Theirs is the second biggest indigenous group, made up of 8,000 people. Pirates, banana companies, the railway, miners and hunters have continually invaded their land since the conquest. The people still preserve their customs, but these are disintegrating. Their crafts include hammocks and *chácaras*, 'string' bags made from pita leaf fibre, baskets, and drums made from tree trunks and iguana (or other animal) skin. Similar drums are made by the Malekus and Ngabës.

The Cabécares
Numbering 10,000 people, the Cabécares make up the country's biggest indigenous group and live on an 80,000-hectare (197,684.3-acre) reserve in Alto Chirripó. Due to this remote location not much is known about them. They still preserve their language and rituals to some extent, although the younger people are losing interest.

Boruca Indians take part in indigenous ritual in Rey Curré.

Like the Bribris, they are from the South American Chibcha family, believe in Sibö , and have matrilineal clans. The Bribri *awá,* or shaman, is the *jawá* of the Cabécares.

The Brunjkas or Borucas

Around 2,000 individuals live on the reserves in Boruca and Rey Curré on both sides of the Interamericana highway. They are famous for their textiles (woven blankets and bags) and masks—used in the famous Fiesta de los Diablitos (*see the section 'Calendar of Events/Fiestas' in* Chapter Seven: Enjoying Costa Rica *on page 203*). Their language is, however, rapidly being lost.

The Teribes

Their reserve is south-east of the bridge over the Río General. Although 1,500 people live there, only 40 per cent are indigenous, and only 25 per cent of the land is in their hands.

A warlike tribe, the Teribe were brought to Costa Rica from Panama by the Spanish in the 18th century in an attempt to pacify them. In Panama, they had killed many colonists and refused to submit. They were forcibly settled in the town of San Francisco de Térraba, built by the Franciscans, but 48 years later, the Teribes burnt it down. Their language, Naso, has already been lost, but they are now undertaking exchanges with the larger Terraba nation in Changuinola, Panama, in an effort to save their culture.

The Guaymíes or Ngabës

This is the biggest indigenous group in the Central American isthmus, with 100,000 individuals in Panama alone. However, there are only 3,000 of them in Costa Rica, divided among four reserves (Coto Brus, Abrojo Montezuma, Conte Burica and Osa) in the Zona Sur.

This group has preserved its traditions more than any other, and its women are the only ones to still wear their traditional dress. They still speak their two languages, Ngäbe and Buglé (Guaymí was the name given them by the conquistadors). Traditionally, they worship the god Ngobö, but now are either Christian, or follow the Mama Chí religion, which blends both pagan and Christian elements.

The Huetares

The original inhabitants of the Valle Central are now reduced to a few thousand people in two tiny reserves in Zapatón and Quitirrisí. They are some of the richest of the country's indigenous people, thanks to their proximity to the capital, and their speed to lobby for their rights. Their language and culture, however, is virtually extinct.

The Chorotegas

Most live in Matambá near Nicoya. They have lost their language, although their traditional art of pottery-making is preserved in Guaitíl (*see the section on 'Guanacastecos' in this chapter, page 80*). Originally Mesoamericans, also found in Nicaragua, they are believed to have been pushed south by conflicts in their Mexican homeland around AD 800.

The Malekus or Guatusos

Their tiny northern reserves are in Palenques El Sol, Margarita, and Tonjibe, areas easily accessible by road. Intermarriage with whites means that there are now only 500 Malekus left. They live in one-family concrete and zinc houses built by the government, and—as most of their lands are actually in the hands of ranch owners—they have to work as *peones* for a low salary. Incredibly, the Maleku language still exists to some extent, as does their works of art—although deforestation has made it very difficult for them to find the wood they need for this.

Ways to Get Involved

- You could easily live for years in Costa Rica and never see an indigenous person. If you have a genuine interest in their culture and the problems they face, one of the best ways to meet these 'invisible' people is to spend some time alongside them on a reserve. Some groups have embraced low-level eco-tourism projects to help boost their income.

- To spend a few days with the Bribris along the Yorkín River on the Panamanian border (one of the groups that still maintains a traditional lifestyle), contact:
  Aisling French at Galería Namu
  Avd 7, Cs 5 & 7, San José
  Tel: (506) 256-3412
  Email: info@galerianamu.com
  (Galería Namu is also the only art store in the country dealing exclusively in Costa Rican indigenous and modern art, http://www.galerianamu.com)

- The non-profit Asociación Talamanqueña de Ecoturismo (ATEC) in Puerto Viejo can also organise visits:
  Tel/fax: (506) 750-0191
  Email:atecmail@sol.racsa.co.cr.

- For more information on indigenous issues in general, contact CONAI at tel: (506) 257-6465.

Guanacastecos or Cholos

Chorotega Indians originally inhabited the large northern province of Guanacaste. The name of the province comes from *cuahuitlnacaztli* in Náhuatl, the language they shared with the Aztecs, meaning 'the place next to trees with ears', referring to the large ear-shaped pods of the area's giant Guanacaste trees.

Guanacaste is renowned for being the only part of the country with a really vibrant culture. Pretty much everything described as Costa Rican folklore is in fact from Guanacaste—including the country's national dance, the 'Punto Guanacasteco' (allegedly invented by a bored musician jailed for drunkenness), national tree and national costume. Guanacaste is the only part of the country where colonial architecture can still be seen intact and traditional ox carts are in use.

In fact, however, Guanacaste only became part of Costa Rica in 1824. Previously the southernmost province of Nicaragua, its inhabitants narrowly voted to leave that country because of the ongoing civil war between the liberal capital, León, and the powerful conservative trading town of Granada following independence from Spain in 1821. Nicaragua did not accept the loss of Guanacaste until 1858, when a border limit treaty was finally signed.

The people of Guanacaste (known by the Meseta Central Ticos as *cholos*) clearly have a richer ethnic mix than most other areas of the country. Their Chorotega Indian heritage is very evident, as is the black blood from African and mulatto slaves brought with the original Spanish settlers. Many still live in colonial houses with central patios and are expert horsemen—a sign of their recent history as *sabaneros* or cowboys, a profession that is fast dying out.

Despite the dash of colour it has given the country, Eduardo, a Guanacasteco in his early 30s, says the region has, however, been regarded with almost as much suspicion as Nicaragua. "Just a few years ago when I studied in Heredia, people still called us *Nicas regalados* (gift Nicaraguans)," he said. "I felt like a foreigner in my own country. I think Ticos have started to travel and get to know their country much better now, though. They can also see that this area is going to become more and more important as tourism grows—and they're going to be coming to look for work here rather than the other way around."

The tourism Eduardo refers to includes some massive tourist developments on the coast, such as the controversial Papagayo Project in Bahía Culebra, once called off on environmental grounds and now re-slated for completion in 2010. It will be a massive complex of hotels, apartments, entertainment parks and shopping zones, which will double the number of hotel rooms available in Costa Rica, and will be the biggest tourist development anywhere in Central America—even bigger than Cancún in Mexico.

"It's going to totally change Guanacaste," Eduardo said. "We need the work, but we're also a very traditional people, and I think this could have drastic effects on our culture and environment. This development is right next to a national park, and we've already had problems with other hotels, which have used vast amounts of water for their golf courses. Guanacaste is almost a desert as it is."

Tourism would seem to be the only option for Guanacaste. Cattle ranching requires very little labour, and in any case many ranches are now uneconomic and closing down. As a result, only 52 per cent of the province's workforce has a steady job, and the unemployment rate (35.5 per cent) is the highest in the country.

Guanacasteco Traditions

Sabaneros, who could break in a wild horse in a matter or hours, led a poor and lonely life. They lived for big fiestas, drinking sprees and the periodic round-ups of cattle herds for branding and sale, in which they would prove their machismo by 'riding' the biggest and angriest bulls. This was the origin of Costa Rica's brand of bullfighting—in which the bull gets to walk away (almost) unscathed.

Unfortunately, the 'real' *sabaneros*, also known as *pamperos* or *bramaderos*, have died out. Cattle these days are often transported in trucks, the plains have been fenced off, and parasite dips and injections for cattle have made the roving cowboys almost superfluous.

For the Sabaneros

The following poem, 'Sabaneros and Bullfights', was dedicated to the once ubiquitous *sabaneros* (cowboys) who would ride straight-backed and inscrutable across the vast Guanacaste plains with a *cacho* (cow horn) of *guaro* (firewater) hanging by their side.

Sabanero, Sabanero
Duerme ya tu sueño entero
Sin trajín ni despertar
Mas tu esfuerzo decidido
Como tu está en el olvido
Y hoy te vengo a rescatar

Sabanero, Sabanero
Dreaming your deep sleep
Without anything to waken you
But your driven determination
Like you, is forgotten
And today I'm coming to rescue you

—Rodolfo Salazar Solórzano

In Guanacaste, horsemanship is still much prized and the spirit of the *sabanero* is romanticised in local folklore and myth. You'll see some children almost too small to walk riding horses, while older kids practise their cowboy skills by lassoing tree stumps.

Traditional bullfights are still also a crucial component of local festivals (*see the section 'Calendar of Events/Festivals in* Chapter Seven: Enjoying Costa Rica *on page 203*).

NICARAGUANS

"Nicaragua and Costa Rica are like the fans of two opposing football teams," a diplomat told me. "They can't survive without each other, but they never have a good word to say about each other either."

These neighbouring countries have had all manner of territorial disputes and border spats. Nicaragua even attempted to invade Costa Rica in 1955, when the Nicaraguan dictator Anastasio Somoza tried to help defeated Costa

Rican ex-president Dr Rafael Angel Calderón Guardia make a comeback. As a result, the Ticos strongly supported the Sandinistas, which toppled Somoza—but soon swapped their support to the US-backed Contras after deciding they didn't really want a communist neighbour. This gives just a small insight into the background to a very dynamic relationship, in which many Ticos paint themselves as sober pacifists and their Nica neighbours as inherently violent.

Nicaraguans are the butt of Tico jokes, much as the Irish are for the English or the Canadians for the Americans. Nica-busting also gives the Ticos an excuse to avoid looking at their own faults.

For example, many Tico jokes about the Nicas focus on domestic violence—conveniently overlooking the fact that domestic violence is rife in Costa Rica too.

Depending on whom you believe, up to one million Nicaraguans have come to Costa Rica in the past two decades, driven by poverty, conflict, natural disasters and chronic unemployment. The official figures are around 400,000, but this number doesn't include the huge numbers of illegal *indocumentados* who easily slip over the border.

What is certain is that Costa Rica has become to Nicaragua what the United States is to Mexico. The staunchly anti-Communist Ticos worry at every mention of a return to power of the Sandinista regime or severe droughts in Nicaragua, which could spark another huge wave of immigration.

If anything, the anti-Nica feeling has intensified in recent years, with 81 per cent of respondents in a 2004 University of Costa Rica survey saying 'something had to be done' to put the brakes on Nicaraguan immigration. Feelings ran extremely high in November 2005 after a Nicaraguan thief was attacked by guard dogs at a property he was attempting to burgle. A crowd gathered to watch as police attempted, for two hours, to fight the dogs off. The man later died in hospital from severe shock and blood loss, leading to fury in Nicaragua, where politicians asked why the police did not simply shoot the animals—the implication being that a dog's life was worth more than a Nicaraguan's.

Although some Ticos gripe that the Nicas are stealing their jobs, in reality, the hard-working Nicaraguans provide the workforce for jobs which most comparatively highly-educated Ticos now refuse to do—domestic help, security and construction work.

San José's Parque de la Merced, now more usually known as the Parque de los Nicas, is full every weekend with Nicaraguans who gather there to meet friends and reminisce about home.

"If we didn't have the Nicas to help at harvest time, our sugar cane and coffee would probably rot in the fields," Tomás, a taxi driver grudgingly admitted. "But they're different from us—they're violent people. I feel sorry for them with all they've been through, but they've brought a lot of crime to the country."

Many Ticos complain that their social security payments go towards supporting Nicas who now have equal access to health and other services. "There are so many of them now that we're going to have to start calling this country Costa Nica," grumbled Tomás. Henry Briceño Barrios, a Nicaraguan working for over a year in Costa Rica, said, "It's true that a few crooks and thieves have come over here, but we're all tarred with the same brush. Most of us just want to work and save some money and go home.

"We would never stay here if it weren't for the terrible conditions we left behind. A lot of Ticos treat us like we're lesser mortals, and make fun of our accent. If we have no documents, employers pay us way below the minimum wage. Many of us aren't educated, and we don't know the law here or our rights so they take advantage of us.

"Our embassy had to complain at international level after the police were rounding up *indocumentados*, stealing their wages and deporting them, without even giving them time to collect their belongings or say goodbye to their families."

GRINGOS

It's estimated that up to 80,000 North Americans, mostly retirees, make their home in Costa Rica—tens of thousands more than the country's entire indigenous population.

It's impossible to know the exact figure as many live in the country as 'perpetual tourists', but what is certain is that the number has grown steadily since the 1960s, thanks to the relatively low cost of living, good climate, political stability and tax breaks. There are now more *gringos* in Costa Rica than in any other country in Central America.

Unlike in many Latin countries (especially Mexico), being called *gringo* is not a term of abuse in Costa Rica. (Originally, the Spanish word *gringo*, meaning 'gibberish', was a contemptuous name for an Englishman or an Anglo-American.)

Not having suffered the kind of US occupations or military interventions of much of the rest of Central America, it is hard to find many Ticos with a bad word to say about Americans. Most locals welcome the influx of American and other foreign firms, that help to diversify the economy.

"I've lived here for 10 years," one American told me, "and this is the only Latin country where my being an American has not once caused any problem. I've never even felt that anyone resents me."

A number of shady American characters, wheelers and dealers, however, have sought refuge in Costa Rica's ever-welcoming bosom and secretive banking laws (*see, for example, Robert Vesco in the 'Heroes and Villains' section of* Chapter Ten: Fast Facts *on page 247*). There is also a fair crop of Vietnam veterans who could not adjust to life in the United States and who can be found slowly drinking themselves to death in Costa Rican girlie bars.

This has dented the *gringo* image somewhat, and people do complain about the steady Americanisation of youth culture, fashion and music. Ticos even have a verb, *agringarse*, for people who take on American styles and habits. Others also lament the changing face of Costa Rica, claiming that *gringos* have bought up large tracts of the best land, or altered particular neighbourhoods. A prime example is Escazú, in San José, now commonly called Gringolandia, where prices have been pushed up to such an extent that none but the richest Ticos can afford to live there.

Many *gringos* live quite closed off from Tico society in wealthy, razor wire-ringed, gated communities and some—

Change in Policy

The immigration agency announced in 2004 that the migratory situation in Costa Rica was 'out of control' and that they would, in future, be restricting residency approvals to the minimum to prevent the phenomenon of 'perpetual tourists', so the growth in *gringo* numbers may now slow down somewhat.

even after decades of living in the country—still struggle to speak Spanish.

A glance at the 'What's On' pages in the English-language *Tico Times* gives an idea of the size and organisation of the American community. More like a flyer from a Californian New Age social group, it offers clubs in such very un-Tico areas as shamanic healing, dowsing, kite-flying, communicating with dolphins and judo for pregnant women.

QUAKERS

One of the smallest, but most interesting, social groups in Costa Rica is made up of the descendants of a group of dairy-farming Quakers from Alabama, USA.

Having been imprisoned in the early 1950s for refusing, on moral grounds, to obey the military draft for the Korean War, they decided, once freed, to start a new life in a more peaceful place. Costa Rica seemed the perfect choice, and they slowly carved the mountain community of Monteverde out of the surrounding cloud forest and set up the cheese factory, which would one day come to make the best cheese in the country.

Their foresight in preserving some of the forest to protect their watershed led to the arrival of biologists who were intrigued by the area's endemic species. Later, intrepid tourists also started to arrive, and as dairy farming became less and less profitable, more and more areas were allowed to revert back to forest. Monteverde is now the second most visited tourist spot in the country, and contains more plant species in 26 sq km (10 sq miles) than the USA and Canada combined.

Several thousand people now live where 50 years ago there was hardly anyone but a few Tico farmers and illegal hooch distillers. The atrocious road leading to Monteverde still acts as a kind of filter. There are now controversial plans afoot to pave the road, however, which, according to Quaker Joe Stuckey, could mean 'one of the final barriers to isolation will fall'.

Only around 50 practising Quakers remain. Several families have left, disillusioned with how their quiet retreat has turned into a tourist attraction, and others have married into Tico families. Those that remain are fairly wary of outside contact. They retain the Friends Meeting House where silent group worship is held, and their children still receive English-language education based on Quaker principles at the village school.

RELIGION AND WITCHCRAFT

Whichever way you look at it, Costa Ricans are overwhelmingly Catholic. Catholicism is the state religion, abortion is illegal and non-Catholics cannot be legally married in their own church without going through a civil ceremony too. The Church is state funded and has always been viewed as one of the strongest and most morally-untainted institutions in the country.

Religion is never far away from Ticos' lips. When you wake up in the morning, you will be asked how you slept: '*Cómo amaneció?*', to which the stock answer is '*Bien, gracias a Dios*' (Well, thank God). People talking about something in the future will often also invoke God, for example, '*Iré mañana, si Dios quiere*' (I'll go tomorrow, if God wills it), and when someone leaves the house, they will be told, '*Que Dios le acompañe*' (May God go with you).

When going to someone's house, instead of knocking on the door Ticos shout, '*Upe*', which is a shortened version of the traditional greeting '*Ave María Purísima Nuestra Señora la Virgen de Guadalupe*' called out by arriving visitors.

Often, when setting out for even a short bus journey or passing a church, Ticos will cross themselves. Many homes are also decorated with pictures of the Last Supper, holograms of the Pope, ornaments of the baby Jesus and palm crosses. New commercial or government offices are blessed by a priest before they open, and roadsides are littered with shrines marking the spot where unlucky motorists died.

The number of believers, however, is clearly on the wane. In a 1995 La Nación poll, 100 per cent of respondents said they believed in God, and 84 per cent said they were Catholics. By 2001, those numbers had fallen to 98 per cent and 70.3 per cent.

Evangelism is making inroads, especially in the city and in indigenous reserves. The Catholic Church has had to become more charismatic, incorporating a lot of clapping and singing, in order to hang on to its congregation. People in the countryside, however, tend to be more traditional and stick with Roman Catholicism.

Even among Catholics, most church-goers are older people, and many of them admit they *muy poco practicante* (don't really practise). The Padre Minor furore (*see the section 'Heroes and Villains' in* Chapter Ten: Fast Facts *on page 247*) was also a big blow to the image of the Church.

As in most Latin American countries, the forcible imposition of Catholicism failed to totally root out indigenous superstitions and practices. Although there is no syncretic religion in Costa Rica today, such as Santería in Cuba or the cult of Maximón in Guatemala, people definitely have a kind of elastic belief system which allows them to pick and choose what suits them best.

Market stalls do a roaring trade in magic herbs and potions, thanks to the faith people have in the supernatural to bring them everything from love, money and luck in the lottery, to revenge against their enemies or a means of getting rid of annoying neighbours.

Many apparently 'normal' people will happily tell you they bathe themselves in magical herbal washes, hang aloe vera or garlic over their doors to suck up bad luck and burn coloured candles to attract love and money, drive away evil spirits or stop gossipy tongues.

They may spread sugar on the floor to keep witches out of the house, or always sweep inwards to keep good luck inside. Just as they use social connections to cut through bureaucracy, Ticos pray to particular saints to intercede with God—Santa Clara can help with business, Santa Apolonia is good for toothache, and San Antonio Abad can help protect pigs.

People buy books of spell 'recipes', adorn themselves with Stars of David and images of the Buddha, have their tarot cards read and tie red ribbons around babies' wrists to protect them from the evil eye.

In this kind of catch-all insurance system, Ticos often say: '*No creo, ni dejo de creer*' (I don't believe—but I don't not believe either).

Although 'witchcraft, sorcery, or any other cult or belief contrary to civilisation or good customs' is technically a jailable offence, many spells are still cast. In a 1996 survey, half of all Catholics said they believed in witchcraft.

Some of the most popular spells include rubbing the back of a black cat with salt at midnight for health and wealth. A surefire means of becoming irresistible to men is to mix together 33 drops of three love perfumes, a piece of gold and hummingbird nest, aloe vera, mint and honey. Leave it in a bottle in the sun for seven days, and then carry it around in your handbag. If you want a man with money, add some myrtle. Most spells involve some aspect of Catholicism, such as prayers to particular saints.

Often inexplicable aches, pains or bad luck are explained by the local *bruja* (witch) as the result of spells or 'bad shadows' cast upon the victim by the envious.

One woman whose daughter was cured of the *mal de ojo* (evil eye) by a witch, told me, "We only went to the lady after conventional medicine wasn't able to do anything. It seemed crazy at first, but we were desperate and would try anything. My daughter had been in a kind of trance, but she was cured. The lady wouldn't accept any money—she just wanted us to pray."

According to *De Que Vuelan... Vuelan!* by May Brenes Marín and Mayra Zapparoli Zecca, people cast bad spells on their enemies by piercing voodoo dolls with nails, burying *aportes* (bags full of nasty substances such as dead toads, chili, entrails, blood and mercury), spraying 'evil' liquids over the entrance to their victim's house, or even simply preparing their food. *Aportes* are often buried in graveyards, where the soil is considered particularly suitable for evil-doing. In the same book, San José General Cemetery official

Escazú

The most famous place in Costa Rica for witchcraft is Escazú where, historically, indigenous people secretly attempted to continue practising their religious and magic rituals in mountain caves. Now a rich suburb of San José full of big houses and fast food restaurants, it looks more like California than Costa Rica. The *brujas*, however, are still to be found—ostensibly reading tarot cards, but often also offering a whole range of other services.

Carlos Rodríguez said his staff find at least one set of *aportes* a month.

Luis 'Billy' Acuña Araya, who runs a magic stall in the San José Mercado Central, told me, "People come a lot to buy the ingredients for *aportes*—particularly to get rid of neighbours they don't like. They put black salt, mercury and other unpleasant things in a red bag along with a message saying 'You will never find happiness until you leave this house' and throw it up on the roof." Even though Billy says that most people use magic for nothing more than attracting love and money, it is not surprising that many people carry some kind of *contra* (amulet) to protect themselves.

Of course many Ticos these days don't resort to magic, herbs or witchcraft, but they are still very superstitious people. For example, if an '88' butterfly (with a mark looking like this number on its wings) flies into their house, they will rush out and buy a lottery ticket with the same number, hoping for a big win.

The following are some of the most important members of the Costa Rican pantheon of popular saints.

La Virgen de Los Angeles

According to tradition, La Negrita—the tiny black virgin, which is Costa Rica's patron saint—first appeared in 1635 to a girl named Juana Pereira on a rock in a forest. Every time the virgin was removed, she miraculously reappeared in the same spot. A shrine was built at the site, and the first pilgrimage took place in 1653 after La Negrita apparently cured a serious illness.

Although black virgins and Christs were popular in Europe in the 17th century, many people believe the appearance of a black virgin was particularly significant, as it allowed the indigenous Costa Ricans to identify with their new religion.

La Negrita was made the nation's patron saint in 1824, displacing the original patron saint and represented the triumph of the *mestizo* religion over Spanish domination.

Today, visitors to the shrine, often patients from the nearby Max Peralta hospital, still 'walk' up the whole aisle of the basilica on their knees. In an ante-room, glass cases house literally thousands of silver *exvotos* or tiny charms, which can be anything from legs, ears and livers to guns, babies and aeroplanes. These graphic requests for miracles are surrounded by thousands more offerings representing thanks for help granted, such as football trophies and university degree certificates. Downstairs at the shrine of the rock, people pray in groups, sometimes with the help of a professional prayer leader.

Every year, on 2 August, around a million people from all over the country, including the president, finish the pilgrimage to Cartago on foot, by horse or on bicycle in order to fulfill their promises to the Virgin.

Dr Moreno Cañas

Dr Moreno Cañas became well known in the 1920s and 1930s as a helper of the poor. He was murdered in 1938, and after his death, he became a mythical figure. People claimed he was communicating with them from beyond the grave, doling out medical advice and occasionally performing supernatural surgery.

Now a popular saint, he has even been officially honoured by being named a *Benemérito de la Patria* and having an obelisk placed in front of the house where he was killed. Special Dr Moreno Cañas photographs and prayers are available for people who want the ghostly doctor to intervene on their behalf. Some people claim a glass of water containing a lemon cut into a cross and placed overnight on a prayer card will be turned by morning into the required medicine.

Sor María Romero

Costa Ricans passionately hold this nun, in the process of being beatified by the Vatican, to be their own, despite the fact she was actually Nicaraguan. In 1989, she was made an honorary citizen of Costa Rica, and her portrait hangs in the Legislative Assembly. Sor María, widely held to have been psychic, came to Costa Rica at the age of 29 and died at 75 in 1977. When her body was exhumed to be relocated 14 years later, it was found to be almost intact. The Pope has accepted as miraculous her cure of a Costa Rican baby with a harelip.

Thousands of people visit her sepulchre in the Casa de la Virgen in San José's Barrio Don Bosco to ask for help (especially on the feast day of María Auxiliadora on 24 May), and many leave with bottles of supposedly miraculous water from the building.

VALUES AND ATTITUDES
Family and Privacy
It is impossible to exaggerate the importance of family in Costa Rica. I lived with one family for three months, and in all that time—although someone popped around to the house virtually every day— only twice was the visitor a non-relative. Nor was this a family of social freaks.

Historically, Ticos lived in isolated mountain hamlets, where they had to rely, above all, on their relatives for working the farm, emotional support and socialising—to the extent that the family is described in the constitution as the 'natural basis of Costa Rican society'.

If you become extremely good friends with a Tico, they will probably describe you as being *como un hermano* (like a brother). Meanwhile, Mother's Day is probably one of the most extravagant holidays in the country, and Father's Day is also seriously celebrated. On the Day of the Dead, graveyards are full of people bringing flowers to relatives' graves and cleaning headstones.

Until very recently, most people lived in the village where they grew up and even now, family members rarely live far apart from each other. A plot of family land is often divided up so that offspring can build their houses right next to their parents.

The irony, however, is that Costa Rica today has a fairly high rate of divorce. This has led to a situation in many families where, for example, one child lives with the mother, another with the father, and a third with a grandparent.

Even when family members do not actually live in the same house, they get together on weekends and holidays for *reuniones* and talk on the telephone to each other constantly. They are not embarrassed to let their relatives know exactly how much they mean to them. One girl I travelled with, who was going to see her mother later that same day, finished a phone call: *'Chao Mamita, la quiero muchísimo, que Dios me la cuide... le mando un beso Madrecita'* (Goodbye Mummy, I love you very much. I'm asking God to take care of you... I'm sending you a kiss Mummykins).

To non-Latinos, this may seem over-the-top to say the least, but this constant love-bombing ensures that Ticos do not feel unloved or awkward with intimacy. Coming from a rather typically inexpressive English family, I was hugely impressed by Tico children, who do not screw up their faces in disgust when asked to kiss grandma, and will happily chat away quite maturely with all generations of family members. Sisters and brothers generally get on with each other a lot better than their counterparts in the United Kingdom or United States.

Such confidence among children is probably due to the fact that they come in for a huge amount of pampering. It's suggested that this is a remnant of the extremely tough early days of Costa Rica, when youngsters were unlikely to survive until the age of five. In order for them to enjoy the little life they might have, they were, and still are *chineados* (spoilt). In some rural areas, you still see babies with red ribbons tied around their wrist, supposed to ward off evil and illness, and during the rainy season, every baby in the land is swaddled in a massive furry rug or quilt—even though the temperature is usually still considerably hotter than a British summer.

Although the country's birth rate, especially in urban areas, has declined sharply in line with the infant mortality rate (from 7.3 children per woman in 1960 to about three today), Ticos love babies. If you haven't had children by your mid-20s, you will be considered strange, and you should fully expect to be roped in as an impromptu babysitter.

Most people live in the family nest much longer than in the United States or United Kingdom, often even after they are married. Students, given the size of the country, obviously don't leave home to study in a distant city, and most young Ticos cannot afford their own home. Ticos rarely rent and house ownership is more than 70 per cent.

Grandparents often also live with their children and older people are well respected, being known as *ciudadanos de oro* (golden citizens). One woman told me, "The fact that we live with our families for so long means that we really get to know our parents as adults. They become like real people to us rather than just parents, and we start to really appreciate everything they have sacrificed for us. That's why, unlike in your culture, it makes it very hard for us to put them in an old people's home."

With home being so sacred for Ticos, it is not surprising that they are often reluctant to allow any but the most intimate of friends into the bosom of their family. This may also have something to do with having to share their house with many family members and the fear of outsiders finding out how modest their living conditions actually are. Middle-class highlanders are definitely more formal and reserved in this sense than those in the countryside, but in general most Ticos would prefer to socialise away from home.

That's not to say you won't be invited to a Tico home, but quite often these invitations are meaningless—intended as a gesture of friendship, but never really serious. Because of this, Ticos invited to someone's house often fail to turn up.

Nicaraguans, who are generally perceived as more open and relaxed than their southern neighbours, joke, 'A Tico is quick to invite you to his home—but it's tough to make him give you the address.'

Juan Carlos, a model, said, "You can't just say to a Tico: 'Pop round to my house any time you like.' That, to a Tico, sounds like you're being nice, but—because of the way we feel about our homes—he would never act on it. You'd have to confirm a specific day and time, probably several times, before a Tico thought you really meant it."

Another man in his 30s added, "When I was growing up, everyone in my family had locks on the inside of their bedroom doors—I never even thought that was strange. I've also got friends I've known all my life, but I've never been in their houses.

"The way I see it is that this is a small country, so the boundaries of privacy are very important to us. The home is a sacred haven pretty much for family only, but even there we need our own space."

Television seems to have had an effect too. Most Ticos are hopelessly addicted to television, particularly *telenovelas* (soap operas). In many middle-class homes, instead of everyone sitting down to watch a programme together, there is a set in every individual's room.

The Rocking Chair

The pace of life in the Costa Rican countryside goes as slowly as possible, and every rural Tico home worth its salt has at least two rocking chairs (*perezosas* or *mesedoras*) on the porch outside. Sometimes these are hand-carved out of wood, with leather backs, or—more usually—made out of woven nylon cords which are much more comfortable than they sound. Here one sits for hours with family members reading the paper, snacking or watching the world go by and chatting to it as it goes.

Infidelity and Machismo

"All the men here think I'm stupid and pathetic," complained my Dutch friend Frans Baas, who was working in a small Tico town.

The outrageous behaviour that had earned him such harsh criticism was not taking up embroidery, hating football or refusing to drink *guaro*, but staying faithful to his girlfriend from home and—even worse—limiting himself to just the one girlfriend.

Frans' Tico friends were continually trying to set him up with local women so he could be suitably macho—a characteristic which itself is said to have come to Costa Rica via the Spanish from the Arabs.

Machismo almost demands that men be unfaithful—leading to Costa Rica's profusion of 'love motels', which offer special short-stay rates for men and their *queridas* or mistresses. These are also used by younger people, who usually live with their families until they are married.

Many men have children with different women and marriage is becoming less and less popular, with couples instead being involved in loose *uniones libres*. There were historically always a certain number of these in the *campo* because of lack of access to churches. Around 51 per cent of children are born to single mothers. The figure in the UK is 44 per cent, but the difference is that many more UK couples actually live together. In response to growing pressure, the government has passed a law allowing women to force their (ex-) lovers to take DNA paternity tests, to enable them to claim child support.

Infidelity, unsurprisingly, breeds jealousy, and although Ticas tend to forgive their men's infidelity, some foreign women living in Costa Rica find it hard to make female friends, as Ticas sometimes view them as a threat. Unfortunately, machismo can also make it hard to find a truly platonic friendship with a man.

One foreign man, who has lived, worked and dated all over Latin America, said, "I find Ticas generally less passionate, open and spontaneous than any other Latinas. They'll be calling you *mi amor* within minutes, but it often seems quite insincere.

"I think this is because they come from a culture in which male infidelity is virtually condoned, and this has made many of them quite mercenary about getting hold of a man who will at least provide them with a comfortable lifestyle while they put up with his affairs. They are not ashamed to admit this."

Consequently, for many Ticas, comparatively wealthy foreign men are an irresistible honey pot.

In any Internet café in San José, you are virtually guaranteed to find several young women searching the web on sites such as http://www.spanisheyescostarica.com and http://www.MyTica.com, looking for *gringo* boyfriends. Such sites post scores of new women each day, and promise wife-hunting Americans that they can meet up to 600 hopefuls during a special six-day reconnaissance trip. In addition, they claim, bringing home a Tica poses fewer immigration difficulties than a wife from Russia or Thailand.

Saray Ramírez, who has had both a Spanish and a Swiss husband, says it is not a question of money. "Ticos are very loving and romantic, but you can't trust them," she said "Foreigners seem to be much colder, but at least they're more sincere. They don't tell you they love you unless they really mean it, and they're also more progressive and open-minded."

Many Ticas are definitely being corrupted by the growth in tourism, and many male holidaymakers come for one thing alone—prostitution, which is legal and widespread. Worryingly, cases of child prostitution and pornography are also on the rise, partly as a result of large-scale crackdowns in other hot spots such as South-east Asia.

However, Bruce Harris, former director (until his ignominious fall from grace—(*see the section 'Heroes and Villains' in* Chapter Ten: Fast Facts *on page 247*) of the Casa Alianza organisation, which fights child abuse across the whole region, says the majority of demand comes from local paedophiles. According to Casa Alianza, up to 3,000 children are being prostituted in San José alone (more than anywhere else in Central America), and hundreds of complaints have been lodged with the special prosecutor. So far, there have been few prosecutions though a big child pornography ring has been broken, and the government has now launched a major publicity campaign to warn tourists that sex with minors is a punishable offence. According to UNICEF, up to 80 per cent of exploited children have been previously sexually abused at home.

Milena Grillo, director of the child advocacy group Paniamor, explained, "We've been too distracted by the popular claims that Costa Rica is a peaceful democracy with no army. This prompts a collective unconscious perception that violence is non-existent. How can society fight a problem it's not willing to recognise?"

The government is legally bound to hand over funds to the Patronato Nacional de la Infancia (PANI), the country's child welfare organisation each year to help address the problem. It has, however, defaulted on the payments in recent years, as it has in its funding to almost every other state-funded welfare and environmental body, claiming that there simply isn't enough money to go around. Casa Alianza has resorted to legal action to try to force payment.

Bruce Harris said, "In the past, the government has swept the situation under the carpet, and attacked us rather than admitting there was a problem, but hopefully things will now change. The first step in getting to the root of this child abuse must be prevention, education, and tackling machismo and violence in the home, as well as training and equipping the people who are going to go after the abusers. It's going to be tough though, in a culture where children can still be married at the age of 14, and where—until the late 1990s—a rapist of an underaged girl could not be prosecuted if he offered to marry the victim."

It is also hard to wonder whether the country's legitimate sex industry is not adding to the problem. Various sex cinemas in San José advertise their films in the national newspapers—with names such as *Adolescentes en Celo* (Teenagers on Heat) and *Cuando las Colegiales se Confiesan* (When Schoolgirls Confess).

National Pride

Ticos LOVE their country. "If we ever go abroad and hear our national anthem, we cry," one macho young Tico told me.

Flag-waving schoolchildren are always at the forefront of patriotic parades, and they are indoctrinated from an early age by teachers and often parents that other countries, beset by violence, envy Costa Rica's lack of military, its stability and high living standards. With up to a quarter of the population having left or fled their own countries to live in Costa Rica, this belief is pretty understandable.

However, many Ticos have travelled surprisingly little around their own tiny country, and of a group of 20 university students I met, not one had visited La Casona, Costa Rica's foremost national monument.

The Teatro Melico Salazar in San José regularly holds popular folkoric dance extravaganzas, which are not solely patronised by tourists, and Radio Nacional broadcasts programmes such as *Aires de mi Tierra* (Melodies of my Land) and *Cantares Campesinos* (Peasant Songs). Even the *páginas amarillas* (telephone directory) starts with several pages of morale-boosting Costa Rican history and statistics about its high standard of living.

Some suggest the strength of national pride comes from the fact that Costa Rica is so small and dependent on the outside world. This makes people feel powerless, and leads to a desire to talk up the national heritage and defend it against foreign influence.

Pobrecito

A deeply Tico trait is to feel sorry for the *pobrecito* (poor little thing)—something which could go a long way to explaining their ready acceptance of thousands of refugees from Cuba, Russia, El Salvador, Colombia, Argentina and Chile over the past couple of decades; and the fact that street begging has become a lucrative profession. Even when it comes to the much-maligned Nicaraguans, Ticos are wont to qualify their criticisms with 'They can't help it, the *pobrecitos*, they've had such a hard time in their country."

People who have done something wrong will often come up with outlandish excuses, often medical, to try to invoke the *pobrecito* reflex of employers or judges. Unsurprisingly, children learn how to exploit this at a young age, and are allowed to get away with murder.

Choteo, Class and Snobbery

If there's anything Ticos hate, it's people who show off or get ideas above their station, and *choteo* is a kind of good-natured mockery that nips any such arrogance firmly in the bud. In Costa Rica, pride always comes before a fall.

Choteo rarely extends beyond friendly irony, but at times can descend to violent attacks, often behind the person's back. Many say *choteo* stems from small-minded envy of those who do well. Ticos are intrinsically conservative and resistant to change; the added prospect of *choteo* can make them fearful of attempting anything outstanding or imaginative.

The flipside of the *choteo* coin, however, is its power to *igualar* (to make everyone the same), that is evident in the general lack of snobbery in Costa Rica. While the popular myth of a classless society is clearly not true, the country's special history, plus decades of social spending by the government, means that there is a massive middle class. While there is obviously a social elite, there are none of the obscene class differences between the very rich and very poor seen in most other Latin countries. Ticos say that in their society people have *roce*, meaning that all the classes mix.

Rich people aren't ostentatious—you don't see any stretch limos or lavish parties here. San José does have a big country club, but many of the members are foreigners. "Really rich Ticos wouldn't join," explained Darren Mora, a bookshop owner. "They see it as a place full of brash, tasteless Americans. In fact, the richer classes traditionally encourage their children to socialise with members of lower classes in order to instill them with a sense of equality."

The president is a regular mortal who usually does not even have bodyguards. "I've met all of the last eight presidents just walking in the street," said Darren. "There's nothing surprising about that."

Ticos value people who are *humilde* (humble) and don't feel that they are any less worthy than someone who is financially better off. The company janitor will feel comfortable striking up a conversation with the CEO, although they wouldn't be likely to socialise.

There is, however, some class-based snobbery. The middle-class like to *aparentar* with nice clothes and possessions—which are often beyond their means and have to be bought on instalment plans.

Many of them until recently *campesinos* themselves, they might look down on both the *maiceros* (rural poor) and *comehuevos* (literally 'egg eaters')—the Costa Rican equivalent of American 'white trash'. *Comehuevos* tend to camp at favourite beaches during holidays, where the sand is often black and volcanic, becoming burning hot in the sun. The *comehuevos*, who can't afford restaurant food, bury eggs in the sand to cook them. They are also seen as loud drunks who leave litter behind. At the other end of the scale, the pampered offspring of rich families are known as *fresas* (strawberries).

Tico Time and Broken Promises

Tico Time means arriving late (around 15–30 minutes for official appointments)—and up to several hours late for meeting friends. Once you have waited in a few lines in Costa Rican government offices, you will soon learn that *ahorita* (right now) in fact means 'maybe never'. The less emphatic, and sadly much less common, *ahora* (now) is actually more immediate.

Increasingly, contact with foreigners has led many Ticos to recognise their lateness as rude, though usually only in the work environment.

"I invited a group of people to dinner recently," said Ray, an American living in San José. "All the Ticos turned up late, some of them four hours late. Incredibly, they were peeved with me for having served dinner before they got there. Others didn't turn up at all, and didn't even call. When I saw one of the no-shows later, they were completely bewildered that I saw their behaviour as a lack of respect."

The Elastic Tico Time
While the Spanish have the Mañana Syndrome, the Costa Ricans have Tico Time. Until around 100 years ago, the fastest you could travel across Costa Rica's treacherous mountain roads was at the speed of your nimblest mule. It took almost a week to reach Puntarenas from San José. As hurrying was senseless in this environment, people unsurprisingly, developed a very elastic sense of time.

"We're really *incumplidos* (unreliable)" my friend Natalia del Valle happily admitted. "We make an arrangement with someone, and at that moment we're genuinely enthused about the idea, but later we forget, or something else comes up.

"We're not used to making arrangements way in advance, and we never think that the other person is taking it very seriously either. The best way to make sure we do something is to call us right then and there and say: 'Hey, are you busy? Let's go for lunch!'"

In 1853, Moritz Wagner and Karl Scherzer, two Germans travelling through Costa Rica, reported on exactly this unhappy kind of culture clash. Coming from one of the most notoriously punctual nations on Earth, you can almost hear the tone of indignant betrayal in their voices: 'One cannot trust the promises and contracts of a Costa Rican. This is the most characteristic trait of his nature. Punctuality and conscientious keeping of one's word are extremely rare.'

Little has changed, and today, some foreigners at the ends of their tethers end up only maintaining friendships with people they can trust to show up on time.

The Lottery
Sometimes it is hard to weave your way through San José's choked streets because of the sheer number of lottery sellers taking up the pavement, either sitting at tables or wandering up and down shouting out the numbers of the cards they're selling. The lottery is hugely popular and becoming more so

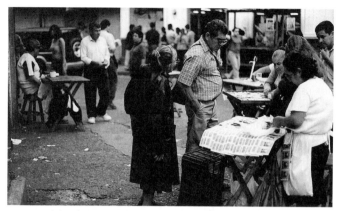

At times it's hard to put a pin between the lottery sellers lining the city streets.

with every passing week, thanks to the slow decrease in the colón's power to purchase imported goods, as it depreciates at a crawling rate against the dollar.

"My wife almost bankrupts us each week, betting everything on the lottery," one taxi driver groaned. "But I can't really blame her—we're getting poorer and poorer, and there's always a chance we could get lucky."

Lottery gamblers don't choose their own numbers, but buy tickets with three pre-printed numbers. Both these, and the series number, must match up with the numbers drawn in order to win. Many people stick to the same 'lucky' numbers week after week.

The lottery itself is played on Sundays, with a top prize of 35 million colones (US$ 100,000), as well as *chances* on Tuesdays and Fridays, with a 10 million colón winning prize. There are also very popular instant scratch cards, or *raspas*.

Salesmen of *tablas mágicas* also do a roaring trade. These tables supposedly tell you your lucky lottery numbers.

WOMEN

Today, Costa Rica has a higher percentage of female politicians (including several former vice presidents) than either the United States or Britain. The majority of university students are female too.

Things, however, have not always been this way. Women only got the vote in 1948, and until 1974, they could only divorce adulterous husbands for 'open and scandalous concubinage'. Interestingly, no such requirement existed for men.

Machismo may be on the decline, but it's far from dead, and while violence in public is minimal, domestic violence is widespread. Women have traditionally been too ashamed or afraid to denounce abusers, and the scale of the problem is only now becoming clear.

A female response to machismo has been *marianismo*, in which women take a kind of long-suffering pride in their strength in dealing with their situation. In fact, many women are now effectively the family breadwinner.

At least two women are killed each month by violent partners. The women's support group Cefemina receives up to 100 calls on its domestic violence hotline every day.

Xinia Vindas of Cefemina said, "Most men think of nothing but work, sleep, football and other women. They expect us to accept their infidelity, because, they say, Tico men are just naturally *muy calientes* (very passionate) and can't help it. Usually we can't leave them even if we want to, because getting financial support for ourselves and our children is like getting blood out of a stone."

Many women's rights advocates also feel the traditionally powerful Catholic Church has been an added fly in the ointment of women's progress. It has historically done its utmost to prevent sex education in schools, which is at least partly to blame for the country's huge number of teenage pregnancies. More than half of all young people use no contraception at all, abortion is illegal, and it's not at all unusual to meet 50-year-old great grandparents.

HOMOSEXUALITY

While Costa Rica is seen as something of a gay Mecca in Central America as there is no explicit official repression of homosexuality, *machista* attitudes still prevail.

In a 2001 survey in the *Tico Times*, Costa Ricans were asked whom they disapproved of most in their society. While

Nicaraguans came in with 13 per cent, well over 30 per cent of respondents pointed the finger at *playos* (homosexuals).

Rick Stern, a psychologist and gay rights activist, who has lived in Costa Rica for 13 years, said there has been no official repression in the country since the Supreme Court ruled in the late 1990s that the police had acted illegally in raiding a gay nightclub. Such raids had been common in the 1970s and 1980s, when police would even shave the heads of those they arrested. "There's still a lot of intolerance among society itself, the family and the Church though," he said "and this means a lot of people, especially in traditional rural areas, remain firmly in the closet."

Many Ticos perceived as being too openly gay have been kicked out of their families and, as in many Latin countries, Costa Rica has traditionally had a large number of 'bisexual marriages', with gay husbands trying to conform to social norms for appearances' sake.

Anti-gay hysteria reached a peak in 1998, when charismatic priest Padre Mínor Calvo, the country's self-proclaimed 'Guardian of Morality' incited the beach community of Quepos to stop the planned visit of a group of gay tourists. He called gay people examples of debauchery and decay, and tried to link homosexuality with child sex tourism. His crusade led to street protests and a bomb threat against Triángulo Rosa, a gay support group. In a bizarre twist, three years later, Calvo was caught by police late one night in a notorious San José gay cruising district, La Sabana, with a young man in his car. The priest insisted he was giving the boy a driving lesson.

Conservatism in Costa Rican society, along with legal prostitution, has also led to a phenomenon which surprises many first-time visitors passing through the area of El Registro by taxi at night—the transvestite prostitute patch. Up to 200 *travestís*, many of whom make disturbingly convincing women, ply their trade on the streets.

"It's the only thing they can do," said Rick Stern. "Latin culture means that young men who want to dress up as women and are not prepared to hide it cannot get any kind of regular job, so they usually start in prostitution as teenagers."

He added that attitudes are changing, and being gay in San José is probably better than being gay in a similarly sized city in the United States—and definitely better than elsewhere in Central America. Despite their machismo, Ticos loathe public violence, meaning open abuse or attacks in the streets are almost non-existent. San José has many gay bars and saunas, as well as a newspaper *Gayness*, which is available in bookshops around the university area.

"We Ticos are quite naïve, and very good at turning a blind eye to uncomfortable realities we don't want to see," Juan Carlos, a gay model, told me. "You can be gay as long as you don't force people to confront it by being too indiscreet. The worst you're likely to experience is some frowning and muttering."

SOCIAL CUSTOMS AND ATTITUDES

'Most Ticos are very conservative individuals who don't usually welcome 'strange' or different ideas. A lot of foreigners view Ticos as lacking initiative and as being passive. They also complain of the lack of punctuality and quick decision-making. However, the positive aspects of Ticos are their friendliness and hospitality. Costa Ricans are also extremely social, and they enjoy gatherings and celebrations of all sorts.'
—InfoCostaRica website (http://infocostarica.com)

DECADES OF INTERNATIONAL IMMIGRATION and exposure to tourism means Ticos are more cosmopolitan than most other peoples in the region, and you are unlikely to make any huge social faux pas or have real difficulty fitting in. Ticos are very open and friendly, and so social etiquette is mostly down to common sense and common courtesy—not going nude on the beach will go a long way, as will attempting to resolve disputes through consensus rather than arguing and making the other party look bad in public. Some other main points to avoid are openly criticising the country or religion, as many people are very religious. However, this country does of course have its own particular customs and attitudes, so here are some pointers on things to look out for.

TO 'QUEDAR BIEN'

Within a very short time of being in Costa Rica, you will start to feel as though you are a pawn in someone else's game of 'Six Degrees of Separation'. Even in San José, you will bump into the same people again and again—and if you are meeting someone for the first time you will, no doubt, discover that they either know, or quite probably are related to, several other people you have already met.

This is not surprising in a small country with only a few million people. Imagine how much worse it must have been in the early 20th century, say, when people hardly ever left their own small community and everyone literally did know everyone else. In this situation, communal in-fighting would have spelled disaster, so Ticos developed a coping mechanism: being nice.

Ticos are internationally renowned for being some of the nicest and most generous people you can meet. Their overuse of *con mucho gusto* is almost as bad as the British obsession with 'please' and 'thank you.' Ticos want to *quedar bien* (pronounced 'kay-DAR bee-EN') with everyone, which means something like 'not rocking the boat, staying on good terms, saving face, and appearing amicable'.

If you want to *quedar bien,* the basic rule is never to be rude or to openly refute what others say. It also means never grovelling; it is a solution that allows everyone to walk away with their pride intact.

Most importantly, you must not shout at, humiliate or criticise anyone, especially in public. Ticos are so proud and easily offended that the criminal code lays down a prison term of up to 50 days for a person who offends another's 'dignity or honour', especially in public.

All of this is, in essence, what gives the Ticos their peaceable reputation, but it also results in what some outsiders regard as hypocritical behaviour.

What's the Fuss About?

Ticos don't like to admit they are wrong, and you will not *quedar bien* with anyone by trying to push the point—as I found out in a particularly stressful incident after someone wiped four hours' worth of work off my computer. I was the one who ended up apparently at fault for having made an unseemly fuss in public.

In order to *quedar bien*, many Ticos say 'yes' when they mean 'no', simply to avoid conflict or offence. The result for outsiders can be, unsurprisingly, infuriating. Long-term civil servant and award-winning author, Carmen Naranjo, even went as far as to publish a list of all the phrases Ticos (especially civil servants) use in order to be non-committal.

Similarly, many people don't like to appear foolish or unhelpful by admitting they don't know something, so you should always ask factual questions rather than ones with yes or no answers. When asking directions, it's always best to check with two or three people just to make sure their answers coincide.

In *The Ticos* by the Biesanz family, playwright Melvin Méndez explained, 'People in other countries can be categorical. Not Ticos. We beat around the bush to avoid saying: 'No', a syllable which seems almost rude to us, and rather than hurt someone, we say one thing and do another.'

Ticos' need to *quedar bien* means that problems must be solved by bargaining and consensus, even within the government. On the plus side, conflict is avoided—but sometimes at the expense of real decision-making.

GESTURES
Greetings

Ticos aren't as big on cheek-kissing as many other Latin Americans. When meeting someone for the first time, it's best to follow their lead rather than lunging in for the embarrassment of a potentially unrequited kiss. You may not reach kissing status until you know someone better. Among non-intimate acquaintances, kissing is more common between women than between men and women—usually reserved more for family members and close friends.

Kissing

When you do find yourself in a kissing situation, remember that double cheek European-style kissing is not the Tico way—instead you kiss just one cheek, making quite a loud lip-smacking noise rather than a 'mwaa' air kiss.

Men greeting other men shake hands firmly. With good friends they swoop in for a giant handshake, with the hand swinging down theatrically from head height. This is often followed up with some hearty shoulder-slapping for good measure.

In the Caribbean, men often greet each other with a tapping of clenched fists, or with an African handshake in which the fingers are slipped out from the 'normal' handshake and the fingertips hooked together, before slipping back into the handshake.

Other Gestures

While someone you've only just met may quite happily prod you in the shoulder to emphasise a point during conversation,

Handshakes and Hugging

The ubiquitous Latin American *abrazo*, or embrace, is not generally done in Costa Rica. A firm handshake is the preferred greeting between men. Women often greet each other by touching the other's forearm lightly. Only women who know each other well will usually kiss each other on the cheeks.

Ticos generally aren't really very big on gesticulating or body contact. Below are some of the gestures you are most likely to come across:

- To beckon someone to come towards you, place your arm straight out in front of you, hand palm down, and flap the hand up and down. Beckoning with the index finger is considered rude. Also rude—but often used for this purpose—is a hiss.
- To ask for the bill across a crowded restaurant, mime signing a cheque to the waiter.
- To signify a place or room being full of people, place the palm towards you with fingers up, then bring all fingertips together.
- To signify something incredible, fast, unbelievable or outrageous, hold the forearm horizontally in front of the chest with palm facing inwards and shake the hand vigorously up and down (often hard enough to make fingers snap loudly against each other).
- To signify that something is finished and you no longer care about it (usually a relationship), place the palms facing each other at chest height and rapidly wipe one palm over the other about three or four times.
- While driving, if the oncoming cars flash their headlights, this means there are police, a landslide, a flood or some other unpleasantness up ahead.
- To say 'cheers' while drinking, Ticos often use the popular Spanish ritual of holding the glass up high and shouting *Arriba!* (up), down low shouting *Abajo!* (down), in the

middle, shouting *Al centro!* and then swallowing the drink, with a *Y adentro!* (inside).

CONVERSATION TOPICS

It's never difficult to strike up conversation with a Tico—in fact you might have to feign sleep on public transport in order to avoid chatting with your neighbour. There are no explicitly off-limits areas, although be aware that many Ticos are quite conservative. If you get a sense of this, it's obviously best to avoid risqué topics such as your impending sex change or fascination with Satanism.

Ticos are big newspaper readers and, being such a small country, generally have a good grasp of affairs in the region and the world. They generally respect the perceived discipline and organisation of the US and Europe, and will be fascinated to find out more about your country and also your opinion of Costa Rica. Score points by reading the local press so you're up to date with what's going on.

Be warned, however. While they're cynical about their own political situation, don't criticise it too much yourself—or anything else in the country for that matter, with the possible exception of the roads. Ticos are enormously patriotic, and while they can be as critical as they like, they may take offence if you do so.

Family is more important to Ticos than just about anything else (with the possible exception of football—the conversation starter par excellence). They will want to tell you all about their relatives, and will expect you to reciprocate. If your family is not with you, carry pictures.

Ticos are only a step removed from their agricultural heritage. Many people will talk for hours about farming, countryside lore and customs, and the weather. Despite the country having only two rather predictable seasons, the onset of climate change

Football is an ideal gambit—especially for men, who will often be invited to join in an informal kick-a-bout. But other hobbies can spark conversation too. Coin collection is very big among Ticos, and they will often want to swap foreign currency with you or show you their collection. If you're lucky, someone will give you one of the beautiful (now phased out) 5-colón bills—with orchids on one side and a copy of the coffee-harvesting painting from the Teatro Nacional on the other.

(which has already had drastic effects in Central America) now means that each downpour and passing cloud has become almost as worthy of comment as in Britain.

INSULTS

Like many Latinos, Ticos love their mothers to the point of worship. Consequently, one of the worst things you can call someone is *hijo'eputa* (son of a bitch), although it really depends upon the tone of voice used. (This term is widely used as an exclamation with no hint of insult.) Some Ticos prefer, *Tu madre puede ser una santa, pero vos sos un hijo'eputa,* meaning to say 'your mother might be a saint, but you're a son of a bitch'. Ticos are quite *delicados* and easily offended. Personal criticism can be taken as a huge insult.

BRIBING AND BARGAINING

The popular respect for law and egalitarianism means Costa Rica has relatively low levels of corruption compared to the rest of the region. While bribery certainly goes on, it is not advisable as a foreigner to get into a situation where you are trying to bribe a police officer or bureaucrat. If really necessary, there are local intermediaries who will do this for you! Likewise, bargaining is not common either, not even in local markets.

FLIRTING AND ROMANCE

"It's harder to find a faithful man in Costa Rica than a Piña Colada in the Sahara," I was told by an earnest young Tico I had met only an hour earlier. He grabbed my hand across the table and looked deep into my eyes, adding, "But I want you to know that I'm really different."

As if this didn't sound fishy enough, it didn't take long to verify with friends that he was, in fact, an incorrigible womaniser. "I'm a Latino," he explained, unabashed, when confronted with the truth. "I have my pride and a reputation to maintain. I'll say anything it takes to get a woman out on a date. Being serious and sincere with a woman like you usually works like a charm."

Ticos love to *dar pelota* (flirt) and do not do so surreptitiously. If you're a woman, men will use any opportunity to smile, blow kisses or strike up a conversation with you, and their heads continually swivel, owl-like and slack-jawed, at passing female pedestrians. The waiter at one restaurant I ate at bombarded me with hopeful little notes telling me, for example, 'Meeting people like you makes me happy to be alive.' Some restaurants and public places even have signs banning *escenas amorosas* (amorous scenes).

"I was quite shocked at first," said Adrian Hepworth, a British photographer living in Costa Rica. "In my country, if you fancy someone, you do your best to ignore them and appear really cool. There's none of that here—if someone likes you they'll make it really obvious. They'll stare and smile at you for ages, or just come up and tell you right out."

Ticos are also very traditional, however. Heaven help the man who expects his date to pick up her half of the tab, or the woman who fails to pamper her boyfriend as if he were a small child. You will also become heavily involved with your opposite number's family at a much earlier stage than in an American or European relationship.

"Before you know it, you will spend every weekend either going to your partner's parents' place, or having them to yours," said a German, who had been dating a Tica for six months. "The first time I met my girlfriend's family, they threw a huge party with 80 family members who had come to check me out! They're wonderful people though, so I don't mind, and it's fun to be part of a close family after growing up in such a different society."

Even though Costa Ricans—both men and women—seem to be more forward than visitors from reserved countries, there is an invisible line beyond which Costa Rican women generally do not go. While men can be very charming, they tend to believe that foreign women have looser morals than Ticas, so female visitors should exercise care with flirtation unless they are really interested. Don't rush things—it's better to take time to develop a proper relationship.

When it comes to that particular brand of (nearly always urban) Costa Rican men who, like the construction workers back home, hang around aiming continual lewd comments and wolf whistles at women, especially blonde tourists, it is good to have the phrase *mal educado*—('badly educated', 'rude') to hand. It might not shame all of them, but it will at least stop you boiling with silent impotence.

GOSSIP

Gossip or *chismes*, is a major part of life in Costa Rica, and the old Spanish saying '*pueblo pequeño, infierno grande*' ('small town, big hell') is still more apt than ever. People really worry about *el que dirán?* (what will people say?).

A hugely popular radio show featuring the ever-nosy character Doña Vina highlighted the issue and spawned a whole new verb, *vinear*, meaning 'to gossip' (a nosy person is *muy vina*), and Samuel Rovinski's play *Las Fisgonas de Paso Ancho* (The Busybodies of Paso Ancho) is obligatory reading in schools.

People from Cartago are particularly renowned as gossips, and are sometimes called *begoñas*, supposedly because they plant begonias in their window boxes as something to hide behind as they spy on their neighbours.

Ticos will happily talk for ages, and in great detail, about the most seemingly insignificant goings-on in the lives of friends, neighbours and television stars—particularly if any whiff of scandal is involved.

My Dutch friend, Frans, who went to work in the small town of Puerto Viejo de Sarapiquí, told me of his arrival there. "The first night, I only met the family I was staying with and didn't leave the house. The next morning I went for a walk around the town and people were going past waving at me and shouting, 'Hello Frans!' I couldn't believe it was possible that word had got around that fast."

Fabrizio Gómez, an actor, said, "People think it's wonderful that we have no army in our country. But why would we need one when we're so good at spying on each other's every move?"

Perhaps it's unsurprising then, that many Ticos have very few friends with whom they would trust their most intimate thoughts or worries, instead relying on family for emotional support.

PIROPOS

Piropos are an old Spanish tradition from the good old days when people would take a *paseo* around the town park every evening, with the single young men walking in the opposite direction from the single young women.

As the *'piroper'* knew the *'piropee'*, the idea was to come up with the most clever or flowery limerick-like *piropo* possible in order to impress the object of your affection. One among dozens that became almost commonplace was:

Del cielo cayó un pañuelo
bordado en sedina negra
decile a tu mamacita
que si quiere ser mi suegra.

From the sky fell a handkerchief
Embroidered in black silk
Go and ask your mummy
If she'd like to be my mother-in-law.

With the growth of cities, migration and greater anonymity, however, the *piropo* went into something of a decline, and often took on more of a clever-dick, often insulting air. The infuriating thing about today's *piropos* is that they're usually muttered as you go past someone, by which time it's too late to come back with a clever retort. Two you are most likely to still hear are: *'Dónde fue el choque?'* (Where was the crash?) and *'Tantas curvas y yo sin frenos!'* (So many curves, and me without brakes!).

Sociologists have compiled various lists of other *piropos* which are still in use, however, such as:

- *Qué vestido más lindo, lástima la percha!*
  (Nice dress, shame about the hanger.)
- *Tanta carne y yo en ayunas!*
  (So much meat, and me on a diet!)
- *Por usted sería capaz de buscar trabajo.*
  (For you I could go out and find a job.)
- *Parece la carreta de Sarchí... solo pintura!*
  (You look like a Sarchí cart (the traditional Tico brightly-coloured ox-drawn coffee cart)... nothing but paint!)
- *Qué dichoso su doctor!*
  (What a lucky man your doctor is.)
- *Quisiera ser bizco, para verla dos veces.*
  (I wish I was cross-eyed so I could see you twice.)

Especially clever plays on words (but which lose all cleverness in English) are:

- *Amor... a mortadela huele tu boca.*
  (My love... your mouth smells of *mortadela*.)
- *Adiós... a Dios le pido que cambie tu cara.*
  (Hello... I pray to God that he changes your face.)

These *piropos* don't have to be just from men to women, although unsurprisingly they usually are, and more often than not you'll just get the kind of construction worker/ truck driver monosyllables you would expect at home. For some men, it seems that articulating even one word is just a bit too tricky, so they have to make do with hissing (poor lambs). At times it seems that you have stepped into a snake pit. Some men even have wolf whistle car horns.

"Of course I don't really like it," one beautiful young Tica told me. "But it's just part of the background noise, and I ignore it like everyone else. The thing that really surprised me was when I went to the United States and no one whistled or hooted at me, I started to think there was something wrong with me."

NAMES AND SURNAMES

Although, like all Hispanic people, Ticos have both a paternal and maternal surname, in daily life the paternal one is often the only one used, which makes life a lot less confusing for non-Latins. For legal purposes or on business cards, they will probably use both (and often their middle name too—usually the name of the saint on whose day they were born).

Confused? Don't be. Ernesto Tomás, son of Daniel Luis Alvarez Gómez and María Fernanda Rodríguez Mora, will be called Ernesto Tomás Alvarez Rodríguez (or just Ernesto Alvarez). Both men and women keep their surnames at birth throughout life, regardless of marriage or divorce, although Ernesto's mother María Rodríguez may at times be referred to as María Rodríguez de Alvarez.

For the dual surname purpose, an illegitimate child may take its mother's paternal surname twice, e.g. Ernesto Rodríguez Rodríguez.

Official Documents and Listings

In a telephone book or in official documentation, surnames usually come first, so Ernesto would be Alvarez Rodríguez Ernesto Tomás.

While religious first names are still popular, the fascination with all things American has ensured a growing number of Anglo-Saxon first names (often bizarrely phonetically spelt), such as Maikol, Randall, Warner and Leidy. Others are nonsensical, such as Email and Pulmitan (a bus company). There is even reportedly one child in Limón who goes round with the name of Usnavi after his parents, with no idea of what it meant, decided they liked the sound of a sign painted on a ship in the bay: 'US Navy'.

NICKNAMES

Ticos delight in nicknames, and Alajuela in particular is famous for them. "Basically, as soon as you set foot in the town you're going to have a nickname—whether you realise it or not," said Daniel, a middle-aged teacher who grew up there.

The people from Alajuela, also famed for their love of practical jokes, even have a nickname for their town's statue of national hero Juan Santamaría, who is called El Erizo (The Hedgehog) because of his frizzy hair. The people of Alajuela and their football team are now known throughout the country as Los Erizos, or Los Manudos because they were traditionally known for their big, rough hands.

Heredianos, and their football team, are called Florenses, as their women are supposed to be the most beautiful 'flowers' in the country.

In race-conscious Costa Rica, a lot of nicknames have to do with skin colour. Daniel, whose skin could hardly be described as darker than sallow, grew up being known as *Tijo* (a type of black bird).

Many times, a whole family will take on a nickname because of the attribute of just one member. "If someone walks like a bird, or is really slow, the whole family may end up being called the *Gallinas* (Chickens) or the *Tortugas* (Tortoises)," said Daniel.

Other nicknames are more ingenious. One man whose parents came from Río Frío (Cold River) and the spa town of Aguas Calientes (Hot Water) was called *Tibio* (Lukewarm).

On a two-day visit to Puerto Viejo de Sarapiquí, I was introduced to a man with some indigenous blood called *Cacique* (Chief), a rather chubby man called *Comeburras* (Packed Lunch Guzzler), and stopped to buy ice cream at a *pulpería* owned by a man with narrow eyes called *El Chino* (the Chinaman).

Often, however, people might be totally oblivious of their nicknames. One Tico friend of mine, who is short with rather goggly eyes, is referred to by everyone as *Sapito* (Little Toad)—although they would never tell him that. On the other hand, a waiter in San José's Vishnu restaurant who is so concerned with his appearance that he even gets his eyebrows trimmed is loudly hailed as *Cejas* (Eyebrows).

While in other cultures Tico nicknames might sound racist, sexist or otherwise politically incorrect, for Ticos they are usually nothing more than a mark of camaraderie. Among Ticos, who don't like to think that anyone is any more special than anyone else, they are also a means of *choteo*. So don't get offended if you hear yourself or others called *Flaco* (Skinny), *Moreno* (Darky), *Gordo* (Fatty), *Güila* (Kid), or if, like me, you have green eyes, *Gato* (Cat).

Spanish names have stock nickname equivalents, such as *Moncha* (from Ramona), *Paco* (Francisco) or *Nacho* (Ignacio). As a foreigner, you may have your name changed with the addition of an—*ito/ita* as a mark of affection, especially if you have a Latin name—for example Teresita, from Teresa.

THE PULPERÍA

The Tico equivalent of a favourite corner shop, *pulperías* have been such a ubiquitous feature of Tico communities that they have even figured in art and literature.

The *pulpería* is not a place where one buys or sells *pulpo* (octopus), but *pulpa* (literally pulp), such as fruit and meat. Since the arrival of supermarkets, *pulperías* have been increasingly confined to the countryside and urban barrios. Unlike supermarkets, however, they represent much more than a place to stock up on groceries.

Some still accept credit or payment in kind, and most double up as a bar, games hall, local bush telegraph and centre for socialising, counselling and advice. They may have a pool table or table football, chess and checkers, and sell everything from ice cream to machetes. The *pulpería* plays a huge role in rural areas where people live quite isolated from each other—it's a place to gather in the evening or at weekends, to sit on benches or in rocking chairs and gossip.

In the poorest areas, it may provide people's only chance to listen to music, watch television or make a telephone call.

DRESS STYLE AND BODY IMAGE

Ticos take a great deal of pride in their appearance, although style is quite a lot more relaxed than in many other Latin American countries—partly as a result of the strong North American influence.

For example, you will see, especially among upper middle-class students, a lot of piercings and tattoos and surf style is massive among the country's youth. However, even if some people look as laid back in style as they do at home, you will notice there is very little sense of individualism. Ticos worry about what other people will think of them, and always try to wear the 'right' label in order to *aparentar*. You are only a little more likely to see a Tico punk than a surfing tapir.

Of course, many Ticos cannot afford Quiksilver or Billabong, and in every town you will find one or more shops selling *Ropa Americana*—cheap, second-hand clothing from the United States. Even if they cannot afford new clothing, however, Ticos' clothes are always spotlessly clean, being washed and ironed after nearly every wearing.

Women take a huge amount of pride in how they look, and beauty contests are popular. While men drink away their evenings in the local *cantina*, women spend hours in the *sala de belleza* (beauty parlour) having their hair dyed or fingernails painted.

The basic female 'look' involves a large amount of make-up, tight-fitting trousers and even tighter-fitting, colourful tops. As in other Latin countries, it's quite unusual to see skirts—apparently because tight trousers are better at emphasising your shapely behind. Short hair for women is almost unheard of in Costa Rica. Ticas make the most of their long, glossy manes and have a huge amount of confidence in their feminine wiles.

With the influx of Western television culture, body image and diet are changing, and cases of anorexia are starting to rise. One rather chubby Tica anthropology student told me this was a senseless paradox in Costa Rica.

"It's really crazy, because that's not how Ticas should be," she said. "In fact, men here prefer women with *figuras rellenitas* (filled-out figures). They've been historically

Dress style on the Caribbean coast of Costa Rica tends to be much more relaxed than in the chillier, more conservative, central plains.

conditioned into it from the days when you wanted a plump and muscular wife to do heavy work and bear healthy children. When I go out at night dressed in a tight outfit, I get a lot more attention than any of my skinny friends."

Men, particularly in the countryside, wear a handlebar moustache, shirt open to show off their chest hair (and if possible several chunky gold chains), cowboy boots (or ankle-length rubber boots in the rainy season), and a cowboy hat. The outfit may be finished off with a leather-sheathed machete slung over the shoulder.

Shorts are not acceptable in the city, unless, of course, they are terminally trendy three-quarter length skateboard shorts. Outside the city, shorts are fine for young people—although dress sense is still fairly proper unless you're in a surfing beach town.

At the beach, conservatism is still the rule. Ticas wear bikinis which can look positively frumpy next to the 'dental floss' G-strings of Brazil and Venezuela, and some even cover up with a T-shirt while swimming.

SURVIVAL SKILLS

'If you ask for something and the answer is ʹ *mañana*' (tomorrow), don't take this literally. ʹ *Mañana*' is best translated as 'not today' and could mean anything from days or weeks to never.' —Austrian tourist, Julia Schmitz, following a five-month trip to Costa Rica.

GETTING THERE

People of most nationalities don't need a visa to enter Costa Rica, but you should check first. With a passport valid for six months, US, Canadian, most western European, Israeli, Japanese and some other citizens will be granted three months' stay. Others may only get 30 days. In any case, if you want to extend your stay, you can easily hop over to Nicaragua or Panama for a couple of days at the end of your time limit and come back in again (although the authorities may soon clamp down on this so-called perpetual tourism). It is certainly not worth overstaying your visa and trying to sort it out later. While the immigration police rarely check tourists, I have met people being deported with no chance of returning within ten years after being caught overstaying their visa by just a couple of weeks.

Visas and Residency

If you want to stay more permanently in the country, the most common types of residency are: *pensionados* (retired residents), *rentistas* (earning residents), *inversionistas* (investor residents), *representantes* (those on company visas), and *residentes* (permanent residents). All can own companies and receive income in Costa Rica, but *pensionados* and *rentistas* may not actually work in the country.

However, in 2004 the immigration agency said that the migratory situation in Costa Rica was 'out of control'. It has started to apply economic criteria to those hoping to obtain residency, stating in some cases that an applicant 'would not add any input to the economy of Costa Rica or create employment for Costa Ricans'.

Currently, a *rentista* applicant must demonstrate a permanent fixed income from investments of at least US$ 1,000 per month. *Pesionados* must show investment income of US$ 600 per month while *inversionistas* must invest a minimum of US$ 200,000. However, these limits could well increase if new laws are passed.

What to Bring on Your Nature Holiday

If you're only coming for a short trip to the country and are heading straight out to the wilds for a nature holiday, the following items would be very useful:

- A good pair of binoculars. Much of the wildlife is virtually invisible without them and even if you hire a guide, it's unlikely you'll be able to borrow theirs before the animal or bird in question has disappeared.
- A good field guide, so you can read more about the animals and birds you have spotted. (Excellent field guides and laminated reference cards showing the country's animals and birds are, however, on sale throughout the country.)
- Plenty of insect repellent, if possible with a high DEET content, for those mosquito-plagued mornings and evenings—especially important in the rainy season or in the jungle. In places where mosquito nets are necessary, most hotels will provide them. Otherwise, they are more easily and cheaply bought in local Costa Rican stores than at home.
- A waterproof jacket or poncho, and an umbrella. Even in the dry season you can get caught in torrential rain.
- Sturdy footwear. You are likely to end up walking up more hills and through more bogs (especially in Monteverde!) than you would have imagined possible.

The Costa Rican immigration service has also introduced a new identity card for all foreigners with legal residency in the country.

WHAT TO BRING FROM HOME

There are few necessities, especially American-made ones, which you can't find in San José. But if you simply can't live without more peculiar local delicacies from home, such as Marmite, or your country's brand of tea or chocolate, it stands to reason that you should bring these with you.

While most things can be found in San José, this is often at a price. Basically, anything not made in the country will be more expensive to buy than elsewhere, due to the shipping costs and/or import taxes (although this could change with the future ratification of CAFTA).

In particular, sound systems (and electronic devices in general) are a lot more expensive in Costa Rica, as are cameras (and film), printer ink cartridges and foreign-made clothes (because of 30 per cent import taxes). However, books are not subject to any import tax (as the government wants people to read) and computers are taxed much less than other electronic devices (as the government wants people to use computers).

Remember that if you're coming from Europe or many other countries outside the Americas, your electrical gadgets will probably not work in Costa Rica as it operates on the American voltage system. Some may be usable with a special adaptor. However, cell phones and video recorders from outside the Americas will probably not work at all.

ACCOMMODATION

Costa Rica has a huge proliferation of hotels, but when you first arrive, one of the best options is a home stay. Much less impersonal than a hotel, and a good means of immersing yourself in the local culture, this will place you with a well-vetted Costa Rican family.

If you want to make your stay permanent, do note that foreigners are allowed to rent and own houses and property in

Costa Rica. Costs vary widely depending on location, and the process for buying a house is highly bureaucratic, with taxes and fees amounting to more than 4 per cent of its value.

In San José, at one end of the scale, you could rent a room in a student house near the universities in the lively area of San Pedro for around US$ 100 per month. At the other end, you could rent a luxurious pad with swimming pool and jacuzzi in flashy Escazú (otherwise known as Gringolandia for its huge number of expat residents) for around US$ 5,000 per month. Areas on the east side, such as Barrio Escalante and San Pedro, are cheaper, cooler and a little more rainy (yes, the climate can really change within just a 15-minute drive here) than the west (Santa Ana and Escazú).

The best areas outside San José in the Meseta Central area are Heredia (Santo Domingo and San Isidro) or Moravia. Somewhat further away (around 45 minutes drive) are Atenas, Grecia and San Ramón. Areas such as Heredia are cheaper than San José and may have a more 'genuine' feel.

Generally, prices to both rent and buy are around half the price you would expect to pay for accommodation of a similar standard in the United States. In the countryside, you can rent a house for around US$ 250 per month and up, and entire farms are for sale from around US$ 200,000. Beachfront locations carry a premium. Condos and other residences on the beach can be bought from around US$ 125,000 up to several million dollars.

Where to Look for Good Deals

Look for the best bargains via the Residents' Association, in local newspapers, or even on supermarket and shop notice boards. Sometimes you will even find free deals in return for house-sitting a foreigner's house for six months while they winter back home. You don't have to be a resident of Costa Rica to own property and you're entitled to the same ownership rights as citizens of Costa Rica. Ownership of real estate in Costa Rica is fully guaranteed by the constitution. However, if you're buying, remember to use the services of a recommended lawyer and notary as there are con artists out there.

A particular scam that came to light in late 2005 involved six notaries (legally required to transfer a property from one owner to another) who were found to have ripped off more than US$ 5 million from would-be investors by forging property deeds for properties that did not belong to them. Two of the six already had criminal records and the others were under investigation for other murky operations. However, there is no requirement for background checks to be carried out on notaries in Costa Rica, and with 10,000 in the country, it is impossible to monitor them all. Even if convicted of fraud they cannot be struck off, but only suspended for ten years.

Information on Notaries

Officials at the National Registry estimate that only around 2 per cent of notaries are involved in fraudulent schemes, but say any potential seller or buyer should make sure they know their notary's history. This can be viewed for free at:

http://www.poder-judicial.go.cr/direccionnacionaldenotariado/ or by contacting the National Registry at tel: (506) 295-3953.

To report a case of real estate fraud, call the fraud department of the OIJ at tel: (506) 295-3312.

Building your own dream house may also involve more red tape than you would anticipate. Land, labour and materials are not expensive (depending on materials, location and size, you can expect to pay from US$ 300–US$ 600 a square metre)—but you may be letting yourself in for delays, unreliable labour, fussy building inspectors, different laws and building codes and other unforeseen problems. It's a good idea to talk to others who have built their own home to get tips and avoid re-inventing the wheel. Importantly, if your heart's set on building on the seafront, remember that the first 50 m of beach from the mean high tide mark is public and cannot be built on. The next 150 m is concession property, on government leasehold, and cannot be leased by a foreigner unless more than half the leasing company is owned by a Costa Rican.

In all cases, beware of squatters. Landless *invasores* frequently move onto property, and may gain 'rights of possession' if they live there for a year and either construct a dwelling or work the land. You will then be unable to sell it. If you have bought a large piece of property and are absent, it's essential to employ a guard.

Plumbing

Don't flush toilet paper down the bowl! Water pressure in Costa Rica is poor, and blockages are frequent. A bin is provided in every bathroom for used paper.

Mail

The recently-privatised Costa Rican mail service isn't bad for Latin America, but that doesn't mean it's great. The general lack of street addresses means that most Ticos have a post office box *(apartado)*—but a much faster and more reliable service is Mail Boxes Etc. Using this, mail is sent to you at an address in Florida, and then couriered down to the Mail Boxes Etc San José office.

Power and Bills

Costs are generally very reasonable—you can expect to pay an average of US$ 20–30 per month if you don't use heating or air conditioning. Costa Rica has the cheapest electricity rate in Central America (mostly generated by local hydro- and geothermal plants) and by far the biggest connection to the power grid in the whole of Central America. The voltage used is 110V AC at 60Hz, the same as the USA.

There is no natural gas supply, but some people use propane gas (either small tanks bought from the supermarket or large 100 litre tanks from local suppliers). If only used for cooking, a small tank will last about one month, a large one a whole year. Gas prices are fixed by the government.

Water is also a government utility (A&A), and bills are usually around US $5 per month.

Bills can be paid in banks, supermarkets and over the Internet, but if you don't pay on time, your service will be cut off, usually within two to three weeks. Although you may be able to negotiate a little, once the service is cut off, you will have to go to the main San José or regional office to pay a fee to get reconnected.

TELECOMMUNICATIONS

Basic telecommunication services are provided by the Instituto Costarricense de Electricidad (ICE). Its subsidiary, Radiográfica Costarricense (RASCA), provides telex, telegraph, video conferencing, data transmission, Internet access, facsimile, data services, etc.

Costa Rica is too small to have telephone codes, and call costs vary with distance. The service is generally good, cheap and calls are half price overnight and on Sundays, as well as on holidays such as Christmas, Valentine's Day and Mother's Day. However, lines can be congested or down due to bad weather, especially in the rainy season.

Also be aware that not everywhere has a phone line. Be extremely wary of buying or renting a house or land that does not already have one installed as, depending on where you are, this can take years. If you must have a phone, be sure to buy real estate with an existing phone line or receive credible assurances that you can have one installed within a given time frame.

Telephone costs are reasonable. A typical monthly phone bill, excluding overseas calls, is about US$ 20 per month. Long distance calls from Costa Rica are very costly though (typically US$ 1 a minute to the US or Canada).

Cell phones can still be difficult to get hold of (though the situation is much better than a few years ago—the British Embassy waited more than a year to get a cell phone in 2000!). There are also promises that the number of lines is going to be greatly expanded. Cell phones cost from a little less than US$ 100 up to around US$ 350. If you don't use your cell phone excessively (and don't make international calls), your monthly fee will probably be less than US$ 30. Watch out if you are not an official resident—you will find that while you can buy a cell phone, you cannot legally get a number for it! A good alternative is renting one, from around

US$ 50 per week. For more information, check Cell Phones Costa Rica at:

http://www.cellphonescr.com

or call tel: (506) 293-5892 or (506) 379-0676.

There are various types of public phones. Chip phones, which take a regular telephone card, and coin phones (put the coin in the slot at the top; it will drop when the phone is answered—do NOT try to push it in!). For coin-operated phones, try to have the correct coins to hand, as they only accept the silver coloured coins and not the newer gold coloured ones.

There are also Colibri or Viajero card phones (197 for local calls, 199 for international calls). These do not accept the Chip cards. You dial 197 or 199, slide the card through an optical reader and then dial the phone number you want to reach. (Until recently, you had to dial a 13-digit code within a specific time limit followed by the telephone number).

On the downside, the service is so cheap that you can often wait for hours for a public phone as the person in front of you chats away. In rural areas too small for payphones, private homes, garages, *pulperías* and bars will often 'rent' their phone.

Internet

There is really no high speed Internet in Costa Rica in the way you would understand the term 'fast' at home—but it's a great deal better than it was only three or four years ago, when it was excruciatingly slow.

If you are an IT professional, business user or an avid Web surfer, however, you will probably be tearing your hair out before long. There are numerous outages, problems with IP addresses being blocked for outgoing email, system slowness and DNS (name server) problems. Many people find they experience at least one of these problems almost every day.

Basically, there are two options on Internet connections, depending on where you live. If you are in the central valley or an urban area, you will probably be able to benefit from the cable Internet services now offered by most cable companies (you must be a customer of their cable TV service). Rates are around US$ 40 per month. Higher speed services are now spreading around the country, and can even be found at the beach areas. However, do not presume that because you know

How to Type @

It is useful to know, when wanting to write @ on a keyboard in Costa Rica, that you must usually simultaneously type Alt and Q; Alt, Ctrl and Q; Alt, Gr and Q, or Alt and 64 (from the number pad on the right hand side of the keyboard).

someone who has ADSL (RSDI in Costa Rica) that it will be available where you live or work—even if that is only a few blocks away.

RACSA (http://www.racsa.co.cr) also provides Internet connection based on a usage cost—US$10 per month for 10 hours, US$ 25 for 25 hours, US$ 35 per month for 90 hours. A new service offers unlimited access for US$15 per month, but this is only available to residence phone lines registered in your name, and connection is only allowed on that phone line. The RACSA service has improved of late, but many customers still complain of poor service and customer care.

You will generally find more reliable and more widely offered services in the Central Valley, and your chances of resolving a support issue in San José are far better than in remote locations. However, be aware that English is not widely spoken at ICE. RACSA may be better, but you still may not be able to find an English-speaking assistant at a moment's notice. Sorting out computer problems over the phone can be tricky unless your Spanish is very good. RACSA and the cable TV services are constantly expanding their services. There are also reasonably-priced Internet cafés nearly everywhere.

Television and Radio

Costa Rica has 13 local TV stations. Cable TV is available depending on where you are—the bigger the city the better the cable service—and costs about US$ 20 per month. Currently the three cable TV providers in the country are AMNET, Cable Tica and Cable América. These companies offer many of the channels available to US cable subscribers.

DirecTV also operates in Costa Rica. The company offers 152 digital TV channels and 33 music channels. The country has 50 AM, 43 FM and 19 short-wave stations.

These companies offer Latin American Spanish language channels and dozens of US channels including CBS, NBC, ABC, Fox, HBO, CNN, ESPN, TNT, the Discovery Channel, etc. There is an initial sign-up fee of around US$ 20 and a monthly charge of about the same amount.

Most radio stations play Latin music. Radio Dos 99.5 FM and Radio 107.5 FM offer 100 per cent rock and also have regular programmes in English.

WHERE THE STREETS HAVE NO NAME...

"I crossed the Atlantic, got all the way to Costa Rica, and then found myself up against the utter necessity to buy... a compass," said Greek academic Constantino Láscaris in his definitive work on the Ticos, *El Costarricense.*

Láscaris was not exaggerating. Finding your way around is one of the most bizarre and infuriating experiences you will have in the country, especially if, like me, you have little sense of direction.

The country was, until recently, largely rural. Villages didn't need street signs as everyone knew where everyone else lived. Unfortunately, this means that today, except in city centres, the streets remain largely nameless and numberless.

Instead, all directions are based on landmarks. You will be told, for example, to look for 'the pink building 200 m east and 50 m north from the south-east corner of the Supreme Court'. Note that 100 m means a city block, 50 m half a block, etc. It often bears no relation to the actual distance, and sometimes metres may not be called *metros* at all, but *varas*.

Even worse, directions are often based on something well known to locals, but which no longer exists—such as the old Coca Cola plant in San José, or a mango tree in Escazú which has been chopped down. One foreigner I met said that in a small village he had been instructed to 'Go 200 m west from where Juan's cow gave birth last year'.

In addition, some people, when going to their house, will say they are going *arriba* (up), or if going to the town centre that they are going *abajo* (down). This is because most Tico towns were built in mountain valleys, with the church and official buildings on the valley floor and houses built up the slopes above. In reality, however, *arriba* may be down and *abajo* up.

Tico directions may be just about manageable if you can tell your cardinal points from the sun (as Ticos, uncannily, do). But what if you arrive in a town you don't know on a cloudy day, or at night?

Of course Ticos are very helpful, so you can always ask. However, they may well give you the wrong direction if they're not really sure, because it might seem rude or embarrassing to admit they don't know. They're also quite likely to tell you it's *a la vueltica* (just around the corner).

If in doubt, there are some handy tips to follow. If you are in the Valle Central, the closest mountain range is always to your south. If you're looking for something near the plaza, it's good to know that the main doors of all Tico churches point to the west.

In towns, where the central streets are numbered and laid out on a grid plan, the situation is initially quite confusing, being made up of *calles* (streets), which run north-south and *avenidas* (avenues) running east-west. The *calle* and *avenida* that cross closest to the town's central plaza are *calle central* (or 0) and *avenida central* (or 0). From there on, the *calles* go in odd numbers (1, 3, 5 etc.) to the east of the plaza, and in even numbers (2, 4, 6 etc.) to the west, while the *avenidas* go in odd numbers to the north and even numbers to the south.

How Addresses are Written

Street addresses are given by the *avenida* or *calle* and the two closest intersecting *avenidas* or *calles*. If you're looking for a building on Calle 13 between Avenidas Central and 2, the address would be written Calle 13, Avenidas Central y 2. In a telephone directory it would be C13, ACtl/2 or C13, A0/2.

Unsurprisingly, although some streets and buildings do have numbers, very few letters in Costa Rica ever get delivered to anyone's door. Nearly everyone has an *apartado postal*, or post office box.

GETTING AROUND
By Car

The Ticos' famed niceness evaporates the second they get behind the wheel of a car. The streets of San José, particularly, are too small for the volume of traffic. The centre is a maze of one-way, traffic-clogged streets noisy with (often unprovoked) horn-blowing. As a driver you need your wits about you. As a pedestrian, be warned that traffic lights turn immediately from red to green with no lip service paid to amber. If you're halfway across the city centre's six-lane Paseo Colón as the lights change, you'll be lucky if the traffic stops to let you get across.

Although you will find large, two or three-laned *autopistas* on the outskirts of San José, once you're outside the city, conditions change drastically. The Interamericana, the biggest road through the country, is single-lane for nearly all its length. Huge tailbacks of traffic stuck behind crawling *camiones* have been very common ever since the railways to Puntarenas and Limón were closed, as all freight is now transported by truck. Other common causes

By Colectivo

In rural areas, *colectivos* are common. These are small trucks or pick-ups, which operate like either a taxi or bus, and will pick up and drop off people as they go.

of hold-ups are landslides, herds of cattle, rainstorms and thick mist (especially passing over the Cerro de la Muerte at 3,491 m/11,454 ft).

Costa Rican roads are also notoriously holey. A popular joke runs: 'How can you spot a drunk driver?' Answer: 'He's the one driving in a straight line.' Although to be fair, the pothole *(hueco)* situation has improved a lot in the past few years.

The excruciating slowness combined with machismo generally leads Ticos to overtake at the slightest opportunity—usually around one of the (very many) blind curves—which in turn leads to one of the world's most horrific accident rates.

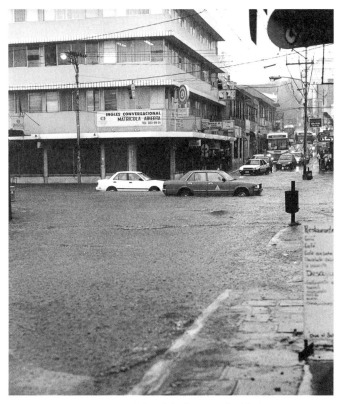

Rains in Costa Rica are torrential, and don't mix well with city centre congestion.

Things are not helped by the fact that driving licences can be bought for US$ 200, while Costa Rica must be one of the only countries in the world to have repealed a previously compulsory seat belt law after the constitutional court ruled in 1997 that it should be a matter of personal choice.

However, the wearing of seat belts was law once again by 2003 and the figures speak for themselves: 321 people died in road accidents in 2004, down from more than 700 in 2000—even though the number of vehicles was increasing by about 30,000 per year. In the years prior to the reintroduction of the seat belt law, the country's laudable life expectancy had actually fallen by one-tenth of a year for men as a result of traffic deaths.

Speed limits are fairly low, a maximum of 100 kmph (62 mph), but generally around 60 kmph (47 mph). Wherever the limit changes, it is painted on the road surface. People exceed the limits whenever possible and often resort to bribing the traffic police if caught. Fines are around 5,000 *colónes* for going up to 20 kmph (12 mph) over the limit and 20,000 *colónes* for anything faster.

Off the main routes, many roads, often along the edge of precipices, have yet to be asphalted and are littered with boulders and potholes. Some are barely passable in the rainy season. For this reason, 4x4 jeeps are by far the best option for off the beaten track driving. In many places people use *cuadriciclos* (all-terrain quad bikes) to get around.

You can drive in Costa Rica with a drivers' licence from your own country. Gasoline is relatively inexpensive, and is available in either regular or super. The price difference between the two grades of petrol is very small.

By Rail

Both lines to the Pacific and the 'Jungle Train' to the Caribbean have been closed down since the earthquake of 1991. However, some sections of the jungle train are still used by tour groups. Plans are allegedly afoot for foreign consortia to fully re-open the lines.

By Plane

Flying is a good alternative to spending hair-raising hours on the road. The two domestic airlines are Sansa (part of Grupo Taca), which flies out of the Juan Santamaría airport in Alajuela, and Travelair, which flies out of the Tobías Bolaños Airport in Pavas, San José. Return flights cost, on average, from US$ 100–250. Book well in advance during the high season as planes are small. Baggage weight is also limited to 12 kg per person.

It's also possible to charter small planes from the Tobías Bolaños Airport, which can be surprisingly economical if you are a group of four or five.

By Bus

Local buses run regularly and have the route (and often the fare) posted on the windscreen. To hail a bus like a Tico, you should stand on the road, arm pointing skywards Saturday Night Fever-style. You nearly always have to pay the full set fare, whether you're going only one stop or the whole route.

In the cities, buses have electronic *barras contadoras*, which count passengers on and off the bus. One of the only times in Costa Rica you are likely to encounter rudeness, or be shouted at, is if you hang around for too long between the bars as you wait for your change—the counting will be screwed up and the driver will have some explaining to do to his supervisors. Angry Tico bus drivers can be surprisingly scary.

When you want the driver to stop, shout *parada* (stop) or, if you have a loud and distinctive whistle, whistle like a Tico. Many bus drivers will drop you off or pick you up wherever you like. In the countryside, local buses are often old yellow US school buses with tiny seats—although you won't have to share your seat with farmyard animals as in most of the rest of Central America.

Long distance buses between Costa Rican towns run regularly and are good value (if slow). For example, a ticket to Bocas del Toro on the Panamanian border will set you back about US$ 10 and take about six hours. However, they all set out from different terminals in San José, in a move intended to cut down on congestion. Taxi drivers know where all the terminals are, and many travel agents have maps of the city showing their location.

If you are travelling to a popular destination, make sure to reserve your ticket well in advance and check the date as tickets are non-refundable.

Most buses do not have toilets or air conditioning, though on long journeys they will stop every few hours for a coffee break. International buses to Nicaragua and Panama are modern, roomy and equipped with savage air conditioning, so remember to take plenty of warm clothes. Most nationalities do not need visas for these Central American countries, although rules do change, so it's worth checking with the embassy before you set off.

By Taxi

Taxis in Costa Rica are all red, and are therefore called *rojos* (although at the airport they are orange). The rates are very good (around US$ 2 for a ride within San José). The taxis have a meter, called a *maría*, which you should make sure the driver switches on at the start of the journey. Taxi rides are also a good opportunity to get to grips with the way Ticos find their way around, as you'll have to give the kind

Travelling by pony cart—the taxi cab of Costa Rica's countryside.

of contorted directions the driver will understand, such as '*de la esquina sureste de la catedral, cincuenta metros al norte*' (50 m to the north from the south-east corner of the cathedral).

By Horse

Many parts of rural Costa Rica are still horse country, where you'll see people riding from the age of about four, often without saddles or shoes. Most horses do not wear bridles with bits, but just a *jáquima* (rope halter). However, the horses are so well-trained and sensitive that the touch of the rope rein on their neck is enough to steer them. If you are used to English-style riding, be aware that you steer one-handed and that the horse moves AWAY from the rope on its neck, so pressure from the right rein on its neck will make the horse turn left. *Monturas* (saddles) when used, are of a semi-Western style. The stirrups are worn long, and often have full leather foot covers designed for barefoot riders.

BUYING A CAR OR BRINGING YOUR CAR TO COSTA RICA

The tax you must pay to bring a car into the country is extraordinarily high—at least 50 per cent of the value of the car. Until a few years ago, the government, in a move to encourage foreign retirees to settle in the country, allowed them to bring a car in tax-free. This allowed people to sell their cars later at a huge profit and live quite comfortably on the earnings. The scheme has now been stopped due to abuse as people were bringing in several cars at a time.

On top of the tax payable, you also have to contend with shipping costs, customs delays etc. It is therefore not advisable to import a car that is not in excellent condition. It's really less of a hassle to buy a car in Costa Rica, although prices are obviously still pretty high (around US$ 20,000 for a five-year-old 4x4, or US$ 10,000 for a five-year-old family car). You will therefore see a lot of old, patched-up cars on the road, and many of the newer cars have actually been 'bought' under hire/purchase schemes.

Due to the high value of cars, vehicle theft is rampant. You should have a car alarm plus another safety device, such as a gear stick lock, installed. Most Ticos keep their car inside a kind of caged garage, or *cochera*. There are protected car parks in the cities, which charge less than a dollar an hour, but there are not enough to meet demand. If you have to park your car on the street, leave it under the watchful eye of a *cuidacarros* or *guachimán* (from the English word 'watchman'), whom you should pay around 300 colones.

Your car will also need to be fitted with a catalytic converter, and get the *marchamo* (obligatory liability insurance—cheaper than in the UK or US) and *ecomarchamo*—a sticker showing that exhaust emissions are within certain limits. In case of breakdown, labour is reasonable but parts may be expensive and hard to find if you drive a car that is not commonly found in the country.

HEALTH

Costa Rica has one of the best health systems in Latin America, and in 2005, recorded an average life expectancy of almost 77 years.

Many people take advantage of the country's relatively cheap, but highly professional, medical care to combine a holiday with medical procedures (often cosmetic) they could not afford at home. For more information on health services available, visit http://www.ticosearch.com/Health.

You are extremely unlikely to get ill while in the country, apart from—at worst—a spot of stomach trouble, but you should, of course, have health insurance.

Most communicable diseases are totally under control, and drinking tap water in the towns is safe (although bottled water tastes better). Food is generally very clean too—to the extent that cutlery in *sodas* and restaurants arrives in miniature plastic bags. However, if you have a weak stomach, it may be sensible to avoid ice in drinks, salads and fruits (apart from bananas and others which can be peeled).

You don't legally need any jabs to enter Costa Rica, though the following are sensible if you're going to spend much time in the region: hepatitis A, typhoid, tetanus, yellow fever and rabies (if you are planning to work with animals or are likely to be exposed to a lot of bats). Don't forget that vaccinations need several weeks to take effect, so see your doctor at least six weeks before you leave.

There have been some very occasional and limited outbreaks of malaria and dengue fever, usually on the Caribbean coast. Prophylactics are a good idea if you are staying in the depths of an affected area for a long time. However, anti-malarial drugs do no favours to your body, and offer no protection against dengue fever. It is important to take precautions to avoid being bitten by mosquitoes (use high DEET content insect repellent, long pants and sleeves, and mosquito nets—all particularly at dusk), and seek medical help in the extremely unlikely event that you do become ill, even if it's months after you left the country.

Watch Out For Creepy Crawlies!

There are all sorts of poisonous creepy crawlies to look out for, particularly snakes—but you would have to be extremely unlucky to receive a fatal bite. The golden rule is to wear boots in forests and to be careful where you put your feet and hands. If someone is bitten by a snake, try to identify the species (important for administering the correct antivenin), immobilise the limb and get help as soon as possible. Do not use tourniquets or slash open the wound—many snake venoms contain anti-coagulants, so the person could bleed to death. Don't try to suck out the venom either—you may end up with two people poisoned instead of one.

Chagas disease is another potential problem, especially if you're staying in old adobe huts with thatched roofs, where the culprit, the 'kissing bug' likes to live. The beetle bites you and tramples its parasite-ridden excrement into the wound. Over the course of many years, the parasites reproduce quietly, leaving you with heart, oesophagus and colon failure. The early, acute stage involves low-grade fever and headaches for a couple of months—seek medical help if you have these symptoms.

Finally, remember that Costa Rica is on the equator, so use high protection sun cream and drink plenty of water.

Natural Remedies

One of the most fascinating aspects of getting to know Ticos is the strong link they still have with the herbal remedies of their rural forebears, many of which were taught to the first Spanish settlers by their indigenous neighbours.

Despite having one of the best free health care systems in the world, many Ticos still swear by natural cures. If you even mention feeling on anything less than tip-top form, chances are you will receive suggestions to boil up a tea of special leaves or bark, or to take a bath in cleansing herbs.

If you have earache, you may be told to find a lactating mother willing to squirt some breast milk in your ear, while preparations from the multi-purpose *guarumo* tree are suggested for both boosting fertility and inducing abortion, as well as ensuring an easy birth for farm animals. A traditional remedy for asthma is the *escarabajo del asma,* a small beetle boiled in milk or eaten alive, which is reputed to open up the airways of the lungs.

Proud San José market stall holder Billy Acuña has a herbal remedy for whatever might ail you, as well as magic potions to spice up your love life.

"We might have a good system now, but you have to remember that until a few decades ago it was almost impossible for someone living in the countryside to get to a doctor," explained Don Daniel, a teacher.

Luis 'Billy' Acuña Araya, whose family has run one of the dozen-or-so medicinal herb stalls in San José Central Market for several generations, said, "Our products are getting more and more popular all the time. People prefer pure, natural products, because they're starting to realise that many conventional drugs can harm their liver or kidneys. Lots of people come to me after drugs from the doctor didn't work or because they can't afford stuff from the pharmacy."

Billy's stall sells everything from aloe vera and rosemary to shark oil and sea urchins. He claims his preparations can cure anything from baldness and constipation to diabetes and cancer. Individual purchases cost less than a dollar, while a specially-prepared *receta*, costs about US$ 5.

Many people go a lot further than simple herbal health cures, and swear by magic and witchcraft too (*see 'Religion and Witchcraft' in* Chapter Three: People *on page 87*).

AIDS

Almost 5,000 cases of AIDS (SIDA in Spanish) have been diagnosed in Costa Rica. Up to four times this many people could be infected with HIV (VIH in Spanish), although many may not yet know it. Around 60 per cent of cases are among the gay community, and many women sufferers have been

infected by gay/bisexual husbands who married to avoid having to come out of the closet.

Problems have also arisen because of Church opposition to the use of condoms (*preservativos*), and the prevalent *machista* attitude that 'real' men don't use them. Central American presidents tried to persuade the Church to tone down this hard line during a 2005 summit to tackle the growing AIDS problem in the region, but they didn't get very far.

Although prostitutes have to have regular health checks and carry a health card, HIV and other conditions may not be picked up by the tests for some time after infection. Many male prostitutes do not have these checks at all.

Stomach Cancer

Costa Rica also has the odd reputation of having the highest rate of stomach cancer in the Western world and ranks fourth in the world after Japan and North and South Korea.

Dr Horacio Solano, head of the government's stomach cancer detection and prevention programme, said, "We really can't say for sure why the rate is so high. Stomach cancer is multi-factorial, but it's definitely got something to do with our diet—we eat a lot of carbohydrate, fat, salt and alcohol and not much in the way of fruit and vegetables."

Other factors could include high nitrogen levels in the volcanic soil (the highest cancer rates are on the volcanic Meseta Central and other countries with a high rate, such as Japan and Chile, also have a lot of volcanoes), as well as bacteria in food and genetics.

Worldwide, stomach cancer incidence and death rates from it are falling—but not in Costa Rica, where 85 per cent of those currently diagnosed will die. It's the top cause of cancer among men and the third among women.

"The problem is we haven't been able to afford early enough detection," said Dr Solano. "Widespread screening is expensive, and the government economists have said our over-burdened social security system can't stretch to it. Now we're trying to persuade them that early detection means less days in hospital, less intervention, and so in the long run will work out cheaper."

Due to its high health indices and First World disease profile (most people die of heart disease, cancer and strokes), Costa Rica is often caught in the Catch 22 situation of being ineligible for foreign aid, but at the same time unable to afford expensive medical techniques. Japan, however, has provided funding and training for Tico doctors to help them set up a broad screening programme—in the early stages of the cancer, the cure rate is over 90 per cent. However, no one knows if the government will be able to afford to keep the programme going.

Alcoholism

Costa Rica has the dubious distinction of having the highest rate of alcoholism in Central America. Up to 20 per cent of the population has a drinking problem ranging from abuse to addiction, and even the tiniest country hamlet has an Alcoholics Anonymous office.

This may seem incredible to visitors, especially those from hard-drinking northern European countries, because in Tico restaurants it is common to see many people—especially women—drinking nothing but fruit juices, and there are also many hard-core teetotalers.

"The thing is that we have a very problematic relationship with alcohol," said Dr Luis Sandí Esquivel, director of the government's Instituto Sobre Alcoholismo y Farmacodependencia (IAFA). "Our actual alcohol consumption is quite low compared with Europe but we don't drink with our meals or regularly throughout the day, as many Europeans do. Instead, people go on a huge binge at the weekend, during football matches, or once a month on pay day with the express aim of getting drunk as quickly as possible. Their bodies have no resistance."

Ticos, traditionally reserved mountain farmers who only saw their neighbours sporadically, needed an alcoholic boost in order to loosen their tongues enough to maintain a conversation, suggests Constantino Láscaris in *El Costarricense*.

While it is quite common, especially in poor barrios, to see dozens of drinkers strewn on the pavements sleeping off the effects of a Sunday spree, and thousands of students swigging pitchers of beer in San Pedro's Calle de la Amargura, it is unusual to see drunkenness descend into public violence. In fact, in the worst drunken behaviour I ever saw, a man who was *muy bien tomado* repeatedly delayed a bullfight by jumping into the ring and dancing in the spotlights, wiggling his bottom like a madman.

A lot of drinking also goes on in the home, and Dr Sandí says one of the most worrying statistics is that 16 per cent of children over the age of 10 already have a drinking problem.

"With both parents working, children are now spending more time alone, and also have more access to money," said Dr Sandí. While in their parents' age group, male drinkers outnumber females by three to one, among the children just as many girls drink as boys.

A third of all traffic accidents in Costa Rica are alcohol-related—the rate of accidents shoots up at weekends—as well as 70 per cent of domestic violence, murder and suicide.

Dr Sandí sees no conflict with the fact that the government itself monopolises alcohol production in the country and makes seven billion colones (US$ 23.3 million) from sales each year. "It's better this way," he said. "If the business was privately-run, production and advertising would probably be even more efficient."

The institution, however, is currently locked in a battle for funds with the government, which legally must give IAFA 15 per cent of its income from alcohol. In 1999, IAFA received 4 per cent, and in 2000 nothing. The government says that in times of limited budgets, it has had to prioritise.

Hospitals and Health Insurance

If you're moving to Costa Rica, you can get health insurance from the Caja Costarricense de Seguro Social (CCSS)—the national socialised medical system. Monthly premiums (very reasonable and almost half price for those over 55) cover all illnesses (including pre-existing conditions) for the member and his or her immediate family.

An alternative choice is the Instituto Nacional de Seguros (INS), the semi-autonomous government insurance company. There is less cover than with the CCSS, but members can choose their own doctor and make appointments with less red tape. Costa Rican hospitals are generally good, and the doctors excellent. Most doctors (although probably not their receptionists) speak English. However, don't forget this is a developing country so lines can be long.

You can also see doctors in private practice, and there are a number of excellent private hospitals

Pharmacies

Unlike many Latin countries, Costa Rica does not have *farmacias de turno*, or pharmacies that stay open overnight on a rotating basis. Many pharmacies are open until 9:00 pm or even midnight, and the pharmacies at the Clínica Bíblica in downtown San José and Hospital La Cima in Escazú are open 24 hours. Pharmacies are well stocked, and you can buy many things over the counter that you would need a prescription for at home, such as strong antibiotics.

BANKING AND MONEY

If you're using your cash card from home, you won't find as many compatible ATMs as in some other countries, although Cirrus and Visa cards can be used in many machines.

> ### Changing Money
>
> For changing money, the rate is the same at all banks but black market changers on the street offer a slightly higher rate. It's very hard to change any dollar bill in Costa Rica that has even the smallest imperfection or tear. You can also actually pay with dollars instead of colones for almost anything.

If you want to set up a bank account, be aware that there are state and private banks. The state-owned banks are the Banco Nacional, Banco de Costa Rica and Banco Crédito Agrícola de Cartago. Money in these banks is guaranteed, and can also be accessed at branches all over the country. Service, however, can be very slow and limited. Lines can extend outside the building, especially on the second and last Fridays of the month—payday for many Ticos. Loans are also expensive and difficult to arrange, so this is not a practical source of capital for a foreign investor.

Service is faster in the private banks, dozens of which have been set up since 1996. Privatisation came after a 1994 scandal when the country's oldest bank, the Banco Anglo-Costarricense, collapsed with the loss of US$ 136 million following huge unsecured loans made by its inexperienced directors on the basis of political favouritism. Banco Elca, for example, takes only five to eight days to cash a foreign cheque, while in Banco Nacional this could take up to a month. However, branches of private banks, and especially ATMs, can be limited outside the Meseta Central.

Most banks offer saving and current accounts in US dollars or colones. Interest rates can vary widely between banks, so shop around. It is much higher on colón accounts, but because of the monthly devaluation against the dollar, you won't be earning as much as you think. Most banks require a deposit of around US$ 500 to set up a current account, and many also require two letters of recommendation. Costa Rica has strong banking secrecy laws.

Inflation and Currency

The colón is devaluing at a creeping rate of about one or two colones per month against the US dollar. In January 1992, there were 138.65 colónes to the dollar. By late November 2005, there were 493.

This is bad news for Ticos as their salaries buy gradually less and less over time and most consumer goods are imported. However, the currency is stable and major shocks and devaluations are unlikely. Inflation is around 13 per cent.

Tax

It is clear that taxes must rise in order to maintain Costa Rica's social security system, and an overhaul of the whole system is expected, probably in 2006.

As a foreign resident, you don't pay any tax on income generated outside Costa Rica, but have to do so on money made within the country— although rates are low. There is no tax for salaries below 215,600 colones per month. Thereafter, it rises from zero up to a maximum of 15 per cent on salaries over 324,100 colones per month. If you are self-employed, the rates after all deductions are: 10 per cent from around 958,000 colones to 1.431 million colones up to 25 per cent above 4.785 million colones.

There is no capital gains tax, but corporations pay 30 per cent income tax on annual earnings, while small enterprises pay tax on income earned within the country of 10 per cent of gross income on revenue up to 13.2 million colones and 20 per cent for any amounts above that.

The tax year ends on 30 September, and forms must be filed and taxes paid by 31 December. Tax evasion, traditionally considered a national sport, is now punishable by a jail term.

Business Hours

- Government offices are open from 8:00 am–4:00 pm.
- Stores are open from 8:00 am–6:00 or 7:00 pm from Mondays to Saturdays. Do take note that there is often a lunch break (sometimes of two hours) especially in rural areas.
- Banks are generally open between 8:30 am–3:30 pm.

SHOPPING

Costa Rica now has more than 20 large, American-style shopping malls. The San Pedro Mall and Multiplaza in Santa Ana are the two biggest in Central America. While these malls and the numerous *gringo*-friendly grocery chains and supermarkets have absolutely everything you can think of under one roof, the country also has many much more interesting shopping options.

On weekend mornings, many Ticos still go to local *ferias*, or open-air fresh produce markets, to buy their vegetables and other goods for the week. These are much cheaper than supermarkets, and much more fun. The vendors arrive early in the morning from the countryside, and sell everything from cashew nuts, coffee beans and pigs' trotters to cut flowers, home-made wine and traditional cakes. Prices are progressively cut during the day, until by the end of the afternoon, goods are almost given away. There are also often musicians on hand for added entertainment.

Shopping in central San José is also fun. The central zone is pedestrianised, and full of buskers, hustlers, beggars and *limpiabotas* (shoe shiners), who for a small charge will not just clean your shoes, but also give you a run-down on what's wrong with the country and the world. If you're lucky, someone may even try to sell you a baby goat or a puppy.

Around the Mercado Central, there are so many stalls selling fruit, umbrellas, cheeses, cheap jewellery and DIY goods that there's hardly any space on the pavement. Inside, the selection is even better, and includes some excellent cheap and cheerful Tico food outlets and fascinating medicinal herb and magic stands.

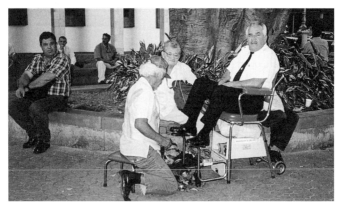

Getting a shoe shine from a *limpiabotas* and putting the world to rights outside San José's Central Post Office.

Every town has a *Ropa Americana* shop, selling a huge amount of cheap second-hand clothes from the United States. If you're the kind of person that loves rummaging through charity shops and jumble sales, you will be in your element.

Increasingly limited budgets also mean that Ticos hate to throw anything away. The country is peppered with hole-in-the-wall tailors, cobblers and odd-job men, who, for a small fee, can and will fix almost anything that would be consigned to the rubbish dump at home.

What To Buy

Coffee

You can buy coffee everywhere from supermarkets to souvenir shops—but be sure you buy export quality coffee as the local brew is of much poorer quality, and often pre-sweetened.

If you're keen to take home a large quantity for family and friends some of the larger coffee companies—such as Café Britt (http://www.cafebritt.com)—provide a service where they will ship home a case for you, for a charge.

Hammocks

Locally-made hammocks are sold in many Costa Rican markets and from stalls along the roadsides of popular tourist routes. They come in a variety of designs and sizes and, if you have the room to take them home, are a great bargain.

Local Crafts and Indigenous Goods

Although Costa Rica doesn't have the same long tradition of crafts as many other Central or South American countries there is still a selection of souvenirs available, mainly made by the country's small indigenous population. The most popular are wooden gifts, including ornaments and bowls made from tropical woods, as well as whistles, masks and embroidery and the unique pottery from Guaitíl.

One-Stop Shop

One of the best one-stop-shops to buy indigenous arts and crafts is:

Galeria Namu

Avd 7, Cs5&7, San José

Tel: (506) 256-3412

Website: http://www.galerianamu.com

Surf Clothes

As Costa Rica's reputation as a surfing Mecca grows, so too does the range of surfing clothes and accessories on sale—many of which are cheaper than those available back home. Clothes shops in the centre of San José offer some of the best bargains and there are also brand name stores in many of the malls.

Wildlife Books

Costa Rica has to be one of the best places on earth to find a really huge and wonderful selection of natural history books on everything from orchids and sea life to birds and butterflies. Many of them are written by top biologists and come with gorgeous plate illustrations by some of the

Other Items

Other products to look out for include Café Rica (Costa Rica's version of Bailey's liqueur), banana paper made with fibres from the banana plant and Cuban cigars—a big attraction for holidaying Americans who can't buy them legally at home.

world's top photographers. These can serve as a great guide during your visits to the country's natural parks, or as a souvenir of your trip to take back home or as gifts for friends and family. The best selection is available at Seventh Street Books in San José, C7 between Avds 0 and 1, tel: (506) 256-8251.

Making Purchases

When doing your daily shopping, be aware that in many stores, particularly bakeries and pharmacies, you select what you want and tell the assistant, who will give you a ticket. You then take this to the *caja* (cash register) where you pay and your purchase is handed over. When clothes shopping, be aware that Ticos generally work in American sizes.

Gifts

If coming from home or abroad, bring something typical or special from your country or the place you've been visiting. Costa Rica is a small country, and Ticos are very interested in the outside world. Be aware though, that US-made goods aren't seen as special or exotic per se as they would be in other Central American countries.

Charity worker Milena Badilla said the best thing would be a gift that could be treasured and wouldn't be thrown away. "An ideal present would be, say, some flowers in a beautiful vase. That way, you can enjoy the flowers, but get to keep the vase. Ticos love to be able to show off and say to friends 'oh, my friend so-and-so from Canada brought me this'. It's something to remember people by."

CRIME

Costa Rica was once a peaceful country, experiencing its first bank robbery only in 1970. Now, like the rest of the world, it is experiencing a rapid rise in crime and by 1993, private guards outnumbered police.

Petty crime is notorious, especially around San José's Central Market, where gangs of young thieves known as *chapulines* (grasshoppers) pounce on their prey and melt away into the thick crowds. When a friend had her handbag stolen in a bar in the city centre, the owner told us this was a regular event. He had the hat stolen from his head that same day as he sat in his car at traffic lights. The week before, investigating a flood, he found thieves had even wrenched out and pilfered the steel pipes from the bar toilet.

Many thieves use a particularly common scam, which I once fell victim to myself: a man started walking ridiculously slowly in front of me while going through a narrow area near a fruit stall. Unable to pass him or turn around, I could feel his 'team mate' opening my rucksack and rummaging through it. Luckily for me, I had my money and documents in my front trouser pocket.

Another common ploy, apparently, is to puncture an unsuspecting driver's tyres. The criminals, posing as Good Samaritans, then turn up apparently to help—and help themselves to everything in the vehicle.

"It's not just the quantity of crime that's changed, it's the type," said Steve Brown of the Residents' Association, an organisation which lobbies for foreign residents' rights. "Fifteen years ago, the worst you could expect was to have your purse snatched, or your washing stolen from the line. Now, things seem to be a lot more violent."

Costa Rica is used as a corridor by narcotic traffickers shipping consignments north from Colombia and Panama. Drugs are often moved through the jungles of Talamanca, and also by boat. Joint patrols by the US Drugs Enforcement Agency and Costa Rican coastguards have been set up to crack down on this trade, though without a great deal of success to date.

The country also has something of a reputation as a haven for foreign crooks. It is weak on extradition, has secretive banking laws, and a big expat community in which it is easy to disappear.

In addition, the burgeoning tourist trade offers an ideal front for the investment of unlaunderable money, with Colombian drugs barons and the Italian mafia reputedly behind the construction of many of the country's biggest hotels and shopping malls. Michel, a shaven-headed French friend travelling the country, told me he had been approached by members of a Corsican organised crime gang asking if he wanted to join their operations in San José.

Steve Brown voiced a disturbing trend. "Today, whenever the police catch criminals, it nearly always seems to be a group of Ticos plus a Guatemalan or a Colombian who has taught them new tricks. While most of the immigrants are entirely legitimate, a lot of criminals have also flooded in, and unfortunately they've had a big impact."

In street crime at least, the figures do not seem to back up this view, as the huge majority of those convicted for such crimes are Costa Ricans. Many feel that the country's much-lauded universal education has in fact bred in Ticos an unwillingness to do low-paying menial jobs, meaning that some people would sooner turn to crime than take on demeaning work. Reduced government spending on education, job cuts and an increasing underclass have only increased the problem.

Whatever the cause, Costa Rica is still safer than the United States or most of Europe, and murder or physical attacks on strangers are extremely rare. In the city, the situation really only requires common sense, while in the countryside honesty and calm still reign—at least for now. Several times I have forgotten something in a café or on a park bench, only to go back half an hour later and find it still there, or even have someone run after me to give it back.

In the capital, most people live behind barred windows, their garden fences festooned with razor wire and broken glass and their properties guarded by big dogs or even geese. Many people will not leave their home untended, and in one house where I stayed all expensive items, such as the television, had a string with bells tied to it to alert the owners if anyone tried to move them.

Many Ticos who grew up in a cocoon of 1960s stability, however, are paranoid about crime. In a 2004 Universidad de Costa Rica survey, 77.8 per cent of those polled reported feeling unsafe in general, and more than half said the government does not care at all about protecting them. Almost all felt that San José was either unsafe or very unsafe.

Guns have become much more commonplace in Costa Rica since the civil wars in Nicaragua and El Salvador, when weapons were smuggled through the country. There are an estimated 30,000 guns in the country today, only one-third of which are legally-owned. To buy a gun legally you only need to show your *cédula* (identity card). You are also supposed to take a course and get a certificate of psychological fitness—but not until after you have already bought the weapon.

In a non-militarised country with a traditional lack of crime, little was invested in training, equipping or paying the 13,000 Costa Rican police officers. This is now changing, however, with numerous armed police now seen on foot or on bicycles in city centres. Professional, non-military training focuses on issues such as human rights and domestic violence.

NEWSPAPERS AND THE MEDIA

Ticos are big newspaper readers (even though a lot of people read little more than the football pages). The conservative *La Nación*, set up in 1936, has the largest circulation of 500,000, about an eighth of Costa Rica's population.

Other papers include the pro-PLN (but also pretty conservative) *La República*, and the more left-wing afternoon paper *La Prensa Libre*. Tabloids, such as *Al Día* and *Diario Extra*, concentrate heavily on sensationalist crime stories and sports. The controversial *Chavespectáculos* is the local equivalent of a girlie newspaper like England's *Sun*, except that it reflects Latin males' tastes by focusing much more on bottoms than breasts.

The Tico Times, the longest-established and largest circulated English-language paper in Central America, is targeted mainly at the older expat audience, with pictures of fluffy animals, recipes, and lightweight opinion columns. *The Tico Times* covers the main bases, but isn't exactly a hotbed of incisive reporting and investigation. All attempts at competition have so far folded.

Of the terrestrial television channels, *Teletica* has the most in-depth local news coverage, while *Sinart* fashions itself as a national cultural channel. The other stations broadcast hefty servings of imported soap operas, football matches and evangelical sermons.

Given the country's credentials in other areas, press freedom is not as progressive as you might expect in Costa Rica. Journalists are expected to verify all information, no matter how impeccable the source, and have no right to keep their sources secret—which seriously hinders investigative journalism.

In an August 2003 survey by *La Nación* newspaper of 184 journalists on their perception of freedom of the press, 41 per cent said they left out information in reporting because of legal concerns, 79 per cent said they felt pressure not to investigate certain issues and 22 per cent claimed that they had received some type of threat during the previous 12 months relating to their job.

Most famously, *La Nación* journalist Mauricio Herrera was sentenced to 160 days' imprisonment for defamation (later commuted to a large fine) for a 1995 article in which he quoted a reputable Belgian newspaper, which had accused a Tico diplomat of links with the mafia. The Inter-American Court later ordered the Costa Rican Government to pay him compensation, but as of 2005 this had still not been paid.

Attitudes started to change when the country was shocked by the hit-style murders of outspoken radio journalist Parmenio Medina (*see the section on 'Heroes and Villains' in* Chapter Ten: Fast Facts *on page 247*) in 2001 and of magazine journalist Ivannia Mora (her former employer and four accomplices were later charged with ordering the killing) in 2003.

By December 2004, 61 per cent of the public felt the press could report freely—up from 33 per cent in 2001. This was attributed to a great deal of investigative reporting of high-level corruption scandals throughout the year, in the face of stiff opposition including from the president himself.

The murders and corruption scandals have prompted widespread calls for a change in heavy-handed treatment of the press and more liberal legislation is expected to be introduced in future.

'Is Costa Rica's reputation for being what *Travel & Leisure* magazine recently called a 'food purgatory' deserved?... Though richer than some of its neighbours, Costa Rica is a poor country and its native residents never had the money to elaborate a sophisticated cookery or dining tradition.'
—*Vacation Cooking Schools Guide*

COSTA RICAN FOOD IS BASED ON two main ingredients: black beans and rice. In most homes, especially in the country, these will crop up in every meal of the day masquerading under various names, and in some places rice and beans are even thrown on newly-weds like confetti. Incredibly, Ticos really do not get bored of this combination. "If my wife doesn't have *gallo pinto* on the table in the morning, I'm really annoyed and she has to give me a pretty good excuse," said a middle aged Tico friend. Unlike Mexican food, Tico fare is not spicy.

BASIC TICO FARE

- **Gallo Pinto**
  Literally 'spotted rooster', this is beans and rice mixed together and fried (traditionally in pork lard) with onion, bell pepper, garlic and herbs. Usually eaten for breakfast, it's often served with eggs, small corn tortillas and *natilla* (sour cream). *Gallo pinto* is pretty much the national dish, even McDonald's serves McPinto. Many Ticos will proudly say they are 'as Tico as *gallo pinto*,' although this is also the national dish of Nicaragua.

- **Casado**
  Literally 'married man', this strictly lunchtime dish is beans and rice (separately this time) served with beef, chicken, fish or liver, along with fried plantain (green banana), salad, tortillas, and maybe some *picadillo* (*see following section 'Popular Dishes' on page 164 for more*

information) and pasta. Yes, if you were at all worried about not getting enough carbohydrates in Costa Rica, your worries will evaporate after a hefty serving of rice, plantain, tortillas AND pasta all on one plate.

- **Arroz Con Frijoles**
  If you're wondering what Ticos eat for their evening meal, it's very often a lighter dish of *arroz con frijoles,* which is—you guessed it—rice and beans.
- **Sopa Negra**
  This soup is made out of black beans, usually with some onion, green pepper, cilantro, a poached egg and a squeeze of lemon juice. It rates along with Alka Seltzer as Costa Rica's number one cure for a *gotera* or *goma* (hangover).

If the above selection makes Tico cuisine sound less than exciting, remember that until recently the country was poor and rural, with a diet designed to keep people going for a day in the fields. Well, the diet simply hasn't kept pace with changing times. These (and the dishes below) are still what you'll find served in *sodas* (cafés) in the country.

Without all that coffee-picking to burn off the calories today, obesity is definitely on the rise, although you still don't see too many rolls of fat forced sausage-like into skin-tight luminous boob tubes—an alarming sight in some other Latino countries. Diet may also play a large role in the fact that Costa Rica suffers from the Western world's highest rate of stomach cancer (*see the section on 'Stomach Cancer' in* Chapter Five: Survival Skills *on page 147*).

In urban areas at least, diets ARE slowly starting to change. "Just ten years ago in San José, if you wanted to eat out you could basically only choose from Chinese and Italian cuisine," said a Tico friend. "Today we have Peruvian, French, Thai restaurants—whatever you can think of." Despite the fact that San José does have some really excellent restaurants, the bulk of eateries are still fast food joints that suit Tico pockets.

Although they love their rice and beans, many younger Ticos are starting to take more care with their diet. A lot are semi-vegetarian, and one of San José's most popular restaurants, Vishnu, serves only vegetarian food.

Another point to remember is that many Tico dishes are family specials to be had only in homes—just as you'd be lucky to find toad-in-the-hole or Lancashire hotpot in any restaurant in the UK. Some delicious dishes Ticos cook up include soups, *picadillos*, meat stews and a huge range of stuffed squashes, pumpkins and gourds, such as *chayote* and *ayote*.

In Costa Rican restaurants, the *entrada* is the appetiser, while the *plato fuerte* or *segundo plato* is the main dish. A good bargain on weekday lunchtimes is to order the *menú ejecutivo,* which usually offers a specific main dish, soft drink or coffee and sometimes dessert, for a reasonable price.

Ticos take their lunch any time between about noon and 2:00 pm, although long Spanish-style lunch hours are no longer the norm. Most people eat their evening meal fairly late, around 8:00 pm or 9:00 pm.

Popular Dishes

- **Arreglados**
  Meat or cheese-stuffed puffed pastry or sandwiches.
- **Ceviche**
  This traditionally Peruvian dish is a firm favourite in Costa Rica. Ceviche is either white fish or seafood marinated in lime juice and spiced up with some onion, garlic, red peppers, and coriander.
- **Chorreada**
  A Guanacaste speciality, this is a big, fat corn pancake, usually served with cheese.
- **Elote**
  Corn-on-the-cob either boiled (*cocinado*) or roasted (*asado*).
- **Empanadas**
  These can be savoury; made from deep-fried corn flour and stuffed with meat, cheese, potato (*papa*), or beans, or sweet; made from baked wheat flour and stuffed with fruit preserves: usually pineapple, guava or chiverre (a kind of stringy melon).
- **Enchiladas**
  Savoury pastries stuffed with potato, sometimes with meat, and a little chilli.

Popular Dishes (cont'd)

- **Gallos**

  A small serving of meat or chicken with tortillas.

- **Olla de Carne**

  Literally 'meat pot', this hearty dish is made of beef, yucca, plantain, corn, ayote and *chayote*.

- **Picadillo**

  Usually made from *chayote*, plantain, or potato, this is a kind of chopped vegetable stew, often with a little meat or egg and flavoured with spices.

- **Pupusa**

  This Salvadorean speciality has become ubiquitous throughout Costa Rica since the large immigration of refugees from war-torn El Salvador during the 1980s. It is a thick grilled tortilla stuffed, usually, with beans, cheese, salad and *chicharrones*—artery-clogging chunks of fatty fried pig skin.

- **Sopa de Mondongo**

  Tripe soup.

- **Tamales**

  Steamed maize dough wrapped up in a corn or banana leaf with meat in the middle.

Meat

Beef is plentiful, thanks to the Guanacaste cattle industry, but can be on the tough/stringy side. *Pollo* (chicken) is good and cheap, often served as *arroz con pollo*—chicken fried rice.

Fish and Seafood

In the Meseta Central, the fish you're most likely to come across is *corvina* (sea bass). The selection

Vegetarians Beware

A word of advice to vegetarians—it is no good asking whether a dish contains *carne* (meat), as in Costa Rica this only refers to beef. If you ask for a dish *sin carne* you run a high risk of being given something containing ham. It's better to say you are *vegetariano/a*—a bizarre concept for many Ticos, especially in the countryside.

is bigger on the coast, but still not huge, featuring a lot of *atún* (tuna) and *pargo* (snapper). *Langosta* (lobster) and *camarón* (shrimp) are available but very expensive as nearly all seafood is exported.

Cheese

Costa Rican cheese is either *blanco* (white) or *amarillo* (yellow), and is generally pretty bland. The Monteverde cheeses (originally made by the Quakers) have become some of the most popular in the country, and include cheddar, cheese spreads and smoked cheeses.

Salad and Condiments

Ticos are not big eaters of greens, and salad is usually a disappointing affair, consisting of some grated cabbage and carrot in vinegar topped with a tomato. Wherever you eat, your table will usually have a big jar of *curtido* (pickled vegetables and chillies) to mix with your food.

Rice is often cooked with garlic and/or red pepper, and sometimes *achiote*, a traditional red food colouring prepared from a native plant. Sandwiches, burgers and *gallos* usually come slathered in *salsa rosa* (Thousand Island dressing), ketchup and mayonnaise.

Bocas

Bocas (literally 'mouths') are snacks traditionally served with alcohol. Somewhat like *tapas* in Spain, *bocas* are sometimes free—although these days you usually pay a small amount extra. *Bocas* could be anything from meatballs to *ceviche*, stuffed tortillas or fried fish and grazing on a few of these as the night progresses is a cheap and delicious way of soaking up excess alcohol. Sometimes turtle eggs—widely held to be an aphrodisiac—are served as *bocas*. Costa Rica is one of the Caribbean's major egg-laying sites for these ancient animals, which are in danger of extinction. A certain quantity of the eggs can be officially harvested, but unfortunately many turtle egg *bocas* are illegal, so it's best to avoid them.

Cakes and Desserts

Ticos, like most Latinos, have an incredibly sweet tooth, and you will come across cake and pastry shops (*pastelerías* or *reposterías*) every few metres selling all manner of sweetmeats, often slathered in bright pink or blue icing.

Merienda, the Tico equivalent of afternoon tea, is an important part of the day, especially in the rainy season, when many people spend hours sitting out the afternoon downpours in *sodas* (cafés) and kitchens.

Some Merienda Favourites

- **Alfajores**
  Shortbread-type round biscuits sandwiched together with *dulce de leche* or fruit jam and dusted in icing sugar.

- **Cachos**
  Literally 'horns'. Tubes of croissant pastry stuffed with cream. Regular shaped croissants are called *cangrejos* or 'crabs'.

- **Churros**
  Six-inch long sticks of deep-fried doughnut mix, usually stuffed with some kind of sweet cream.

- **Dulce de Leche**
  Mind-blowingly sweet concoction of milk and sugar boiled together to the consistency of condensed milk. Sometimes eaten alone as a treat, used to sandwich together cakes such as *torta chilena,* or used as a cake filling—often sweetened still further by mixing with, say, guava jelly.

- **Ensalada de Frutas**
  Fruit salad; a healthier option, though it's often out of a tin and accompanied by *gelatina* (jelly) and *helado* (ice cream).

- **Orejas**
  Literally 'ears'. Dinner plate-sized pastry covered in sugar.

- **Púdin**
  Heavy, moist, bread pudding.

- **Queque Seco**
  Literally 'dry cake'. Basically a sponge cake cooked in a ring shape.

- **Suspiros**
  Meringues.

- **Tamales Asados**
  Sweet corn *tamal* made with sour cream and sugar.

- **Tres Leches**
  Incredibly sweet and soggy cake steeped in boiled milk and sugar.

SWEET STANDS

Roadside stalls and street vendors also sell a colourful variety of home-made sweetmeats, which are great for a snack if you're off on a long road journey. These include:

- **Bananos a la Leña**
  Wood-smoked bananas.
- **Bolis**
  Frozen flavoured ices in a tubular plastic bag, made either with water or milk.
- **Cajeta**
  Basically fudge, which can contain nuts, raisins, dried fruit, or coconut and is often coloured pink.
- **Copos**
  A cup of ice shaved off a huge block and mixed with milk powder, condensed milk and a choice of brightly-coloured fruit syrups.
- **Higos and Toronja**
  Preserved, sugared figs and grapefruit.
- **Tarteletas**
  Little coconut tarts.

FRUITS AND VEGETABLES

Ticos might not be huge vegetable eaters, but they love to snack on fruits. The most fun kind of fruits are those you pick yourself. Often, travelling with Ticos, you will find they screech to a halt by the side of a road, whooping with delight,

THE VEGETABLES ARE THERE SIR

to collect *jocotes* or throw rocks and sticks into mango or guava trees in an effort to bring down the fruit. Be warned that in the countryside howler monkeys often hang out in mango trees and will mercilessly pelt you with unripe fruit if you try to steal their mangoes. If you bother them too much they will urinate on you... or worse! If your efforts are fruitless, there are always plenty of roadside stalls selling just what you were looking for.

- **Carámbola**
  Starfruit.

- **Cas**
  A small, many-seeded fruit, which is almost unbearably sour when eaten raw. Ticos add salt to make it more palatable, but as a soft drink, with plenty of sugar, it is refreshingly delicious.

- **Guaba**
  This is not guava (which is *guayaba*), but instead the giant brown pod from a leguminous tree. The idea is to break them open and suck the sweet fluff off the shiny seeds, which are sometimes used to make jewellery.

- **Jocotes**
  Reddish plum-sized fruit with a dry, tart flavour. The tree is often used as a living fence—its cut branches being stuck in the ground as posts, where they take root and grow. Ticos love them as they're ideal for roadside-picking.

- **Mamones Chinos**
Rambutans, whose hairy red covering is removed to reveal a white, lychee-like fruit.
- **Manzanas de Agua**
Asian water apples, a dark pink fruit which looks like a small bell pepper, with a delicious, refreshing texture.
- **Manzanas Rosas**
Again from Asia, these are rose apples. Small pinkish-white fruits with a highly perfumed flavour.
- **Marañón**
The fruit of the cashew nut. It's a large, capsicum-sized fruit with the nut dangling from the end. The delicately perfumed fruit is used for jams and wines. The nut is poisonous until roasted.
- **Nances**
Tiny yellow berries whose indescribable taste is both bitter and sour. Often pickled or made into wines.
- **Pejibaye**
An indigenous staple, this fruit comes from the same palm whose growing shoot provides *palmitos* (palm hearts)—a salad ingredient grown in plantations in some parts of the country. You will find *pejibaye* cooking in big metal pots on roadsides or in supermarkets (they must be boiled for about four hours). Tasting like a cross between chestnut and potato, they're usually eaten with mayonnaise.
- **Pitahaya**
Known as the strawberry pear, this baroque-looking dark pink fruit comes from a cactus. Found most commonly in the north.
- **Plátanos**
Giant green bananas or plantains. When roasted or fried, these have a delicious starchy, sweet flavour.
- **Zapote**
Orange-fleshed fruit with a huge, black, avocado-like stone and dusty brown skin. The taste and texture is rather like an orange sweet potato.

You'll also see a lot of stalls selling nothing but apples and grapes. These are hard to grow in Costa Rica and are mostly imported from the United States—an expensive treat.

AFRO-CARIBBEAN FOOD

On the Caribbean coast, food reflects the West African, Jamaican and British traditions. At the market in Limón you can buy turtle meat and salt cod, a huge range of roots such as yam, cassava and sweet potato, as well as breadfruit and *ackee*. Food is generally a lot spicier than anything you'll find in the highlands, often flavoured with cumin, chilies, cloves and groundspice. Coconut milk is also used a lot.

- **Ackee**
  The national fruit of Jamaica, it is known in Spanish as *seso vegetal* (vegetable brain) as it looks a lot like a small brain. The fruit comes in three-inch pods and is poisonous until the pods have opened. When boiled, the yellowish fruit has the taste and consistency of scrambled eggs. It's often served with fish—a favourite dish is *ackee* and codfish.

- **Calalu**
  Stewed leaf vegetables.

- **JonnyCcakes**
  Originally from 'journey cakes', these are heavy, dry bread buns, ideal for taking along for a day's walking.

- **Pan Bon**
  The name comes from either the French 'good bread', or is a corruption of the English 'bun'. It's a heavy, glazed gingery-spiced fruit cake.

- **Patacones**
  Deep-fried green banana chips.

- **Rice and Beans/peas**
  This is the Afro-Caribbean version of *gallo pinto*—you can't get away from it anywhere in the country. In the Caribbean, however, it's cooked with coconut milk, which gives a very different, aromatic flavour.

- **Ron don**
  Really delicious, hearty meal, which is cooked slowly for several hours. Either meat or seafood stewed with root vegetables and breadfruit in coconut milk.

COFFEE

Given the historical importance of coffee to Costa Rica, a surprising number of city dwellers these days prefer herbal teas. Ticos, however, still have one of the highest per capita caffeine consumption rates in the world. Most people have a coffee shot up to three times a day—often even just before bedtime, and coffee dispensers can be found in banks, book shops and supermarkets. Ticos will tell you that 'coffee is good for you', for example using black coffee as a migraine cure; the caffeine apparently opens up constricted blood vessels in the brain.

Coffee normally comes very heavily sugared and is either *negro* (black) or *con leche* (milky) in a tall glass. *Agua chacha* is coffee with a lot of milk. You will hardly ever find an espresso, cappuccino or frothy milk, and in many homes coffee is still prepared using a *chorreador*, a kind of muslin sock supported on a wooden frame. The coffee filters through this and into the cup.

Despite their world-class coffee, Ticos regularly commit crimes against coffee that would never be tolerated in places such as Venezuela, where each cup is prepared individually in a gleaming coffee machine. In Costa Rica, cold coffee is often re-heated and (horrors!) some people even use instant.

While there is a difference in the price and quality between export coffees (such as Café Britt and Volio) and those for local consumption (such as Rey), you won't find any foreign brands on sale here. Costa Rica's coffee always tastes great as it is generally grown over a mile above sea level, where low air pressure results in hard beans. (Soft beans burn when roasted, creating a bitter taste.)

Coffee Tasters

Coffee tasters, or *catadores*, who decide which coffees to buy, are as important in Costa Rica as wine tasters in France. They train for five years to learn exactly how to slurp the coffee off a big spoon onto their taste buds, and they taste it cold—a good coffee should taste just as good cold as hot.

Coffee still gives many Ticos a feeling of pride and cultural tradition. The landscape of hillsides is covered in the shiny-leaved plants. At blooming time they are covered in white flowers called *nieve* (snow). The only kind you'll see in this Switzerland of Latin America and a classic image of the Meseta Central. Until recently, children would work during school holidays in the coffee fields, which were a place of healthy fun and fresh air flirting. These days, however, Costa Rica relies almost entirely on Nicaraguan workers to pick the coffee crop, as highly educated young Ticos are no longer interested in the hard work and low pay involved.

Historically, by law, Ticos could grow only Arabica beans, in order to maintain a special market niche. Today, however, many higher-yielding hybrids are grown. Most coffee plants can produce beans for 30 years, and Costa Rica produces more coffee per square metre than any other place in the world. The processing of a red coffee berry picked from the bush takes a week, involving pressing, peeling, fermenting, sun drying, raking and roasting at about 250°C. The least roasted beans give a light roast coffee and the longest a French roast.

Other Drinks

Ticos really excel on the soft drink front. Every house, no matter how humble, has a liquidiser, which is usually used to whip up fantastic and delicious fruit concoctions. Some of the best are made out of fruits such as *guanábana* (soursop), papaya, *piña* (pineapple), mango, *tamarindo* (tamarind), *banano* (banana), *sandía* (watermelon), *mora* (blackberry) or *fresa* (strawberry), and can be made with either *agua* (water) or *leche* (milk). Fruit juices may have salt added.

You will find drinks such as *chan* and *mozote* particularly in the countryside. *Chan* is made from small black seeds, which have both the look and consistency of frogspawn—definitely an acquired taste. *Mozote* is a rather acrid drink made from the bark of a tree. *Pipas* (coconuts), are sold with a hole tapped through the shell so you can dri°nk the milk. *Caldo de caña* is sugar cane juice crushed from the cane in a kind of giant mangle, and *agua dulce* (sweet water) is made from raw cane sugar dissolved in water. The big, brown slabs of cane sugar called *dulce*, are sold in supermarkets.

In Guanacaste, corn is a much bigger part of the diet, and many drinks are based on this and other cereals. Some drinks are milky, such as *horchata* (ground rice and cinnamon), *resbaladera* (barley, rice and cinnamon) and *pinolillo* (maize and cocoa). Others include *avena* (oats), *cebada* (barley) and *linaza* (linseed).

Ticos also drink a lot of carbonated bottled drinks. One of the most popular is ginger ale, which is confusingly known as *gin*. If you want to take a soft drink away from a *pulpería* or soda, it will be poured into a plastic bag so that the salesman can claim the refund on the bottle.

On the Caribbean coast, tea and herb teas are more popular than coffee. Traditional wild 'bush' teas include sorrel, lemon grass, ginger, wild peppermint and soursop.

Alcohol

The Costa Rican government has a near monopoly on the country's alcohol production, producing both beer and *guaro*, a rough firewater made from sugar cane. The most popular brands of beer are Imperial (also called Aguila for the unfortunately Nazi-looking eagle on the label), Bavaria and Pilsen.

Guaro can be pretty deadly stuff, and is often known by its brand name of Cacique. It is staple fare in cantinas, usually knocked back neat, or with salt and lemon, like tequila. In more classy establishments, you can order a *guaro* with any mixer. On the coast, a shot of *guaro* may be mixed with *pipa* (coconut juice) to make a *coco loco*. A stiff *guaro* with lemon juice is also taken by many as a cold treatment. It might not cure you, but it will definitely numb the misery! A small glass of neat *guaro* is ordered as *techo bajo* (low roof); a full glass is *techo alto* (high roof).

On the Caribbean coast, rum is more popular than *guaro*, and is often drunk with fresh milk or coconut milk.

A typical Guanacaste alcoholic drink is *vino de coyol*, which comes from the sap of the coyol palm. Traditionally, it must be cut only during certain phases of the moon, and ranges from *vino dulce* (sweet wine) after 24 hours of fermentation to *vino fuerte* (strong wine) at eight to 22 days. After that, it's vinegar.

DINING AND ENTERTAINMENT ETIQUETTE

For Ticos, their home is their castle, and so don't be insulted if you find you're not being invited for meals or drinks in Costa Rican acquaintances' homes. In fact, few invite anyone except family and extremely close friends to come over for a meal. You'll find that most entertaining is instead done in bars and restaurants. As there is a wide range of international and local restaurants in the country, especially in San José, this is not a problem!

Tipping

There is not a big culture of tipping in Costa Rica, and Ticos rarely do it. A service charge of 10–15 per cent is usually already included in restaurant bills, as well as the 13 per cent sales tax levied on all goods and services. Most menus have two columns— one for the actual price of the dish, and another for the price including tax. If service was really great, tip 5 per cent.

There are also lots of bars. In general, sitting on bar stools is a 'signal' that you're open to conversation with others (until fairly recently not acceptable for women). People choose tables and booths more for intimate conversations or to carry out business. The best area of San José to find a really good variety of bars and unusual cafés and eateries is the San Pedro university area. Bear in mind that many of the people you meet may primarily be keen to practise their English on you!

An exception on the home entertainment front is business dinners, which may often be held in people's homes, generally in the evening. Ticos very rarely arrive on time—a safe bet would be to arrive 15–30 minutes late in order to avoid catching your host hopping out of the shower. Spouses are generally welcome at such dinners. When sending invitations, include only those with whom you are negotiating and expect spouses to be included in an invitation either way. If you are a guest in a home, expect to be seated at the head of the table. As a first-time guest, you should stay only around an hour or less after the meal is finished; good friends can stay longer. If dining in a home without domestic help, offering to help is greatly appreciated. In such circles, it is generally considered impolite for women to drink anything stronger than wine or beer.

You should bring a gift when going to someone's house for dinner. Unless you know your host fairly well, it is advisable not to give alcohol. The family may be teetotal, or a family member may be an (recovering) alcoholic. If this is not an issue, fine wines and Scotch would be appreciated, as well as chocolates, other delicacies and flowers—but don't give calla lilies, which are associated with funerals. Costa Rican women generally appreciate perfume or silk scarves.

When initiating conversation, Costa Ricans appreciate being asked about their families—particularly their children—local culture and history. They enjoy discussing the beauty of Costa Rica and politics, so it's worth brushing up on your Central American and Costa Rican politics and especially why former president Oscar Arias won the Nobel Peace Prize. As Costa Ricans have a deep sense of personal honour, care should be taken not to say anything that could be remotely construed as disrespectful. Don't ask a woman about her job unless you are certain she works outside of the home.

ENJOYING COSTA RICA

'The Sele (the national soccer team) has become the affective, emotional and spiritual refuge of Costa Rica.'
—José Rodríguez, General Director of private polling firm Demoscopia following a 2001 study that showed high levels of public pessimism towards political and church leaders, with people believing the country's sporting celebrities to have greater morality.

CULTURAL BACKGROUND

Even being generous, it is hard to describe the country's historical cultural production as more than pitiful. Poor, rural and with a tiny population (less than 200,000 by 1860), Costa Rica has little architecture left from the colonial period, as most buildings from then were made from straw and adobe.

Costa Rica did not get its first printing press until 1830 (compared to 1539 in Mexico and 1660 in Guatemala), so it's not surprising that writing was slow to develop. The country certainly didn't produce any literary giants, and in fact, apart from Manuel González Zeledón and Aquileo Echeverría, hardly anyone appears to have made a stab at anything very creative until the 20th century.

What did happen, however, was that from around 1860 onwards the country started to have more contact with all things European as a result of the coffee trade and development of the railway. The children of newly rich families were sent away to be educated in Europe, creating an intellectual class obsessed with imitating European—especially French—styles. At this point, any homegrown innovation would have been sneered at.

San José's beautiful Teatro Nacional, built in 1897, and described soon after by foreign visitors as 'a jewel in a mud hole', was designed and built by French and Italian artists. Every stone, pane of glass, and lick of gold paint was brought from Europe too.

European-style marble tombs still dominate San José's main cemetary.

An exact small-scale copy of Paris' Opéra Comique, the Teatro Nacional was built with funds raised by the coffee barons through a self-imposed export tax. The tax was implemented after Italian opera singer Adelina Patti, who was touring Central America, refused to sing in Costa Rica as she felt that there was no venue worthy of her.

Likewise, the General Cemetery in San José is full of European-style marble angels, replica pyramids and Greek temples carved by Costa Rican sculptors who had trained in Italy.

In fact, the only truly Tico invention was the intricately hand-painted *carreta* (ox-cart) used to transport coffee. Covered in geometric designs reminiscent of Moorish art in southern Spain, replicas of the carts are now the most ubiquitous example of creole *artesanía*, and are available as souvenirs in the tourist town of Sarchí.

In this environment, innovative artists, such as the great sculptor Franciso Zúñiga, found themselves with little choice but to leave the country because of the prevailing belief that everything foreign was better. Zúñiga settled in Mexico, where his modern styles made him one of the most famous artists of his era.

University of Costa Rica anthropologist Sergio Chávez said, "The problem is that we're passive and self-congratulating.

We've never had to fight for anything. We didn't have an independence struggle from Spain or the ravages of a guerrilla war in the 1970s. We're relentlessly middle class, and that's just not the kind of background that favours the development of new art forms."

Minds did start to broaden in the 20th century, and a great debate arose over whether art and literature should continue to be influenced by foreign styles, or rather reflect the realities of the country. With greater consciousness of the exploitation of peasants by wealthy landowners and foreign companies, daily life started to figure more heavily in local art, and literature became peppered with *costumbrismo* (rural color and dialect). The arts, however, remained the preserve of the elite until 1960, when the state-funded publishing house Editorial Costa Rica opened doors for many new authors.

A Modern Cultural Revolution
In the early 1970s, during his third presidential term, José Figueres announced, "Why should we have tractors if we don't have violins?", and sparked what Ticos like to call their cultural revolution, by setting up the Ministry of Culture and the National Theatre Company.

The arts blossomed. In the new climate, Costa Rica developed a huge national library with 300,000 volumes in nine languages and dozens of museums and galleries. In San José, some of these (including the National Museum) are housed in former jails or military barracks.

Samuel Rovinski, a top Costa Rican author and advisor to UNESCO said, "What took 300 years to develop in Europe developed in 30 years here. We went through all the phases in extreme acceleration, and the whole national mindset has been permanently changed."

Today, in something of a reversal of history, many foreign artists actually settle in Costa Rica to make the most of the relaxed pace of life, stunning scenery and clear air. Many Ticos earn a living making artwork for sale to tourists (although much of this is cheap, tacky and not particularly original).

The all-pervasive globalising influence of Hollywood and MTV is seen as the biggest threat to Costa Rican cultural development today.

Rovinski said, "It might seem impossible that we can survive any real and concrete competition from the US, the biggest empire in the history of the world. However, the Romans absorbed Greek culture without it destroying them, so let's hope our encounter can also be enriching rather than destructive."

Theatre

The capital has at least 14 theatres, around as many per capita as in London or New York. Costa Rican theatre has been important even in continental terms—especially during the 1970s and 1980s, when playwrights fleeing as refugees from dictatorships in Argentina, Chile, and Uruguay took up residence, although the oldest theatre troupe is the English-speaking Little Theater Group. Opening nights are packed, and while it's hard to imagine that there could be sufficient audiences in San José to keep a play running for more than a few days, the *Teatro de Barrios* programme took many plays all around the country, swelling the average audience size from 2,000 to 30,000 or more.

Although state funding of the arts has fallen dramatically since the economic crisis of the 1980s, pushing many actors, directors, and writers into more populist work such as television sitcoms, the show still goes on. While many theatres concentrate on risqué sex comedies, there are always classics showing by Moliere, for example, or even Ancient Greeks such as Aristophanes. On Sundays, bands play for free in parks all over the country, while flyers posted on lamp posts advertise discussions on philosophy or politics.

Art

One of the best Tico painters to look out for is Isidro Con Wong, who started life as a poor farmer of Mongolian descent. Painting with little more than his fingers and *achiote* (a red vegetable paste), his works can now be found in several permanent museum collections in the United States and France, and sell for many tens of thousands of dollars. Other top artists are Max Jiménez, Francisco Amighetti, Margarita Bertheau, Luisa González de Sáenz, César Valverde, Rafa Fernández, and Ricardo 'Negrín' Rodríguez Córdoba, a black artist from Limón. Top sculptors are Francisco Zúñiga and Jorge Jiménez Deredia.

Today, the government-subsidised House of Arts helps to sponsor art by giving free painting and sculpture lessons, while the Ministry of Culture sponsors art classes and exhibitions in city parks on Sundays. Other art exhibits and installations can be found in the Museo de Arte Costarricense, and the many other smaller galleries throughout the capital. Meanwhile, the Center for Creative Arts, opened in 1991 in Santa Ana, offers courses and studio space for local and visiting artists, [tel: (506) 282-6556/8769].

Literature

The government, private donors and *La Nación* newspaper sponsor annual literature prizes. However, without having suffered the often terribly traumatic, battles, wars and upheavals that provided the inspiration for the literary giants of other Latin American countries, Costa Rican literature generally continues to lack the humour, satire, style and insight of writers such as Gabriel García Márquez and Isabel Allende.

The country's most important authors are Fabián Dobles (look out for his archetypal 'proletarian' novel *Ese Que Llaman Pueblo* and *Historias de Tata Mundo*), Joaquín Gutiérrez (*La Hoja de Aire*), Carlos Luis Fallas (especially *Mamita Yunai*, his classic tale of oppression and misery among 1930s banana plantation workers), José León Sánchez (wrongly imprisoned on the notorious prison island of San Lucas—most famous is *La Isla de los Hombres Solos*), Carmen Naranjo (Costa Rica's foremost female writer—look out for *Los Perros no Ladraron, Sobrepunto,* and *There Never Was Once Upon a Time)*, Carmen Lyra *(Mi Tía Panchita,* based on traditional tales told in the Caribbean by African slaves), and Samuel Rovinski (especially plays such as *Las Fisgonas de Paso Ancho).* Quince Duncan is the country's major black writer and Eulalia Bernard *(Ritmohéroe, Negritud, My Black King* and *Griot*) the top black poet. (*For more literary suggestions, see* Further Reading *on page 290.*)

Music

Revitalised by José Figueres in 1970 when it was on the point of collapse, the National Symphony Orchestra is now world class, with soloists playing all over the globe, while the state-funded Youth Orchestra (the only one in the Western world) has wowed audiences at the White House and the United Nations.

The National Symphony Orchestra performs in the National Theatre from April to November, with concerts on Thursday and Friday evenings, plus Saturday matinees.

There is also the Sura Chamber Choir, the first professional choir in Central America, which was founded in 1989 with musicians and vocalists from the country's two state universities.

Classical music evenings are periodically held by the Goethe Institute, Alliance Française, the Museo de Arte Costarricense and the Costa Rican-North American Cultural Center, The country also hosts an annual international music festival in the last two weeks of August.

In terms of modern music, some of the most popular bands and singers are Editus (who has won two Grammies), Marfa, the Brillanticos, Calle Ocho, and the newcomer Debbie Nova, who has sung internationally with the Black Eyed Peas and Ricky Martin. On the Caribbean coast, look out for Shanty (Calypso), Charro Limonense and Chakra.

GUANACASTECO CULTURE
Bull Riding

Most traditional Costa Rican culture is, in fact, from Guanacaste, and much of this centres around the region's history in cattle ranching. One of the most important expressions of this culture is the *tope* or horse fair (*see the section on 'Fiestas' in this chapter, page 202),* and another is bull riding.

While *corridas de toros*, in which young men get a testosterone rush by taunting a small cow in a ring, can be seen at festivals all over the country, bulls are only ridden in Guanacaste.

Calderón, a former bull-rider, or *montador*, told me, "Bull-riding became like an addiction for me. It's impossible to explain the adrenalin rush you get when that huge animal is leaping around under you, and you're just desperately hanging on—and then the crazy scramble to get away from under the hooves once you fall off. It meant I was always a huge success with the ladies, but unfortunately I had to stop after I got gored through my knee."

Many *montadores*, mostly males who do it professionally, have died or been permanently disabled. Some women, called *chigüinas*, also ride the bulls, animals which weigh in at up to 770 kg (1,700 lbs). Female participation, however, is generally frowned upon.

Today's bulls are no longer the wild creatures of the days when they roamed the plains unchecked, and so have a *verijera* or *mecate* tied tightly around their groin to enrage them into serious bucking.

The bulls have innocuous names like Pineapple Juice or Holy Spirit, and wait in holding pens while the *mecate* is fixed and the rider gets on. *Montadores* either ride bareback or on a leather *albarda* (saddle)—sometimes two at the same time, facing each other.

A *cimarrona* (literally 'untamed') band plays crashing, discordant music as the spectators wait for the bull to come leaping out of the booth. *Montadores* are lucky if they manage to stay on top of the bull for a whole minute. Once they have fallen off, the real fun (for the young machos in the crowd) begins. While the bull snorts and paws the ground, the boys leap into the ring to wave red capes at it and poke it with electric cattle prods. Those that think themselves really tough will dart past it, touching its head or pulling its tail. If the bull chases you, the best option is to get to the bars around the ring and climb up them as quickly as possible!

Once the bull is tired, horsemen come into the ring to lasso it and haul it out—although this may not be necessary, as these days most animals have caught on, and wait by the exit gate, desperate to get out.

Guaitíl Pottery

In the small villages of Guaitíl and San Vicente on the Nicoya Peninsula, more than 90 per cent of the inhabitants make their living from pottery making. Children learn to

Firing pottery the traditional way in Guaitíl.

make ceramics exactly like those used by their indigenous Chorotega ancestors, which are now on display in the country's museums (although the traditional designs—outlawed by the Spanish as pagan—are only now being re-discovered).

These once-controversial designs feature animal forms and the deities that the Chorotegas once shared with the Aztecs, such as Quetzalcóatl, the feathered serpent; Tezcatlipoca, the smoking mirror; and Tlaloc, the god of rain and fertility.

The whole pot-making process takes days, requiring special clay, sand and natural red, black and white curiol dyes, carried in from miles away. The clay is pounded in a massive wooden *pilón*—a kind of mortar and pestle, dried several times in the sun, and fired in wood-burning dome-shaped kilns at high temperatures.

A special jade-type stone called a *guaca* (often found in the graves of Chorotegas) is still used to bring up a gleaming shine on the finished ceramics. Nowadays, some people resort to using shampoo and plastic brushes. Unfortunately, the supply of crucial dark clay on public land is now running out, and the potters are trying to negotiate with local landowners to secure a new supply.

For information and pictures of other indigenous arts from Costa Rica, visit:

http://www.galerianamu.com.

Folkloric Dancing

Guanacaste is the only place where you'll really find folkloric music and dancing in Costa Rica. Pre-Columbian instruments such as the *chirimia* (oboe) and *quijongo* (a single-string bow with gourd resonator) are still used as backing for traditional Chorotega Indian dances such as the *Danza del Sol* and *Danza de la Luna* (dances of the sun and moon). You are more likely to see dances such as the energetic *Cambute* and *Botijuela Tamborito*, with much flurrying of lacy petticoats by the ladies and yelping by the men.

Several folkloric dance troupes tour the country, while others perform year-round at the Melíco Salazar Theatre, the Aduana Theatre and the National Dance Workshop headquarters in San José.

Bombas

A peculiarly Guanacasteco fiesta custom, these short, humorous rhymes are recited as interruptions during traditional dances. The idea is to shout '*bomba!*' to stop the music, before saying your rhyme. (Unfortunately much is lost in translation...)

> *Ayer pasé por tu casa*
> *Y en la puerta un burro había*
> *Y pensando que eras vos*
> *Le dije: Adiós, vida mía!*

> Yesterday I went past your house
> And in the doorway there was a donkey
> Thinking it was you
> I called out: 'Hello, my love!'

> *El zapatito me aprieta*
> *La media me da calor*
> *El muchacho de enfrente*
> *Me tiene loca de amor*

> My shoe is too tight
> My sock is too hot
> I've got a crazy crush on
> The boy from across the street.

SPORTS

Many Ticos are reasonably fit, and although most people can't afford to join a gym, the Sabana park is always full of people playing basketball, soccer, tennis, volleyball, baseball, or just jogging.It hasn't always been this way though. According to the Biesanzes in *The Ticos*, one man was even arrested in a highland village in 1976 after police caught him running, and deduced that he must be mad.

They're also interested in boxing and cycling. There's plenty of coverage of both in the papers, and you'll often see people training or meeting for cycling competitions along major roads. There is even an annual Tour de Costa Rica.

Soccer is a popular pastime and Costa Ricans, both young and old, enjoy watching and playing the game.

Football (Soccer)

If a Costa Rican male approaches you, holding one hand limp-wristed and palm down, slapping the back of it with the other hand, don't panic! He is not accusing you of being gay, but is actually inviting you to join in a *mejenga*, or informal football (soccer) game.

Likewise, there's no cause for alarm at the sound of an enormous, almost inhuman roar coming from the bowels of your neighbourhood *cantina* (well, not on a Sunday or a Wednesday night anyway). This, or a sudden chorus of frenzied horn honking from surrounding traffic, is a guarantee that a favoured team has just scored. People who can't be at the match or in the bar will be listening in on car radios.

Costa Ricans are, quite simply, obsessed with *fútbol*, which has even altered the structure of many Tico towns. A settlement without a soccer pitch can't legally qualify as a political district. In a large number of towns, the shady trees that once graced the Spanish-style central plazas have been uprooted and replaced with a grass pitch and goalposts, sometimes made from bamboo.

'Perdemos, pero somos los mejores.' (We lose, but we're still the best.)
—Anonymous soccer fan

The social life in some small towns has been quite drastically changed by soccer. The young people, both boys and girls, are happy enough practising their dribbling, but many older folk complain that there's now nowhere to have a *paseo* on Sunday after Mass, or to sit out in the evening with an ice cream and watch the world go by.

Football coverage in the local press is massive, often to the total exclusion of any other sport, and sometimes to the exclusion of the news itself. Sandwiched between baseball-mad Panama and Nicaragua, Costa Rica is the only Central American country, aside from Honduras, with a big tradition of soccer. The sport was introduced to the country in the early 1900s, by the sons of rich coffee barons who attended school in England.

Football is now such a big part of the culture that sociological texts have been written on its impact. Sociologist Sergio Villena Fiengo, the author of one such tract, says soccer is not just a game for Ticos, it also gives them a sense of 'anonymous belonging' and a means of venting emotions which are normally repressed in this relatively reserved society. Combined with a strong sense of national pride and patriotism, matches are, he said, "moments highly charged with tension, but at the same time free of social controls, which create a kind of social catharsis."

Getting to the 1990 World cup quarter-finals was one of the proudest moments in Costa Rica's soccer history, leading the president to declare a national holiday. People still talk about the eventof more than a decade ago with misty eyes. The Ticos reached the World Cup again in 2002, although they failed to get through to the last 16.

Before international matches, newspapers are flooded with letters from fans to their favourite players, as if they were warriors going away to war. These letters often praise the players for their *humildad*, that top Tico trait of humility.

The country has produced some international-level players, such as Paulo 'Chope' Wanchope, who has played for Manchester City and other clubs in England, Hernán Medford, Ronald Gómez, Wilson Muñoz and Jafet Soto. The press follows the fortunes of the players' foreign teams in minute detail, and the players, said Villena, are expected to fulfill a symbolic function even more important than that entrusted to ambassadors.

Back at home, however, players frequently actually threaten to go on strike, claiming they have to work too hard, that the season is too long and that they want their own union. This griping may not be quite as petulant as it sounds. With so many teams in the country, there are 56 matches in the national league alone.

Ticos boast that they're the best players in the region, and often attribute their fairly frequent defeats not to any failing on their own part, but like so many of the country's other problems, to external factors. Villena said, "The referee picked on us, it was too cold, it was too hot, the pitch was in a bad state... people nearly always say: 'We lost, but we're still the best', 'We have talent, it's just organisation we lack.'" Universidad de Costa Rica anthropologist Sergio Chávez added, "We're too anarchic and individualistic to be good team players as everyone wants to be the star."

The best way to make up your mind about such criticism is by attending a game, a frenzied and near-deafening experience. The season runs from August to May, and seats are cheaper and the atmosphere crazier in *sol* (sun) than in *sombra* (shade). For the few weeks when the local teams are not playing on home turf, Ticos make do with watching them playing abroad in international contests and qualifiers.

Like Europe, Costa Rica has its share of *barras* or hooligan gangs, such as the Ultras and the Doces. In the finals of the national championships in 1993, fighting between the supporters of Cartago and Heredia got so out of hand that the National Guard had to be called in, and the match was abandoned in chaos. It later had to be replayed in an empty stadium. Generally though, in typical Tico fashion, actual violence is very rare. Pregnant women and children attend soccer matches without any worries, although one important point to bear in mind is to duck if someone shouts: "*Suelo! Suelo!*" (floor)—Tico fans don't like to have their view of the game blocked.

Usually, the worst kind of post-match violence reported by police is between two groups of *barras* pelting each other with fruit. Several injuries were reported after Costa Rica's defeat of Honduras in the 2001 World Cup qualifiers, although these were mostly broken ankles suffered by people who had indulged in too much joyful jumping. Traffic in San José also came to a standstill for almost an hour as fans sat in the street doing Mexican waves.

One ex-*barra* member told me, "We were never really interested in real violence. Sometimes we'd throw a bag full of wasps at the other side's fans. Other times we'd throw rotten eggs or pods from the pica-pica plant, which has irritating hairs which get into the skin and itch like crazy."

For many supporters, alcohol is a big part of the soccer experience. Unfortunately, but tellingly, indices of both alcohol-fuelled car accidents and domestic violence shoot up after matches and announcements are even flashed on television screens during football matches saying '*mantengamos la paz familiar*' to remind fans not to take their frustrations out on their spouses.

The biggest rivalries are between supporters of the two top clubs. Saprissa (the San José team) is also known as Los Morados (purples) for the colour of its strip, while Alajuela is called Los Manudos (big hands) or Los Erizos (hedgehogs), the nickname for people from Alajuela. The other major top team is Heredia or Los Florenses—so called as women from Heredia are supposed to be the most beautiful 'flowers' in the country. A new team on the scene is Las Brujas (witches) from Escazú. As of 2005, Alajuela had won the National League 24 times, followed by Saprissa (23) and Heredia (21). However, Heredia, which won the first ever championship in 1921, has not won since the 1992/93 season.

The teams are divided into two divisions, with 12 teams in each. At the end of the season, the bottom team from the first division is relegated to the second, while the top team from the second division is boosted up. The 11th team in the First Division and the runner-up in the Second Division also have a play-off to determine which division they will play in the next season.

Team Colours

The colours of the top Costa Rican teams are:

- Club Sport Herediano   red and yellow
- Deportivo Saprissa   purple
- Liga Deportiva Alajuelense   red and black

The official Costa Rican football website, with all the latest news and fixtures, is:

http://www.unafut.com

Surfing

Although Costa Rica has the perfect conditions for surfing, the sport only really started to take off among locals in the early 1990s. Now it has become, for many, a passion.

José, a sun-bleached, dreadlocked surfer who lives in a hut right on the beach in Jacó so he can be in the sea in seconds, said, "We're more organised now, with competitions and stuff. Before, everyone in Costa Rica thought surfers were just layabouts and drug addicts."

The attitude in surf towns is the most laid-back you will find anywhere in Costa Rica, and is in particularly sharp contrast with the conservatism of the Meseta Central. Surf towns are also some of the places where you're most likely to come across the open sale of illegal drugs—mainly *mota* (marijuana), *perico* (cocaine) and *piedra* (crack), all served up by the *doctor* (dealer).

Those that pride themselves on being 'real' surfers will not take drugs, or even smoke or drink, because they have to be up and alert for the best waves early in the morning. They also have a tendency to sport tattoos, eat macrobiotic food, and sit on the beach, waxing their boards and staring out to sea with a faraway look in their eyes.

"It just gives you a really different outlook on life," said Oscar Arguedas, one of the country's pioneer surfers and arguably the most mellow human being on the planet. "My wife left me, my dog was run over, and I was duped out of US$ 750,000 by a friend. But when you go out there and confront death in the middle of those huge waves, you get the kind of adrenalin rush that makes all the bad things just melt away."

While all the surfers tend to spout the same kind of New Age philosophy, their simple way of life can be very seductive. It's also usually easy to find someone to give you some tips or lend you a board. Be very careful, however. Many Costa Rican beaches are riddled with *corrientes* (rip tides), and several people drown each year.

Traditionally, some of the best surfing was in the Caribbean (particularly the famous and enormous *salsa brava* wave in Puerto Viejo). The 1991 earthquake, however, pushed the reef up in some areas, making surfing difficult or dangerous. Most of the big surf areas are now on the Pacific coast.

While Tico surfers, like all Ticos, are polite and hate confrontations, you should remember that surf etiquette applies just as much here as elsewhere. Gringo surfers have a bad reputation, and the locals will not take kindly to you stealing their wave (although they probably won't say anything to your face).

FREE TIME

Ticos are experts at enjoying free time, although this often means doing nothing much at all. They are happy to spend hours hanging around, chatting, telling jokes (most people have an enormous repertoire) or playing practical jokes. This is often called *matando la culebra* (killing the snake)—a banana workers' excuse for idleness to their overseers.

When not enjoying a *reunión* at home, Ticos like to go out in large, giggling, screaming herds of friends or family. In the dry season, they visit parks, springs *(ojos de agua),* and beaches, where they often turn up the sound level still further with a radio played at full volume. (Unfortunately many Ticos still can't swim, and several drown each year in the country's rip tide-plagued waters). In San José, one of the busiest places on a weekend (for people who can't get to the beach) is the big Sabana Park, which is full of families flying kites, having picnics and taking horse rides.

In the rainy season, people spend more time lingering over coffee and cakes in cafés, window-shopping or going to the cinema. The cinema is popular, although Hollywood films tend to arrive pretty late (so operators can pay lower licence fees). The Sala Garbo in San José also shows European art house movies, as do some university cinemas.

Nightlife

Ticos, especially those living in San José, like to go out to eat, drink, listen to live music or dance. They'll do this pretty much any night, but the busiest evenings are from Wednesdays to Saturdays.

Away from the bright lights of the US-style city centre bars and the clubs of the San Pedro university area, however, most drinking goes on in the ubiquitous *cantina*. The *cantina* is an almost exclusively male preserve, and can be recognised by the doorway, which will be either shrouded by a beaded curtain, swinging Wild West-style saloon doors, or a large advertising hoarding. Inside, aside from the odd peeling pornographic calendar, decoration is limited to say the least, with metal chairs often welded to the floor.

While you might be expected to drink a few shots of *guaro* and engage in discussion about football or women, you are very unlikely to get into an ugly Mexican-style tequila-drinking contest with the locals. You would, however, offend or confuse your fellow drinkers if you turned down the offer of at least a first drink.

There's not a huge amount of nightlife in the countryside, where many bars are housed under traditional indigenous rancho roofs, huge conical thatched structures around 10 m high. Apart from this, there might not be a lot else to do apart from karaoke.

ACTIVITIES, HOBBIES AND SPORTS TO PICK UP

There are not really any specifically home-grown, local activities of note (unless of course you fancy taking your life in your hands by leaping into the bull ring during local festivals), but Costa Rica does provide a huge range of sports and other activities, most of which will enable you to enjoy its great outdoors to the full.

Golf

The golf scene in Costa Rica is growing fast and attracting many visitors from overseas. In response to this, the existing clubs are upgrading their facilities and improving their courses.

Some of the Best Golf Courses

- **Rancho las Colinas Golf and Country Club**
  An 18-hole course in Playa Grande, Guanacaste.
  Tel: (506) 383-3759
- **Garra de Leon Golf Club**
  On Playa Conchal, also in Guanacaste. This has beautiful vistas, and sweeping fairways. Stiff sea breezes make the course, and the choosing of clubs, a challenge.
  Tel: (506) 683-0303 / 0304
- **Parque Valle del Sol**
  Located in the San José area near the Juan Santamaria International Airport, this course is a big plus for holidaymakers and residents alike. It has a very interesting layout with lots of water—lagoons and wetlands.
  Tel: (506) 282-9222 / 2333
- **Cariari Country Club**
  Located in the San José area, this is the country's premier golf course. A challenging championship course, it was the site of two former PGA events.
  Tel: (506) 239-0022

For a more complete list of the country's courses, see
http://www.golf-man.com/courses/cricagcs.html.

Before you take to the green, however, you may want to bear in mind that golf courses generally require a great deal of water for irrigation and are thus environmentally controversial—especially those in the dry north Pacific area, such as Guanacaste. Most golf courses have a fairly strict dress code, not allowing shorts or T-shirts.

Bicycle Touring

There are lots of hills in Costa Rica, so this will get you fit! However, it's a wonderful way to get off the beaten track and meet the Ticos. Costa Rican drivers also seem to respect bicyclists more than pedestrians. However, truck and bus drivers may be less courteous.

If you plan to see the country from the top of a bicycle, your life will be easier if you peddle a good machine with at least 21 gears. Be aware that you'll be outdoors at high altitudes so bring along a windbreaker and some warm clothes; and don't forget your emergency kit with water, tyre patching gear and a few basic tools.

Bicycling Equipment

For bicycling equipment, try:

- Mundo del Ciclismo in San José
  Tel: (506) 233-7070
- Deportes Garabito in Esparza
  Tel: (506) 635-5863

Surfing

The best Pacific breaks in Costa Rica are near its northern and southern borders, while the central beaches are probably Costa Rica's most consistent surf spots, with few completely flat days per year.

Playa Hermosa, south of Jacó, is the place to head if there isn't a big swell in Guanacaste or on the Caribbean. Even if the water is flat here, you can always find something rideable at one of the various breaks to be found 10–45 minutes' drive in either direction. Manuel Antonio, about an hour south of Hermosa, has many other attractions to complement the surf. If it's flat you can enjoy sea kayaking, snorkelling or a white water paddle down the Savegre River. Dominical, further to the south, tends to get better waves. The Atlantic coast has suffered some serious storms and subsequent flooding in past years, but Puerto Viejo's legendary *salsa brava* usually gets hit by some great surf in January and February. But as is all too often true of legendary breaks, it can also get crowded during those months.

Remember if swimming at surf beaches that they can be very dangerous and have rip tides. Few beaches have lifeguards. For information on all your surfing needs, including wave forecasts and tide times, visit:
http://www.crsurf.com/.

Life in the Treetops

Another exciting outdoor adventure you can experience in Costa Rica is a tree top canopy tour, available in places such as Monteverde and Rincón de la Vieja. This allows you to see nature from a monkey's eye viewpoint while enjoying a white-knuckle ride on zip lines through the treetops. Fitted with gloves and a harness, you are clipped to various cables and whiz from platform to platform many metres above the ground. If you manage to prise your eyes open, and haven't scared all the local creatures off with your screams, you will be amazed by the variety of plant, insect and bird life you can see from this unusual angle. Not to be recommended for the overweight, young children, or those with a fear of heights. A much more sedate option (and, to be honest, an option far more likely to give you a good long look at the forest canopy's monkeys, birds and orchids, is to take a walk on the raised walkways through the treetops in Monteverde and some other forest reserves.

Scuba

The top spot, without a doubt, is the mysterious Cocos Island—if you can afford it! Hiring a boat for a week's trip will set you back around US$ 3,000—as well as the US$ 25 daily park entrance charge. The diving here is challenging to say the least, with strong currents and, despite the ravages of Asian shark fishing fleets, lots of sharks. This is one of the very top diving spots and last true wilderness on the planet. It is the only offshore land mass in hundreds of miles, and so has generated its own eco-system, attracting huge numbers of sharks, including hammerheads, and massive rays.

The best dive spot in mainland Costa Rica is Caño Island, which is also home to an amazing variety of marine life. The Gulf of Papagayo, on the north-west Pacific coast, meanwhile, is surrounded by an abundance of dive sites, where you can get up close and personal to white tip reef sharks, giant schools of grunt, yellowtails, spotted eagle rays, turtles, stingrays, angel fish, octopuses, sea horses, starfish, frog fish and many species of eels.

Information on Scuba Diving

- Costa Rica Adventure Divers
  Tel: (506) 236-5637 / (506) 371-1598
  Website: http://www.costaricadiving.com
- Bill Beard's Costa Rica: Scuba Diving and Adventure Tours
  Website: http://www.billbeardcostarica.com/.

Windsurfing

Steady 96 kmph (60 mph) winds sweep across Lake Arenal during the dry season (mid-December to May), allowing for some of the best windsurfing in the world. Windsurfing aficionados from all around the world flock to Lake Arenal to whip across this magnificent, 35-km- (22-mile-) long lake.

Nowhere else in the world would you be able to enjoy top-notch windsurfing conditions while witnessing a pyrotechnic show of incandescent rock and lava flowing down the sides of a volcano!

Rafting

Dozens of jungle-lined tropical rivers offer churning white water almost year-round. The wet season (from May to November) is best because there's always plenty of water. In fact, some rivers get too high to run during the rains. In the dry season, you are limited to the wetter Atlantic slope, but that still leaves plenty to choose from. However, be aware that several tourists have died in rafting accidents in Costa Rica in recent years. Make sure you only use reputable tour companies.

The country's most popular rafting river is the Atlantic slope Río Reventazón ('bursting river'), which certainly lives up to its name and offers year-round water, being controlled by the Cachí Dam. The Reventazón is divided into four sections of various degrees of difficulty.

The Río Pacuare, meanwhile, is a regular on lists of the world's top-ten rafting and kayaking rivers. It is both beautiful and exciting, winding through densely forested gorges with many waterfalls.

The scenic Río Corobicí is a gentle 'float' rather than an adrenalin-pumping thrill, and is a must for nature lovers. More than 300 hundred species of birds have been identified in the area, and slipping by unobtrusively on a raft is one of the best ways to see them, not to mention howler monkeys, iguanas, river otters and various other mammals and reptiles.

Information on Rafting

You can easily find out about white water rafting trips from:

Instituto Costarricense de Turismo

Tel: (506) 223-1733

Website: http://www.tourism-costarica.com

However, for the true daredevil adventurer, Costa Rica has many more stretches of white water never visited by commercial tour operations, either because they are too difficult or too remote. *The Rivers of Costa Rica: A Canoeing, Kayaking and Rafting Guide* by Michael W Mayfield and Rafael E Gallo describes them all in loving, and sometimes scary, detail.

Sport Fishing

Two oceans, beautiful lakes and hundreds of rivers all add up to some of the best fishing for more species at any time of the year than you're likely to find in such a small and easily accessible area anywhere else in the world.

The main fishing areas are Cabo Blanco to the Gulf of Papagayo on the Northern Pacific Coast, Cabo Blanco to Drake Bay in the Central Pacific, and Golfito and Playa Zancudo in the Southern Pacific, where you may encounter marlin, dorado, tuna, sailfish, wahoo, roosterfish, snook and jacks, runners, mackerel, amberjacks, groupers, barracuda, corbina or snappers inshore.

On the Caribbean coast, look out for tarpon when the surf is up, barracuda, jacks, kingfish, sierra, tripletail, cubera, grouper, jewfish, wahoo, big tuna and the occasional Atlantic sailfish and blue marlin. With la ight tackle, you might catch rainbow bass *(guapote)*, mojarra, vieja, machaca, catfish, drum and alligator gar.

Some operators provide houseboats that serve as floating lodges to get you into the miles of jungle rivers and small hidden lakes that others rarely fish.

Lake Arenal, at the base of the active Arenal Volcano, is easily the most popular inland fishing destination. The lake is home to *guapote*, or rainbow bass. There is a daily limit of five fish, which can weigh in at up to 9 lbs. A number of lodges around the lake offer boats and guides.

There is also fishing available on many of the country's rivers. However, be aware that closed seasons in some waters may vary from year to year, and a valid Costa Rican fishing license is required for all freshwater fishing in the country.

Information

For more information on tropical fishing, see:
- Tropical Fishing Adventures
  Website: http://www.tropicalfishing.com/costarica.html
- Costa RicaL: Sportfishing
  Website: http://centralamerica.com/cr/fish/.

Horse Riding

Even though Costa Rica's cowboys or *sabaneros* are a dying breed, horses are still very much a functional part of daily life in rural parts of the country. This is one of the most beautiful places to ride too—from cantering through the surf along the long, long beaches of the Nicoya Peninsula to wandering through along forest trails (you get a much better look at the wildlife than on foot).

One of the most authentic horse riding experiences is at Buenavista Lodge (email: info@buenavistacr.com) in the heart of Guanacaste, Costa Rica's cowboy province. This working cattle ranch has basic lodges and hearty food where, with a cowboy as your guide, you can ride up to sulphur springs, remote waterfalls and try your hand at spotting everything from howler monkeys and toucans to coatis.

Dance

Ticos might not dance it up quite as much as the Cubans, but they very definitely leave their supposed reserve at home when they go out dancing. Nearly everybody has the kind of fluid footwork and hip movements that will make all but the most advanced salsa dancers blush, feel horribly inadequate, or both. If you fancy having a go yourself though, you'll have some of the best fun of your life—although be warned that it can be surprisingly tiring!

When you head out for a night on the tiles, be warned that a nightclub is called a *discoteca*, while what is called a nightclub is, in fact, a strip joint!

Classes

If you want to learn, you'll be welcomed at a class either on your own or with a partner. Try:

- Bailes Latinos in the Costa Rican Institute of Language and Latin Dance in San José
  Tel: (506) 233-8938
- Danza Viva
  Tel: (506) 253-3110
  This place offers courses in *salsa*, *meringue* (the two most popular disco dances), the *lambada*, the more formal *bolero* and *marcado* and the Caribbean *mambo*, as well as ballet, jazz and modern dance.

Salsa 54 on Calle 3, Avenida 11/3 is the best place to dance—or just watch—in San José, although most discos mix in a lot of salsa numbers with contemporary tunes.

Courses

For those who are more than normally enchanted by Costa Rica's wonderful wildlife, you can take a range of courses to broaden your knowledge in subjects such as birding and tropical dendrology (the study of trees) at the Centro Científico Tropical in Monteverde, tel: (506) 645-5122 or email: montever@sol.racsa.co.cr

Photography

With everything from exploding volcanoes to flitting hummingbirds, mysterious cloud forest and raging rivers, Costa Rica is a photographer's dream.

Other Activites

For other options—from scrabble contests to yoga and social clubs to football match fixtures—look at the *Tico Times'* weekly 'What's Doing' section and the 'Viva' section of *La Nación*.

Really get the most out of your camera with guided photo safaris led by experts, which offer you both guidance and an itinerary to some of the country's most photogenic spots. More information at:

http://www.photographyincostarica.com/
photosafaris/aboutus.htm.

FIESTAS

Ticos love an excuse for a party. All towns and villages have a fiesta at least once a year. These may be to mark the town's saint's day or the end of the year (traditionally a good time as the coffee harvest is in and everyone had been paid their Christmas bonus). Local parishes also have *turnos* (smaller fiestas) to raise money for the church.

Most fiestas last for at least a week, and start each day with rockets at dawn. They usually include fairground rides, local bands, folkloric parades, dances, beauty contests, *corridas de toros* (bull fights), sports events and plenty of eating and drinking. Classic fiesta food includes Chinese *chop suey* and *vigorón* which is made of yucca, *chicharrones* (fried pig skin) and cabbage.

No fiesta would be a fiesta without the presence of *Los Gigantes*—a group of giant figures on stilts which run around taunting (and being taunted by) the local children. The giants

Fiesta *gigantes* taunting children—or is it the other way round?

The *tope* is an essential part of any Tico fiesta.

usually include *La Giganta* (the giant woman), *El Gamonal* (the chief), *El Diablo* (the devil), *La Negra* (the black woman) and *La Bruja* (the witch)—although their traditional violence has now been officially limited.

"When I was a kid, the *gigantes* used to go around with sticks and try to catch you," said Max, an engineer. "Sometimes they'd really whack you, but it was all part of the excitement. Now it's been made illegal because of people bleating about child abuse."

Another inevitable part of a Tico festival is the *tope*, or horse parade. Horsemen—often hundreds from all over the country—come to parade through the streets on their *caballos de paso;* highly-strung and specially-bred, high-stepping horses. Decked out in incredibly ornate and be-tasselled tack, they prance and skitter all over the streets, sometimes almost standing on the onlookers who let out high-pitched Speedy González-type screams of excitement.

CALENDAR OF EVENTS/FIESTAS
January
- **Copa de Café, San José (First week)**
  This is a big international junior tennis tour event at the Costa Rica Country Club.
- **Fiesta de Santa Cruz, Guanacaste (Mid-January)**
  A celebration in honour of the famous Guatemalan Black Christ of Esquipulas, supposedly discovered here in colonial times after a Guatemalan miracle-peddler

abandoned it. It features a two-week pilgrimage around the district, culminating in folk dancing, *marimba*-playing and bullfights.

February
- **Fiesta de los Diablitos (Dates vary)**
  Masked dancing among the Boruca Indian community of Rey Curré. Very similar to the other Boruca festival in December.

March
- **Día del Boyero, San Antonio de Escazú, San José (Second Sunday)**
  The country's ox-cart drivers gather for a colorful parade and contest, and priests bless the oxen.
- **Día de San José (19 March)**
  Celebration of the capital's patron saint.
- **National Orchid Show, San José (Dates vary)**

April
- **Holy Week (Week leading up to Easter)**
  Religious processions are held in towns across the country, and many Ticos make the most of the Thursday and Friday holidays by going to the beach.
- **Juan Santamaría Day, Alajuela (11 April)**
  Ticos celebrate the bravery of their national hero with parades, concerts, and dances.
- **Día del Aborígen (19 April)**
  National celebration of Costa Rica's indigenous population, history, and culture.

May
- **Labour Day (1 May)**
  It is particularly celebrated in Limón, with dances and cricket matches.
- **Carrera de San Juan (17 May)**
  Costa Rica's biggest marathon, starting from near Cartago and passing through the mountains to San José.

- **Día de María Auxiliadora (24 May)**
'Miraculous' nun Sor María Romero (*see the section 'Religion and Witchcraft'* in Chapter Three: People *on page 87*) was a big devotee of this virgin, and this is now the second biggest religious festival in the country. Novenas are said for nine nights, culminating in a 4:00 am procession and Mass every hour at the Casa de la Virgen in San José's Barrio Don Bosco, where Sor María's remains lie.

July
- **Fiesta de la Virgen del Mar, Puntarenas (Saturday closest to 16 July)**
A fiesta to give thanks to Our Lady of Carmen who miraculously saved storm-stricken fishermen from a shipwreck in 1913. A procession of boats decorated with yellow and white ribbons (the colours of the Catholic Church) carries the statue.
- **Guanacaste Day (25 July)**
A week of festivities in towns across the province leads up to the big day on 25 July, in honour of the annexation of Guanacaste in 1824. Festivities include massive *topes*, bullfights and rodeos, folkloric processions, dancing etc. The biggest events are in the provincial capital, Liberia.

August
- **Fiesta de la Virgen de los Angeles, Cartago (2 August)**
Around a million Ticos make the pilgrimage, or *romería* to the Basílica de Nuestra Señora de Los Angeles to pay homage to the country's patron saint, La Negrita (*see the section 'Religion and Witchcraft'* in Chapter Three: People *on page 87*). Some *romeros* walk—many barefoot—cycle or ride on horseback, from as far away as Guanacaste. They camp overnight outside the church before making their way to the altar on their knees to give thanks to the Virgin for miracles, or to ask for help in the coming year.
- **Mother's Day (15 August)**
This is not a simple day for giving *mamá* a bunch of flowers and a card. Shops are crowded out for weeks before with

The Basílica de Nuestra Señora de Los Angeles is home to Costa Rica's patron saint and the scene of massive pilgrimages every August.

Ticos looking for gifts—more often than not a new washing machine or car. Some people even plunge themselves into debt in an effort to out-do their siblings or friends. This is a big family day, where mothers are thoroughly pampered. People whose mothers have passed away visit their graves with flowers and gifts.

- **Independence Day (15 September)**
  Various festivities are held throughout the day, culminating in a children's lantern-lit parades at night.
- **International Beach Clean-Up Day (Third Saturday)**

October

- **Carnaval de Limón (Week leading up to 12 October)**
  Uniquely in Latin America (where carnival is generally celebrated the week before Lent), in Limón it marks Columbus' arrival in Costa Rica. The carnival was originally the brainchild of Arthur King, who brought back tales of colourful celebrations after a stint working in Panama. This massive party mixes Tico fiesta traditions, Afro-Caribbean music and hordes of outlandish, often skimpily-clad Rio-style street paraders.
- **Fiesta del Maíz, Upala, Guanacaste (12 October)**
  A celebration of all things related to corn. The highlight is a pageant, with the local beauty queens parading in outfits fashioned from the crop.

November
- **Día de los Muertos (2 November.**
  As in most of the Latin world, on the Day of the Dead, Tico families visit their deceased relatives in graveyards around the country and stage religious processions.

December
- **Día de la Pólvora, San Antonio de Belén and Jesus María de San Mateo (8 December)**
  This celebration, in which fireworks are let off, honours Our Lady of Immaculate Conception.
- **Fiesta de la Yegüita, Nicoya (12 December)**
  According to legend, two drunken men were fighting with machetes and one of their wives prayed to the Virgin of Guadelupe to intervene. A horse appeared, biting and kicking the men until they stopped. Today's festival, along with the usual fiesta activities, involves the parade of a wooden horse *(yegua)* and the virgin, accompanied by whistle music. Some people still use the occasion to settle scores, and the horse intervenes as necessary.
- **Las Posadas (Begins 15 December)**
  Country-wide event in which children and adults, re-enacting Joseph and Mary's search for lodging in Bethlehem, go from house to house in their neighbourhood singing carols.
- **Festejos Populares (Begins 31 December)**
  These are held around the country, but particularly in San José, where there are bullfights, a *tope*, a carnival, and fairground rides in Zapote. On New Year's Eve, there is a dance in the Parque Central.
- **Fiesta de los Diablitos**
  Indians in the Boruca reserve perform this traditional masked dance over three days, in which the Spaniards are represented by a bull. The animal vanquishes the Indians, or *diablitos* (little devils), but—wishfully departing from historical fact—they come back in the night and symbolically kill it.

LEARNING THE
LANGUAGE

'If someone is speaking to you, appears agitated, and you hear '...*tu madre*...' the speaker is probably not inquiring about the health of your mother, as you might suppose!'
—Message posted on travel website
giving Costa Rican language tips

ONE OF THE MOST COMMONLY BANDIED-AROUND MISCONCEPTIONS about Spanish is that it is an 'easy' language. Of course, it is much easier, if you are a native English speaker than, say, Japanese. But while it is reasonably easy to learn to speak basic survival Spanish, it can take longer than you might expect to learn to speak it well unless you can already speak another Latin language. Sadly, many people become disillusioned or give up after being initially told how 'easy' it was.

The major problem, for English speakers, is that Spanish has a LOT of grammar, including two noun genders, two different verbs for 'to be' and a verb mood that can be very hard to grasp (the subjunctive). With verb conjugations, there are generally only four possible permutations in English, e.g. 'say', 'says', 'said' and 'saying'. With Spanish verbs, there are nearly 50. In addition, Spanish in Costa Rica varies widely from both the Spanish spoken in Spain and most other Spanish-speaking countries, in terms of both pronunciation and vocabulary.

But don't get downhearted! On the plus side, Spanish, unlike English, is at least based on rules, which can be learned. It's also 100 per cent phonetic—so you'll never agonise over the pronunciation of the Spanish equivalents of 'enough', 'cough' and 'thorough'. Costa Rican Spanish is spoken relatively slowly and clearly, and, along with that of Colombia, is usually recognised as the best in the whole of Latin America (usually put down to the high levels of education in both countries).

There are dozens of very good Spanish schools in the country, and most educated younger Costa Ricans—especially in the urban areas—can speak at least a smattering of English. This can be a huge help at the beginning when you get stumped. Ticos are also endlessly patient. Most of them have had to deal with so many English-speaking tourists or residents who can't or won't even say '*gracias*', that they are delighted at anyone making the effort, however ham-fistedly, to speak their language.

Unless you're pretty fluent in Spanish, Ticos may try to help you out by reverting to English. I've known some foreigners who are really determined to speak only in Spanish and so tell a white lie, saying they don't speak English. Of course, if you are asked where you're from, this means you'll have to plump for somewhere unusual like Norway—and hope no-one asks you to teach them any Norwegian!

Once your Spanish skills improve, you will find that soap operas can be a good way of picking up (admittedly rather melodramatic) conversational slang. Another big help is that Hollywood movies in Costa Rica are always subtitled into Spanish—reading the subtitles while you hear the dialogue can be a massive learning boost.

It is beyond the scope of this section to provide more than the most basic of pointers for readers who can't yet speak Spanish—a good phrase book, dictionary and, if possible, a few weeks in a Spanish school are strongly recommended. Much of the information in this section is aimed at people who already speak some Spanish and want to learn some of the peculiarities of the language as spoken in Costa Rica.

As already mentioned, Costa Rican pronunciation is good. Outside the Meseta Central, however, you will find that people often speak much faster. In Guanacaste, the accent is the same as in Nicaragua—very fast, and with only an aspirated pronunciation of the letter 's'.

Much 'realistic' Costa Rican literature, especially from the early 20th century, faithfully reproduces countryside pronunciation that you will still hear today. For example, many words starting with a consonant followed by **ue**, such as *huevo*, *fue* or *vuelvo*, may sound more like 'güevo', 'güe' or 'güelvo'. Less educated Ticos may also leave out various consonants, running words together—so that *entonces* (then, well, so) sounds more like 'to'es', while *de nada* (you're welcome) becomes 'e-na'a'. In coastal areas, people often replace a final **r** with an *l* sound, for example the verb *decir* (to say) becomes 'decil'.

Stress

The stress comes on the last syllable if the word ends in a consonant other than **n** or **s** e.g. *la mujer* (woman), or *universal*. If the word ends in a vowel, an **n** or an **s**, the stress comes on the penultimate syllable, e.g. *la cama* (bed), la *imagen* (image) or *interesante* (interesting). An accent above a vowel, e.g. *difícil* (difficult) or *la química* (chemistry), shows irregular stress, that is placed on the accented syllable. For words ending in **io** or **ia**, these letters are pronounced as a diphthong, i.e. one syllable, (e.g. in *el misterio*, where the stress is on the **e**), unless a stress accent shows differently (e.g. *la panadería* meaning bakery).

Cognates

Though English is a Germanic language, more than 50 per cent of all its vocabulary actually has Latin roots. This gives rise (helpfully) to thousands of related words in Spanish and English, which means a beginner can expand his or her vocabulary very quickly.

For example, hundreds of words in Spanish ending in -**dad** end in -ty in English, e.g. *libertad* (liberty), *posibilidad* (possibility), while words ending in -tion in English end in -**ción** in Spanish, such as *información* (information) and *violación* (violation).

English words ending with -ly are often like Spanish words ending in -**mente**, such as *realmente* (really) and *naturalmente* (naturally), while those ending with -ry in English end in -**rio** in Spanish, such as *territorio* (territory) and *comentario* (commentary). -Ism in English becomes -**ismo** in Spanish, e.g. *comunismo* (communism) and *individualismo* (individualism).

There are many other cognate forms. Be warned, however, of many 'false friends' e.g. *actualmente*, which means 'currently' rather than 'actually', and *sensible*, which means 'sensitive', not 'sensible'. When I was first learning Spanish, I regularly caused hilarity by saying '*Estoy embarazada*', whenever I was embarrassed—not for a moment intending to announce that I was pregnant!

Gender

In Spanish, nouns are either masculine (mostly ending in **o**) or feminine (mostly ending in **a**), e.g. *la muchacha* (the girl), *el muchacho* (the boy). There are exceptions to the above, e.g. *el programa, el planeta, el problema* and *la mano* (hand), *la foto* and *la dínamo.*

Nouns ending in **-ión** or **-dad** are also feminine (e.g. *la organización* and *la unidad*). Those ending in any other letter simply have to be learned e.g. *la piel* (skin), but *el nivel* (level), and *la mujer* (woman), but *el amor* (love).

Commas and Points

Be aware that Costa Ricans reverse the commas and points in numbers that English speakers are used to. For example 4,982 (four thousand, nine hundred and eighty two) in Costa Rica is written 4.982 or 4.982,00. You will even see this with dates, for example the year 2.003.

Pronunciation Guide

Vowels

- **a**   like the *a* in *cat*
- **e**   like the *e* in *bed*
- **i**   like the *ee* in *meet*
- **o**   like the *o* in *top*
- **u**   a short *oo*, as in *Oops!*

Consonants

Most consonants are pronounced like their English counterparts. Exceptions are:

- **c**   like the hard *c* in *cat* before **a**, **o** and **u**;
  like the soft *c* in *centre* before **e** and **i**
- **d**   like the *d* in *dog* at the start of a word;
  like the *th* in *this* elsewhere
- **g**   like the hard *g* in *give* before **a**, **o** and **u**;
  like the *h* in *his* before **e** and **i**
- **gu**   like the hard *g* before **e** and **i**;
  like the *gw* in *Gwen* before **a**, **o** and **u**—but pronounced
  more softly, almost like a *w*
- **gü**   the same soft *gw* as above, but used before **e** and **i**
- **h**   silent
- **j**   like the *h* in *his*
- **ll**   like the *y* in *yellow*
- **qu**   like the *k* in *kite*
- **r**   in the middle of a word, sounds like the lazy *tt* in the
  American pronunciation of *butter*;
  at the start of a word, is should be rolled. However, if
  you have problems with rolling the Spanish **r**, worry
  not! Uniquely, many Ticos, especially older Ticos, do not
  roll it either. Instead it is a rounded *r* pronounced pretty
  much as it would be by an American or an Englishman
  with a Westcountry burr
- **rr**   rolled, as above
- **s**   like the *s* in *soap*
- **y**   at the start of a word, pronounced like *j* in *jam*;
  elsewhere pronounced like *y* in *yellow*
- **z**   like the *s* in *soap*

> **Important Points of Grammar**
>
> Unlike English, adjectives nearly always follow the noun, e.g. *un programa interesante* is 'an interesting programme'. They also agree in gender and number with the noun, e.g. *el gato negro* ('the black cat'), but *las vacas blancas* ('the white cows').
>
> Spanish has two verbs 'to be': *ser* and *estar*. *Ser* refers to a permanent state, and *estar* to a temporary state or location. For example, *el perro es gris* (*ser*) means 'the dog is grey' and is a permanent state, but *el perro está fuera* (*estar*) meaning 'the dog is outside' refers to a location. *Es aburrido* (*ser*) means 'he is boring' while *está aburrido* (*estar*) means 'he is bored'.

VOSEO

Vos is an archaic form of 'you', which is now only widely used in Argentina, Uruguay, Nicaragua and Costa Rica, where it is an intimate, informal means of address (the formal form is *usted*), used instead of *tú*.

Originally, however, the *voseo*—which descends from the Golden Age and was used in Spain until the 19th century—was actually the polite second person singular form, equivalent to 'thou' in English. It was the way in which the *hidalgos*, or noblemen, who settled Costa Rica, addressed each other.

For those who have studied Peninsular Spanish, *vos* conjugates exactly like *vosotros* (the informal plural 'you' of Spain). The only difference is that where verbs in *vosotros* end in **-áis**, **-éis** or **-ís**, in *vos* they end in **-ás**, **-és** or **-ís**, always maintaining the same stress as the *vosotros* form.

Alternatively, you can usually take the *tú* form and just stress the last syllable, e.g. *tú miras* becomes *vos mirás*. *Vos* uses the infinitive as a root, so doesn't share the irregularities of *tú*. So:

- *Tú entiendes* (*vosotros entendéis*) is *vos entendés* (you understand)
- *Tú piensas* (*vosotros pensáis*) is *vos pensás* (you think)
- *Tú dices* (*vosotros decís*) is *vos decís* (you say)

Importantly, note *vos sos* (*tú eres/vosotros sois*) or 'you are'. In the simple past, *vos* adds an 's' to the *tú* form, so *tú supiste* (you knew) would become *vos supistes* (*vosotros supisteis*).

In the imperative, *vos* simply removes the 'r' of the infinitive (or the 'd' of the *vosotros* imperative):

Tú	Vosotros	Vos	English
pon	*poned*	*poné*	put!
mira	*mirad*	*mirá*	look!
ven	*venid*	*vení*	come!

Unlike *vosotros*, *vos* takes 'te' rather than 'os' in the reflexive, e.g. *Tenés que vestirte enseguida* (You have to get dressed straightaway).

VOS OR USTED

The use of *vos* is becoming something of a hot potato in Costa Rica. While you'll still hear it a lot in the countryside, you will rarely hear *vos* these days in the city. Many, many people in Costa Rica now exclusively use *usted*, even with family members, children and pets.

Some people may switch from *vos* to *usted* and back again during the course of a conversation to emphasise a slight change in mood. Unlike most other Spanish-speaking countries, there may well not be a symbolic moment in your relationship with a Tico when you cross the intimacy threshold from *usted* to *vos*—particularly among middle-class Ticos, who like to be thought of as cultured and educated. If you hear someone saying *vos*, there's a good chance they may be from Nicaragua, where it's still used more widely.

Some towns are also more likely to use *vos* than others. Two Tico friends, university students Rebeca, from Cartago, and Ariana, from San José, have known each other for years, but while Ariana always calls Rebeca *vos*, for Rebeca, Ariana will always be *usted*.

"*Vos* sounds nice and old-fashioned, but it's the way I think of farmers speaking," a San José taxi driver said. "It's just way too informal for me. I don't really have any kind of relationships where I'd be comfortable calling someone *vos*." Ticos will not expect you to know how to use *vos*. *Tú* is fine for a foreigner, unless you're planning on staying for a long time.

If you do use *vos*, it goes without saying that you should never do so with people much older than yourself. It's really easiest to avoid the whole minefield by sticking with *usted* until the Tico you're talking to suggests you change.

In addition, *tú* is slowly starting to appear in the country through the influence of foreign movies and soap operas, with occasional Ticos using it as a 'classier' alternative to *vos*. There is a big backlash against this, however.

"If another Costa Rican called me *tú*, I wouldn't even respond to them," said Ariana. "It's not part of our language or culture—it just smacks of people trying to be something they're not."

Many multinational companies, such as Burger King, take such strength of feeling on board, changing their advertising for Costa Rica from *tú* to *vos*.

TIQUISMOS

Despite being such a small country, Costa Rica has as much or more country-specific vocabulary and slang than many other much bigger nations. Many of these *Tiquismos* arose because of the country's historic isolation, and have their roots in farming or religion, or more recently, in the Ticos' unusually heavy exposure to English.

Of course you will also find many diminutives ending in *ito* or *ico* (the very reason for the Costa Ricans being called Ticos), either for emphasis, or to make words sound more cute or friendly; such as *ahorita* from *ahora* (now/right now), *despuesito* (afterwards), *hasta lueguito* (bye), *chiquitico* (teeny) from *chiquito* (tiny) and ultimately *chico* (small), and *a la vueltica* (just around the corner).

This is a list of some of the most common *Tiquismos* (a few are used more widely throughout the region), but it's not exhaustive. There are hundreds more though, lots of them used by speakers of *pachucho*, a kind of street slang.

Adiós!	Hi! (when passing someone in the street, especially in rural areas), usually means 'goodbye'.
Andar	To have (literally 'to walk'), e.g. *Sólo ando cien colones*

Apear	To get down (used instead of *bajar*)
Birra	Beer (usually *cerveza*). Also *rubia* (literally blonde)
Blanco	Cigarette (usually *cigarro*)
Bomba	Petrol station
Brete	Job (*bretear* means to work)
Buenas	Short for *buenos días, buenas tardes* or *buenas noches*
Cabra/o	Girlfriend, boyfriend (literally 'goat')
Cachos	Shoes (literally 'horns')
Campo	Space, e.g. on a bus (literally 'field'). *Hay campo?* means 'Is there space?'
Cerrado	Stupid, pig-headed (literally 'closed')
Chamaco/chavalo	Child/kid
Chepe	San José
Chile	A (usually sexual or scatalogical) joke
Chinamo	A street stall
Chiva/chivísima	Brilliant, cool (literally 'goat'). Used mainly by younger people
Cien metros	One city block
Chorizo	Illegal business (literally 'sausage')
Chunche	Thing
Diay!	Crucial Tico interjection, which can mean anything from 'hey!' to 'what a shame' to 'hmm...'
Que dicha/por dicha	Thankfully, luckily
Este	Often a drawn-out 'eeeeeste...' Used much as 'like' in lazy English, to fill a space while you're thinking of what to say
Gato	Person with light-coloured eyes (cat)

Güeison	Bad quality. This originally comes from the phrase *buey sólo*, or 'single ox'. A pair of oxen are needed to pull a cart, so a *buey sólo* is something that's pretty useless.
Güevón	Literally 'big egg' (or big testicle). Term of address used between men, often insultingly.
Güila	Child/kid. Be careful as this means prostitute in Mexico!
Hijo'eputa	Literally 'son of a bitch'. Widely used as an expression of surprise or annoyance, and sometimes toned down to *juepucha*.
Jale!	Let's go!
Jupa	Head
Limpio/quedarse limpio	To have no money
Macho/a	Light-skinned or haired person
Maicero	Hick
Maje (usually *ma'e*)	Literally 'crazy' or 'stupid'. This word is the equivalent of 'mate' in English, *tío* in Spain or *che* in Argentina.
Maso	Short for *más o menos* meaning 'more or less', 'pretty much'.
Nerdo	Nerd
Nota	As in *que buena nota*, or *que mala nota* meaning fantastic or what a pain
Ocupar	Used instead of *necesitar* (to need), e.g. *ocupo ir al banco* (I need to go to the bank).
Platero	a gold digger
Porta amí?	What do I care? So what?
Que pereza!	What a pain! How boring!

Pesos	Colones
Playo	Homosexual (another word is *guineo* which is a type of small banana)
Porfa	Please (short for *por favor*)
Pura vida	The absolutely ubiquitous Tiquismo. Literally 'pure life', it can mean cool, great or thanks, and even be used as a greeting. It can be applied to people, places, events, etc.
Regalar	Literally 'to give as a gift'. This is widely used instead of *dar* (to give). Asking for a beer in a bar, for example, you would say *regáleme una cerveza, por favor*.
Roco	Old man
Rojo	1,000 colón note. Literally 'red' (the colour of the bill). This also means a taxi as Tico taxis are red.
Salado	An unlucky person. Literally 'salty'.
Suave/suave un toque!	Hang on/wait a minute
Teja, tejita	100 colón bill
Tomado	Drunk
Torta	A big cock-up
Tuanis	From 'too nice' in English. Basically 'cool!' Can also be used as a greeting.
Tucán	5,000 colón bill (it has a toucan on it)
Tugurio	Shanty town
La U	University (especially UCR)
Upe!	Greeting/warning shouted when approaching someone's house instead of knocking on the door

Vacilar	To have a good time/pull someone's leg; *vacilón* is 'funny' (person, experience)
Vieras que...	You should see..., or you wouldn't believe...
Vina	Nosy, *vinear* is 'to gossip, try to find out about something'

AFRO-CARIBBEAN ENGLISH

Most black people in the Caribbean, at least among older generations, speak English much better than Spanish. Younger people tend to speak more and more Spanish, however—often to the chagrin of their parents.

However, there are two kinds of English: One is perfectly intelligible, though with a Caribbean lilt. The other is *mekatelyu* ('make I tell you'), more a kind of code language originally designed to bamboozle British slave masters. This is a mixture of Victorian English with some Spanish, French and completely invented words—all spoken at break-neck speed with a strong Jamaican accent. It has evolved individually to some point at least in Costa Rica, as people cannot always communicate perfectly with the black speakers of *guari-guari* just over the border in Bocas del Toro in Panama.

The most ubiquitous phrase you'll hear in the Caribbean is: *Wh'apin*? (What happen?), which can mean anything from 'how are you?' to 'what's up' and 'what's wrong?'. It can also be used in explanation, like *lo que pasa es que...* in Spanish, e.g. 'Wh'apin, rain wet me up and I catch a draft.'

You'll also hear a hooting '*cho man!*', used to express disbelief, disgust or surprise; '*go good!*' for 'goodbye'; and some bizarre grammar—e.g. 'his friends' would be '*him friends dem*'.

An equivalent of the Spanish *don* and *doña* is used for politeness with older people, who are called 'Mr Edwin', 'Miss Edith,' etc. (not 'Mrs'). Black Costa Ricans speaking Spanish may well affectionately call you *mami* or *papi*.

BUSINESS PRACTICE AND CUSTOMS

'Costa Rica is centrally located between two of
the largest consumer markets in the world and,
with all the neat, new technology, business can be
done from here as easily as from Peoria, Illinois or
Patagonia, Argentina! Costa Rica's government is as
stable as one could want (in Central America) and
the Costa Rican people are simply 'a cut above.''
—Ed Underwood,
president of Central American Consulting Services, Inc.

FOREIGN INVESTORS FLOCK TO COSTA RICA for several reasons: its stable politics, relatively low costs (though more expensive than most of the rest of the region), peaceful labour relations, and well-educated workforce, much of it bilingual. There is now an education initiative to build on this by turning Costa Rica into a country with a population fluent in high grade technical English.

The infrastructure is good too. The country has a self-sufficient power supply with the highest level of connection and cheapest rates in the region. It also has two international airports and ports on both the Pacific and Caribbean coasts.

All this adds up to make Costa Rica the easiest working environment in Central America. The 2004 World Investment Report showed that it had the third highest level of foreign investment in the whole of Latin America. In addition, it has a young, mainly urban population, which means the productive workforce and consumer group are set to grow rapidly.

The country is fast moving towards an economy dependent on tourism and high technology industries. This, however, doesn't spell new opportunity for everyone. In fact, the changes brought by the apparently terminal decline of coffee prices and huge workforce reduction of the government bureaucracy since the 1980s means a large part of the population is getting steadily poorer. Currently, about 18 per cent of Costa Ricans do not earn enough to support themselves.

More than a fifth of the labour force is employed in the informal sector, working as anything from shoe shiners, street vendors and prostitutes to scavengers, door-to-door salesmen or illegal taxi drivers (*piratas*). Many people *camaronear* (literally 'go shrimping'), looking for various small jobs on the side, which usually pay below the minimum wage, in order to help them make ends meet.

Despite local opposition, Costa Rica has worked (through the urgent need to tackle its massive internal debt) to open up its traditionally protectionist economy to foreign investment and competition. It is a signatory to many regional and international trade agreements, such as the General Agreement on Tariffs and Trade (GATT), the World Trade Organisation (WTO), and the Association of Caribbean States. It has been granted preferential conditions in the USA and Europe, and has signed bilateral trade agreements with several countries in the region. It also has bilateral investment treaties with many countries (mostly European).

The next big step will be the ratification of CAFTA (the Central American Free Trade Association), which will liberalise agriculture and other export sectors, services, intellectual property, labour laws and areas involving natural resources.

Resistance to the free trade deal with the United States has been high in Costa Rica, as in many other countries in the region. There have been several large demonstrations against CAFTA—mainly against the opening up of the telecommunications and insurance government monopolies—seen by many Ticos as untouchable national patrimony—to foreign capital. There are fears that services, such as the unprofitable provision of power and communications to poor rural areas, would be cut, and that Costa Rica's social security system (CCSS), which provides universal health coverage, could no longer be able to buy some medicines. However, there now seems to be a feeling of general unhappy acceptance to the agreement, as people realise there is really no option.

WHAT KIND OF BUSINESS?

The Costa Rican economy is changing rapidly, with agriculture being downgraded and clothing factories declining in the face of cheaper competition from Asia. The country is now trying to re-model itself as a suitable location for high technology industries, foreign companies' operation centres for human resources, call centres, conferences and conventions.

In 1988, Intel opened a huge microprocessor plant in the country (the country's GDP figures are now given both 'with' and 'without' Intel), while Procter and Gamble has set up its services and payroll division here to cover all its operations from Alaska to Tierra del Fuego. Lucent Technologies, Panasonic, Siemens and many others have their bases here too.

As an investor, it's important to think extremely carefully about the sort of business you want to set up, especially if your scope is small. In particular, remember that you can't set up anything that will compete with a government monopoly (of which there are several in Costa Rica—at least until the ratification of CAFTA).

In fact, for nearly all small foreign investors, the safest bet is tourism—one of the fastest growing areas of the economy.

That's not to say that other businesses are doomed to failure, but long-term San José resident and bar owner Julian Smith, offered some warning, "This is a small market, and local consumers don't have a lot of money. You need to decide what clientele you're aiming for—the small, rich class or the much larger, but poorer, middle class. Having seen many people try and fail, I would say the classic mistake is to come here on holiday, see something that's missing compared to what you have at home, and automatically think that it would go down well here. It's hard to make money here, and it's crucial to find out if there is a real demand for your product."

Ricardo Rouillon, a jet-setting Peruvian entrepreneur who tried to import high quality foods such as gourmet asparagus and octopus, learned the hard way about the need for good market analysis.

"Basic food here, if you look at it charitably, is simple. Uncharitably, it's a disaster—rice and beans in the home, and fast food if you eat out," he said. "I would have thought my products would go down a storm among wealthy people with more refined tastes. But in fact, it turns out that rich people here are not at all ostentatious and they live very simply. Costa Rica is rarely what it seems on the surface, and I have never had to do so much research in any other country."

There are other factors to be taken into account when investing in the country. Absentee ownership is particularly inadvisable. "You really must be here, unless you have a manager you would trust with your life—especially if your business involves a property," said Lynda Solar, executive director of the Costa Rican-American Chamber of Commerce (Amcham). "There are problems here with squatters, because they gain all rights to your land after a year and you will then be unable to return to it or sell it."

She also warned against the investment programmes that have proliferated in recent years in Costa Rica, such as teak plantations offering huge returns within a few years. Many people buy into these to fund their (often early) planned retirement in the country, but frequently find the dividends a lot less than they were led to believe, or even non-existent.

Opportunities from the Dismantling of Government Monopolies

While it still maintains monopolies in many areas, the government is keen to offload many of these responsibilities as part of its long-term scheme to bring down internal debt. This will have to happen, in any case, under CAFTA, and will provide many new options for foreign investors.

Current government monopolies include alcohol distilleries, telecommunications, insurance, newspapers, radio, television broadcasting, electricity and petroleum refining. For the moment, foreign participation in these is either forbidden or, at best, has to be part of a joint venture with a Costa Rican majority shareholding partner.

The dismantling of the National Insurance Institute (INS) would create definite business opportunities in an almost untapped market, and another institution that would provide great opportunities for private investment is the Instituto Costarricense de Electricidad (ICE).

Although widespread riots in 2000 scuppered the 'ICE Combo' plan to break up this monopoly (followed by other similar riots in 2003 when liberalisation was once again mooted), the government simply no longer has the funds to invest in major new infrastructure projects, such as hydroelectric plants (nearly 80 per cent of the country's power comes from hydroelectricity).

A proposed (and ecologically extremely controversial) dam to be built in Boruca would enable the government to meet the country's power needs over the coming decades, as well as to export more power to its neighbours in the region. Costing about US$ 2 billion, the project would be impossible without private sector participation.

In the meantime, small private power companies are currently allowed to generate and sell electricity to ICE on a long-term build-operate-transfer (BOT) basis.

RED TAPE FOR FOREIGN WORKERS IN COSTA RICA

State protectionism means that, as a foreigner, you may own a business but you cannot legally work in it or anywhere else—unless you are a legal resident. Becoming a resident itself is not a simple task. You must either be married to a Tico, have children born in the country, or have held one of the other types of Visas (*see the section on 'Visas and Residency' in the* Chapter Five: Settling In, *page 125*) for at least two years.

Once you have a residence permit, you still cannot work without a work permit—and this may take up to 60 days to be approved. It is only valid for a year and must be renewed annually. It may also be hard to get a job unless you're working in your own business. Foreigners cannot occupy jobs for which Costa Rica nationals are available unless they get special permission. In any case it may be hard to find work—Ticos are not generally used to the idea of foreigners seeking local employment, and local wages are not likely to be attractive either. All of this means you are generally left able to do only a limited number of jobs, for example teaching English or writing for an English-language newspaper.

Of course many, many people work illegally; often in bars, hotels, or with travel companies, and usually with no problem—especially in areas furthest away from the capital. If you do this and get caught, do be aware that you run the risk of deportation.

If you have your own business, there are even greater limitations in some areas. For example, with such a large number of foreign-owned businesses being involved in tourism, it is important to be aware that 50 per cent of the capital for beachfront development concessions must come from nationals and that foreigners wishing to be joint partners must have resided in Costa Rica for at least five years.

Foreign companies registered in Costa Rica, meanwhile, may obtain temporary residence permits (annually renewable) to bring in foreign technicians, executives or managers, and a company with more than 30 employees can also apply for a general work permit to bring in specialist foreign workers without the need to make an individual application for each person. This permit is also valid for one year and must also be renewed annually.

A branch of a foreign company operating in Costa Rica must appoint a Costa Rican resident as its legal representative with full power of attorney on matters concerning the business of the branch.

The labour code limits the percentage of foreigners working in each corporation, specifying that at least 90 per cent must be local and that 85 per cent of salaries paid by a company must go to Costa Rican nationals.

NGOs and Volunteering

With all these problems in getting paid work, many people choose to work as a volunteer while in Costa Rica. Most projects are focused on environmental conservation, and you could end up involved in anything from dolphin data collection or turtle tagging to rainforest conservation, organic farming or sustainable forest management. You could also get plenty of wildlife-spotting opportunities working in one of the national parks, (possibly digging on archaeological sites, protecting nesting turtles, doing lifeguard duty on a park beach—but more usually cleaning and heavy work). There are also many opportunities on social projects, for example working with street children or women prisoners, or teaching English to the disadvantaged. (*See the Resource Guide, page 288, for NGO contact details.*)

TYPES OF COMPANIES

Four forms of business organisation are recognised in Costa Rica: a corporation (*sociedad anónima*), limited liability company (*sociedad de responsabilidad limitada*), limited partnership (*sociedad en comandita simple*), and general partnership (*sociedad en nombre colectivo*). Corporations are by far the most common and most flexible. They must be formed by at least two parties, although one party may obtain 100 per cent of the stock immediately afterwards.

Legal and Other Requirements for Setting Up a Business

The first step for setting up a business in Costa Rica is to get in touch with a notary public—the only person allowed to register a company with the Costa Rican Mercantile Registry. Without this registration, a company cannot operate legally. All information about the new company and the people who will administer it must be submitted. This includes names, nationalities, the legal form of the business being organised, the company's purpose, amount of capital and how this will be paid.

An extract of this registration is then published in *La Gaceta*, the official legal journal, and payment on initial equity (usually ranging from US$ 100–1,000) must be deposited in colones with a local bank until registration is complete.

There is usually no minimum investment required to set up a Costa Rican business corporation, except of course in the financial or banking sectors.

Companies may also have to secure a municipal patent or permit. Any foreign business with branches in Costa Rica, or which intends to open branches, must appoint and retain a legal representative with full power of attorney regarding the business or branch.

Recording fees for the registry are low but lawyers' fees can vary greatly. Lynda Solar of Amcham, which represents 400 North American, Costa Rican and multinational companies, advised, "You really cannot cut corners in this country, and it's worth paying extra for a real professional, if possible bilingual, not only to set up the business, but also to find distributors or buyers. A good lawyer will help you to avoid potentially costly confusion over technical legal terms, and to get a business set up in a week rather than a month. If you get a cheap lawyer, you'll get a cheap job done."

Another requirement to be aware of is that new companies must secure an environmental impact certificate before they start operations. These are generally strictly enforced—building work was stopped for some time during the construction of the massive Intel plant outside San José after archaeological remains were found at the site. Foreign firms might find they get especially tough treatment in this respect.

Legal Contacts

For recommendations of good local lawyers, approach the commercial office of your embassy or Amcham. For more in-depth legal advice, as well as other information on how to estimate operating costs, tax and other investment questions, contact CINDE (Costa Rican Coalition for Development Initiatives) or PROCOMER (Costa Rican Foreign Trade Corporation). (*See the Resource Guide, page 284, for details.*)

RULES FOR EMPLOYERS

After years of state paternalism, Costa Rican labour laws are very protective of the employee and Ticos jealously hang on to their various benefits—even though these can, at times, reduce a firm's competitiveness. Ridley Scott, director of the Columbus movie *1492: Conquest of Paradise*, which was filmed in Costa Rica, was baffled when local extras refused to work 12-hour days, even after having signed contracts agreeing to the long shifts.

Lynda Solar said, "Workers here are very savvy when it comes to their rights. Labour codes here are stricter than in the United States, although thankfully the rules are much clearer and easier to understand than they once were. You must follow the rules or you could easily find a complaint lodged against you with the Ministry of Labour."

It's also important to be aware that the rules governing child labour are very strict too, unlike in many other Central American countries where minors commonly work in factories. Although you do see young children who have been sent out by their parents to work selling chicks or pencils on the street, it is absolutely illegal to hire them to work in the formal sector.

In terms of workers' benefits, all salaried employees must be registered with the CCSS, and the employer pays 26.5 per cent of the employee's total salary amount to the government for various social security contributions, such as health insurance, pensions and family welfare programmes. An additional 9 per cent is deducted from the employee.

The minimum monthly wage (in late 2005) ranged from approximately US$ 250 for unskilled workers rising to US$ 570 for employees with a university degree. Starting salaries are dependent on an employee's academic level.

Workers also get a big Christmas bonus or *aguinaldo* (8.33 per cent of salary) and hefty severance pay if they are laid off after three months or more of service. Pregnant women are entitled to four months' maternity leave, while new mothers get an hour a day for breastfeeding. All Ticos must have a one-hour lunch break, plus 15 minutes in the morning and afternoon for coffee.

In many offices, people come dressed casually on a Friday in order to 'get ready for the weekend'.

Vacation Time and Holidays

Workers are also entitled to two weeks' vacation per year, as well as the national holidays listed below.

- 1 January — New Year's Day
- April — Thursday and Friday of Holy Week
- 11 April — Juan Santamaría Day (Costa Rica's national hero)
- 1 May — International Workers' Day
- 25 July — Guanacaste Day
- 2 August — Day of Nuestra Señora de los Angeles (Costa Rica's patron saint)
- 15 September — Independence Day
- 12 October — Día de la Raza (to mark Columbus' 'discovery' of the New World)
- 8 December — Immaculate Conception Day
- 24 December — Christmas

BUSINESS CUSTOMS

Business customs in Costa Rica are not wildly different from anything you'd expect at home, largely because of the influence of the country's large North American population over many years. There are, however, hints on dealing with local partners and workforce, which will help any business venture run more smoothly and fruitfully.

Doing Business a la Tica

With Costa Rica being so small, virtually all the big firms involved in import or export belong to the handful of inter-related, old money families that still run the country. This can make it hard to break in with any kind of serious competition, so you must be very resilient.

It seems that most people are more concerned with price than anything else. There is only a very small market for quality products, and for many buyers, quality means a label saying 'Made in the USA'.

How can you sell anything in such an environment? It is possible, said Ricardo Rouillon, but you will make life a lot easier for yourself if you play by the Ticos' rules.

"In this country, an aggressive sales pitch will turn people off straight away," he said. "You have to be humble, but get the balance just right. If you look too eager to sell, or offer it at a low price, people will not buy it either; they think there is something wrong with it.

"After some time, I finally learned that one of the most useful tricks is to make yourself out to be more important than you are. If I tell a prospective client I have been knocking on doors here for two years, it could take me weeks or months to get an appointment.

"They'll be much more impressed and see me straight away if I say I have just flown in for a few days and am leaving soon for a meeting in Europe. In my experience, people here do not value your time. They will turn up late for meetings, and sit around drinking coffee without getting to the point.

"I take a leaf out of the Ticos' book, and never give away too much about myself; I keep them guessing. It's not really being untruthful, because nearly everyone here presents him or herself as having more authority than they actually do. This means you should know the chain of command in a target company, or you could waste a lot of time talking to the wrong person."

THE BUSINESS ENVIRONMENT

Before heading for a business meeting, be fully prepared for the fact that you could become a victim of 'Tico Time' and

The heart of San José may look low-rise and low-key, but in fact its one of the best places in the region to do business.

be left hanging around kicking your heels waiting for the other parties to arrive.

If this does happen, don't complain over wasted time as it will get you nowhere—you are likely to lose credibility by losing your temper, and Ticos are much more punctual in the business environment (though not the social one!) than other people in the region. There's certainly no point getting off on the wrong foot with people who simply have less of a cultural sense of urgency. Costa Rica's business community is small and your reputation, good or bad, is likely to travel before you. Instead, try to keep your schedule fairly open by not planning too many back-to-back meetings.

Lynda Solar said that such delays are thankfully becoming less and less acceptable among the business community. "There are so many American companies working here that we really work under US culture in Costa Rica now. While an 8:00 am meeting in the US may begin at 7:45 am, we're still not at that stage here. It would generally start at 8:00 am or at the latest 8:10 am here rather than at 9:00 am as would be the case in many other Latin countries."

In general, personal relationships and conversation are valued more highly than punctuality, and there is usually quite a bit of friendly chit-chat before business meetings get seriously started. Getting straight down to business as you would at home might seem rather rude or brusque. There are few topics off-limits when talking with Ticos, but don't waste the opportunity to strengthen your new business relationships by moaning about their country, bureaucracy or government. Ticos may well do this themselves, but if a foreigner starts carping too much, they may take offence.

On punctuality, it is not only in terms of meetings that foreigners tend to become impatient. Costa Ricans are notoriously conservative and risk-averse in business. Decisions are usually made by consensus, which can tend to make processes very slow. Tico companies are also often late in paying bills, so you should establish payment methods in advance. Time estimates for deadlines are rarely reliable.

Costa Rica is a very business card-oriented culture, and everyone from your taxi driver to a company president will whip out a card *(tarjeta de negocio)* at the slightest opportunity. It's a nice touch to have your card printed in both English and Spanish. Costa Ricans set a great deal less store on formality than many other Latin countries. While many people's cards will show the person's educational status, for example *licenciado* (graduate) or doctor (PhD), this is not the norm, it is not vital to greet anyone in this fashion in a business setting as you would do elsewhere in Latin America.

You should, however, use *Señor, Señora* or *Señorita* (the equivalent of Mr, Mrs or Miss), plus the person's surname, when you first meet them. If the person is of really high status, such as a minister, you should of course exchange *Ministro* for *Señor*! Once your relationship becomes closer, it is okay to swap to their first name, although you should prefix the terms of respect *don* or *doña* for people appreciably older than yourself (*señorita* plus first name for an unmarried woman). Similarly, address people as *usted* instead of *tú*, unless or until they tell you to swap to the less formal form of 'you'.

In terms of business dress style, it is best to go for formal, i.e. suit and tie, especially in San José. Altitude and clouds can make weather in the capital surprisingly chilly for a country so close to the equator, so it's wise not to scrimp on a jacket. Trouser suits or skirts are fine for women, although Tica style is dressier than in America or Europe.

Outside San José, most foreign businesspeople are involved in tourism, in which case dress codes are obviously much more relaxed. In the hotter coastal areas, men very occasionally wear *guayaberas* (traditional, embroidered shirts with four patch pockets) that are not tucked into the trousers.

As with everything else in tiny Costa Rica, networking is the key, so you should have good people skills. Although many Ticos, especially in the business community, have been educated abroad and speak excellent English, any effort to speak some Spanish on your part will definitely be appreciated. You should try to learn at least enough to be polite.

Lynda Solar said, "In a small business community, there are a lot of opportunities for people who know how to work the system, but this will often depend upon who you know."

But how do you actually get to meet the people in the know? Tico society is generally more reserved than in most other Central American countries and the United States, and you're unlikely to be invited to a business colleague's house. There are, however, several business chambers such as Amcham many of which organise events such as golf contests—a lot of business in Costa Rica gets done on the fairway.

They also host plenty of social events where, as anywhere else, alcohol can be an important part of the bonding process. But Lynda Solar said, "Unlike some other Latin countries, you won't be expected to get roaring drunk, or even to drink at all. Alcohol consumption is definitely not a vital part of doing business here, and not nearly as prevalent as it once was."

She added that although Costa Rica is a Latin, often *machista* country, there is little sexism in business, especially at the higher levels. "In Latin America, Costa Rica is the vanguard in terms of participation of women in the business community," she said. "It has a lot to do with the level of education. More than half this country's university population is female, and we have a lot of female CEOs."

Workforce

"One of Costa Rica's greatest untapped resources is its workforce," said Julian Smith. "I have had no problems at all with staff. If you treat people well, they really appreciate it—especially women, who may be subject to sexual harassment in a locally-owned workplace."

A foreign bistro owner agrees. "One of the nicest things about working here is the great respect Ticos have for themselves and others. Ticos are very humane and equality-conscious and my dish-washer will feel quite comfortable talking to me on an equal footing."

But, as he points out, this also underpins one of the most important issues for maintaining good relations with your staff: Ticos are proud and reluctant to accept criticism.

He said, "If you're going to criticise someone, you must never embarrass them by doing so in front of others. However much you may be itching to shout at someone who has done something seriously wrong, doing so will just result in them and their co-workers losing all respect for you. You must find a more consensual solution."

Ricardo Rouillon agreed. "You really cannot exploit people here the way you can in poorer Latin American countries. They simply will not accept it.

"This is a good thing, of course, but you must be very careful about how you tell your workers what to do. My head waiter resigned in a huff because I told him to set the tables my way, rather than the way he had always done it. People here get very upset by directness and confrontation. They go all around the houses to make everyone happy and save face."

Julian explained how to get around the problem, "Our company van was damaged after the driver allowed his underage son to drive it. Even though it might seem ridiculous, the correct solution was to start off by admitting that I was partly at fault for not having made it clear that we only wanted him to drive it."

At the other end of the scale, he points out, being too nice may lead people to take advantage of you so you must find a happy medium.

Similarly, if you want an employee to work harder, Julian says, the best approach is to appeal to their sense of *pobrecito*, or 'poor old you'. "I would make them feel that they're doing me a real favour," he explained. "I would say, for example, that we've been having a really awful month, and so could they please help me to get the work finished quickly."

Bribery and Dodgy Dealings

By Latin American standards, Costa Rica is very 'clean' when it comes to corruption, although it did slip in the stakes from being the least corrupt country in South America in 2000 to the third least corrupt country in 2004—behind Uruguay and Chile—in a Transparency International survey. However, bribery still exists, people still pay *mordidas* (literally 'bites'), and underpaid, overworked public employees look for illegal income in the form of *chorizos* (literally 'sausages').

Julian Smith said, "The country is so small that anyone with access to the president or other avenues of power is constantly besieged by people wanting favours. This can easily result in bribery and corruption."

Another American businessman added: "No official person has ever even insinuated to me that unless I paid a bribe the work wouldn't get done, but I have bribed people in order to speed things up, particularly tax issues and getting things cleared through customs. I have always been the one to suggest the payment, but no one has ever been offended or refused to accept."

Everyone agrees that excessive red tape is one of the major causes of corruption, with desperate businessmen willing to pay bribes in order to cut through the morass of bureaucratic delays to simply get work done. For example, all contracts must be scrutinised and approved by a government office called the *controlaría*. The intention is to ensure that no money is changing hands. In reality, however, it just makes things proceed at a frustrating snail's pace and breeds more corruption than it prevents.

The government is now making serious efforts to slim down bureaucracy, having set up an office called the *Programa de Simplificación de Trámites,* which had introduced more than 70 reform projects by mid-2005.

Irene Vizcaíno, an official in this department, said, "*Mordidas* have become common because of the hundreds of hoops people had to jump through. You'd go to one office only to be told to go to another and then another. Any procedure could take months, and you never knew how long it actually should be taking.

"The idea behind this was that the greater the bureaucracy, the greater the safeguards against corruption. But in fact, it just created a kind of Kafka-esque nightmare for businessmen, with lawyers and middlemen being the only winners."

The office is now working to weed out duplications and unnecessary procedures, and has also produced an excellent CD and information pack laying out exactly what the steps are in setting up a business, the maximum time limits for completion of each procedure, investors' rights and options for legal action. (*For contact details of this office, see the* Resource Guide *on page 285.*)

Irene Vizcaíno said that, with the Costa Rican economy attempting to diversify, the streamlining plan is deliberately aimed at attracting more foreign investment. However, with a huge backlog of papers waiting to be cleared, it could take years to get the system running smoothly, she warned. She added that bribery has always

US Law

Do take note that US law has a 'Foreign Corrupt Practices Act' which means that an American businessman could be charged in the US for bribing a Costa Rican official.

been, and still is, very definitely illegal and punishable by jail and/or deportation.

In the meantime, in order to minimise the amount of bureaucratic pain you may suffer, most businessmen recommend the use of a *despachante* or *gavilán* ('hawk'), so called because they make a profession out of spending hours waiting around in government offices or banks and then swooping down to collect important papers. These people know all the ins and outs of the system, are fairly reasonably-priced and indispensable, unless you want to wait yourself in interminable lines only to find out you're in the wrong office, or to be told to 'come back tomorrow'.

Shady Characters

Tens of thousands of foreigners do business happily in Costa Rica—but it's also good to be aware that the country has its fair share of fraudsters and con artists (most famously Robert Vesco (*see the 'Heroes and Villains' section in* Chapter Ten: Fast Facts *on page 247*). These characters often come to hide from the law back home and are attracted by the country's secretive banking laws, vagueness concerning extradition and large expat community, which provides an ideal environment to hide in.

A foreign bookshop owner said, "Most of my worst business experiences have actually been with other foreigners. In less than nine years, we've had six attempts to con us out of money by professional con artists in 'bust out' scams.

"Another problem is that the legal system here is labyrinthine. It's very hard to pierce the corporate veil, and with the legal system based on the Napoleonic code, there is no case law as in the US or UK. This means there has to be a specific law for absolutely every eventuality—if a law has not been written to address your particular issue, then it's simply not covered.

"An example of one of the legal deficiencies is that someone can run out of cash, shut down their business and start another one in another name across the street. The current system means their debts will all be erased. If that person owes you money, it will be impossible to get it back. I can't tell you how important it is in this country to have a good, trustworthy lawyer."

Tax Incentives

Costa Rica offers major tax incentives in key industry areas where it is trying to attract investment. These are significant in a country where import taxes can be very high.

- Import taxes are waived on materials to be used in tourism developments.
- For forest conservation, land and asset taxes are exempted and special police anti-squatter protection is guaranteed if landowners can certify that no lumbering has taken place during the two previous years and will not take place over at least the next 20 years. The same benefits are offered to those who replant deforested land.
- Import duty and other taxes are also waived for businesses involved in mining or agriculture.
- For income tax rates etc., see Chapter Five: Survival Skills on page 152. Be aware that the entire tax regime is likely to be overhauled in the near future, with increased taxation at some levels. However, corporate income tax is expected to fall from 30 per cent to 25 per cent for small, medium and 'pioneering' businesses. Note that strict punishments are now imposed for tax evasion, including a prison term of up to ten years. Such sanctions were until recently unknown.

Unions

The first union was set up in 1916. However, since the banana strike of 1934, employers have tended to see union activity as tantamount to communism—anathema in Costa Rica.

In 1995, unions represented only one worker in 16 in the private sector but three out of five in the public sector. In the private sector, potential union activists are frightened of being sacked, while workers often view union leaders as corrupt and self-serving. Unsurprisingly, nearly all strikes are among public sector workers, which can effectively hold the state to ransom.

As a result, private sector workers often organise around *solidarista* associations, which are little more than management-controlled savings and low-interest loan bodies financed by payroll deductions.

There are also 22 *colegios* (guilds) of professions such as lawyers, doctors and architects. These regulate the people allowed to work in each profession, and are often also required to oversee contracts and procedures in their speciality area.

Personal and Business Security

Amcham advises businesspeople to take the same kind of sensible precautions they would take at home.

Lynda Solar said, "Despite the rise in petty crime and car theft, Costa Rica, unlike the rest of Central America, does not suffer from kidnapping or other violent crime against businesspeople. The *Organismo de Investigación Judicial* (Costa Rica's equivalent of the FBI) is overworked, but generally does a good job."

Remember that in businesses where you're taking cash, for example restaurants and stores, it's extremely important to have an ultra-violet bill checker. There are many professionally counterfeited bank notes in circulation.

Intellectual Property Rights

Intellectual property rights laws in Costa Rica are far from perfect, especially in terms of the policing infrastructure. As in so many areas, Costa Rica has forward-looking legislation that meets WTO requirements, but no means of implementing it. Even the Supreme Court admitted in 2001 that it was still using some unlicensed software.

"With the boom of high-tech businesses in the country, biotechnology and software could become fantastic industries here," said Lynda Solar. "But if patents and other rights are not respected, the country is going to find it is shooting itself in the foot."

Getting the Latest News

The chambers of commerce provide an ideal venue for getting the most up-to-date news on changes in the situation as well as legislation regarding intellectual property rights and other issues.

Translation

Although you can get by to a large extent with English in Costa Rica, a good translator is fundamental and well worth the cost (around US$ 100–150 per day, ask your embassy or chamber of commerce for recommendations). Business jargon can be quite different from conversational language, and you don't want to lose out on a deal by missing the point. Legal documents that must be recorded in the National Registry or logged in a Notary Protocol book MUST be written in Spanish. However, foreign businesses have done leases in English with an official Spanish translation, and have litigated these leases in court in Costa Rica.

Translation is also crucial if your company plans to produce local brochures or advertise in the widely read Costa Rican media—a good way of drumming up business. You don't want to blow your chances with badly worded Spanish, which is a possibility unless you speak with perfect fluency.

In addition, you will probably attract more customers by using local Tico slang words, which you may not know. For example, many Ticos hate the creeping infiltration of *tú* (the informal word for 'you') instead of *vos* (the local equivalent). As a result, many international companies have changed the grammar on their adverts in Costa Rica, and you would be advised to do the same.

Stock Exchange

The *Bolsa Nacional de Valores* (stock exchange) is the biggest in Central America, having operated since 1976, and trading is focused almost entirely on government securities. Daily trading volume of approximately US$ 50 million in 1999 had risen to US$ 137 million by the end of 2004, with market capitalisation standing at US$ 1.97 billion. There are in excess of 2,500 listings on the exchange. Its index (IBNV) reached a high of 4,800 in mid-2003, but fell back to below 3,500 by the end of 2004. There are currently 28 brokerages permitted to trade securities on the BNV, employing more than 200 individual stockbrokers. The trading process is completely automated. The BNV publishes daily, weekly, and monthly bulletins with complete disclosure of all transactions. (*For contact details of the BNV, see the* Resource Guide, *page 285.*)

Free Trade Zones

There are 12 *zonas francas* or special business parks (six of them privately managed) in which major tax incentives (virtually 100 per cent exemptions) are offered to companies involved in manufacturing goods for export, or those involved in services, processing, science or technology and making new investments in the country of at least US$ 150,000. (Companies setting up anywhere in Costa Rica with an investment of at least US$ 2 million are also eligible for the *zonas francas* benefits). Government finance is also available for the training of employees. Some of the *zonas francas* subsidies and benefits are scheduled to expire at the end of 2007.

Another benefit for exporters is the simplified customs and trade procedures. Several hundred companies—around half of them from the United States—now operate within these zones, with a total combined export value of well over US$ 2 billion.

FAST FACTS

'Many foreigners who decide to make Costa Rica home
believe that because they have had a wonderful time
here as a tourist that the transition to full-time life in
Costa Rica will be smooth. ... This is a grave error,
because the majority of people who decide to go back
home don't do it because they couldn't find a refrigerator
or a car—but because they couldn't adjust to the culture.'
—Eric Liljenstolpe,
president of the Global Solutions Group in Costa Ricato come

Official Name
Republic of Costa Rica

Capital
San José

Flag
Five horizontal stripes of blue, white, red, white and blue (from top to bottom). All are equal bands except the centre red stripe, which is twice the height of the rest and contains, to the left side, the coat of arms with a white outline.

National Anthem
Costa Rica

Time
Greenwich Mean Time minus 6 hours (GMT -0600)

Telephone Country Code
506

Land
Located in Central America, Costa Rica lies between Nicaragua (to the north) and Panama (to the south). It is bordered to the east by the Caribbean Sea and to the west by the North Pacific Ocean.

Area
51,100 sq km (19,729.8 sq miles)

Highest Point
Cerro Chirripó (3,810 m / 12,500 ft)

Climate
Costa Rica has a mixture of tropical and sub-tropical weather, with cooler temperatures in the highlands. December to April is the dry season while May to November is the rainy season.

Natural Resources
Hydropower

Population
4,016,173 (July 2005 est)

Ethnic Groups
White, including *mestizo* (94 per cent), Black (3 per cent), Amerindian (1 per cent), Chinese (1 per cent) and others (1 per cent)

Religion
Roman Catholic (76.3 per cent), Evangelical (13.7 per cent), Jehovah's Witness (1.3 per cent), other Protestant denominations (0.7 per cent), others (4.8 per cent), none (3.2 per cent)

Official Languages
Spanish

Government Structure
Democratic republic

Administrative Divisions
7 provinces: Alajuela, Cartago, Guanacaste, Heredia, Limón, Puntarenas, San José

Currency
Costa Rican colón (CRC)

Gross Domestic Product (GDP)
US$ 37.97 billion (2004 est.)

Agricultural Products
Bananas, beans, coffee, corn, pineapples, potatoes, rice, sugar

Other Products
Beef and timber

Industries
Microprocessors, tourism, construction materials, fertilisers, food processing, plastic products and textiles

Exports
Bananas, coffee, electronic components, medical equipment, pineapples, sugar and textiles

Imports
Capital equipment, consumer goods, petroleum and raw materials

Airports
Estimated total of 149, of which 30 have paved runways. The main international airport is in San José.

HEROES AND VILLAINS
Ticos are very proud of the achievements of their compatriots, and are really appreciative if a foreigner knows anything about them. The following list (including some non-Ticos who have had a major impact on the country) provides a brief rundown of some of the most famous goodies and baddies in Costa Rica, past and present.

Claudia Poll Ahrens
Costa Rica's Olympic medal-winning swimmer. Born in Managua, Nicaragua, she grew up in Costa Rica and is a

Tico citizen. She won her first Olympic gold medal in 1996 in Atlanta, and has established many new national, Latin American, international and world records. In June 2000, Claudia tested positive for an illegal, performance-enhancing steroid and was suspended from competition for four years. She claims innocence.

Laureano Alban

A poet chosen by the Spanish government to write an official poem 'El Viaje Interminable' to mark the 500th anniversary of Christopher Columbus' discovery of the New World. The poem presents Columbus' journey as a metaphor for the human confrontation of the unknown.

Padre Mínor Calvo

A Catholic priest, famous for his crusades against homosexuality, who was plunged into controversy after the police surprised him in his car with a young male passenger late one night in a notorious gay cruising area of San José. The scandal grew as details of this event—along with the alleged financial management of the Catholic station Radio María, which he ran—were repeatedly broadcast by journalist Parmenio Medina. Supposedly sent to Italy by his superiors in the Church after the closure of Radio María, Calvo was found to be hiding out on a farm in Cartago following Medina's brutal and mysterious murder. He was later charged with having ordered the murder and is due to go on trial in 2006.

Pancho Carrasco

Costa Rica's first heroine. In 1856, she enlisted as a cook in President Juan Rafael Mora's army fighting the American freebooter William Walker. Unusual for a woman of her time, Pancho was literate, and served as the president's secretary.

In the famous Battle of Rivas, she fired at an enemy soldier, forcing him to abandon his cannon and flee, and was carried victoriously on her companions' shoulders. She later worked with sick and dying soldiers, and after the war received a medal for heroism. At her funeral in 1891, she received the military honours of a general.

Jorge Jiménez Deredia

Famous Tico sculptor selected to produce a sculpture of Saint Marcelino de Champagnat, founder of the Marist brothers, to mark 150 years of diplomatic relations between Costa Rica and the Vatican. The 4.5-m (15-ft) tall marble sculpture is situated in the left transept of Saint Peter's Basilica, and was blessed by the Pope in September 2000.

Dr Franklin R Chang-Díaz

Costa Rica's very own astronaut. One of 19 people chosen from 4,000 hopefuls and the first Latin American to be accepted by NASA (although this required him to become an American citizen). He has made numerous space flights and headed investigations into subjects as varied as Chagas disease and anti-matter. Most famously, his work on a plasma rocket is hoped to get the voyage time to Mars down to seven months.

Jorge Debravo

Brilliant young poet born into an extremely poor family who went without shoes throughout his childhood. He spent all the money he earned harvesting corn on a dictionary, and a teacher helped him win a scholarship to get through primary school. His first poems were published in a local newspaper shortly afterwards. Debravo died in a car accident in 1967 at the age of 29.

Fabián Dobles

He wrote about 20 books of poetry, novels and short stories, most famous of which were his 25 tales of Costa Rican life in *Historias de Tata Mundo*. Dobles often wrote using the *campesino* language of the countryside and peasants, and won the Magón National Culture Prize in 1986.

Quince Duncan

The country's top black writer. A prolific writer of academic works, essays and novels about the Afro-Caribbean experience in Costa Rica.

Editus

A popular Tico musical trio whose eclectic music combines violin, guitar, Afro-Caribbean percussion and sounds from the rain forest. They accompanied Panamanian *salsa* legend Rubén Blades on his European tour, and produced a record with him, Tiempo, that won a 1999 Grammy Award.

Geovanny Escalante

Saxophone player from the famous Tico band Marfil, who broke Kenny G's world record for holding a single saxophone note in 1998. After three months of training in the gym, the 24-year-old held the note for 90 minutes and 45 seconds, nearly double Kenny G's timing.

Carlos Luis 'Calufa' Fallas

He grew up desperately poor and started to work on a banana plantation at the age of 16. As well as being a notorious womaniser, he went on to become a Communist Party leader who led the first big strike of banana workers against the United Fruit Company in 1934. Most of his literary works were gritty pieces focusing on the tough conditions suffered by the poor. The most famous of his works, *Mamita Yunai*, was a 'denunciation of the abuses' suffered by the country's mainly black banana workers. He won the prestigious Magón National Culture Prize in 1965 and died the following year.

José 'Don Pepe' Figueres Ferrer

Coffee farmer who led the civil war of 1948 and became the architect of the present Costa Rican state and constitution. A virulent anti-communist, Don Pepe served as president three times, and was responsible for abolishing the army, nationalising the banks, giving the vote to women and blacks and overseeing the country's 1970s cultural revolution. He died in 1990.

Carlos Gagini

An intellectual, anti-imperialist and linguist, he was a proponent of the international language Esperanto and compiled a dictionary of the Costa Rican indigenous Térraba language. In the 1910s, he wrote *La Caída del Aguila*, or *The Fall of the Eagle*, a spookily prescient novel about a world war involving an alliance between Germany and Japan. In the Jules Verne tradition, the book also featured a submarine base under the Isla del Coco. He died in 1925.

Dr Marcus Mosiah Garvey

Founder of the black Back to Africa movement, whose slogan was 'Up you mighty race, you can accomplish what you will'. Born in Jamaica, Garvey developed many of his ideas after working in a Costa Rican banana plantation and seeing the misery and exploitation suffered by his fellow workers. In 1919, he set up the Black Star Line to buy ships to return several million of his followers to the homeland, and the following year proclaimed himself provisional president of Africa. This move was supported by many white supremacists, such as the Ku Klux Klan. He suffered a series of economic disasters, however, and in 1922 was arrested for having tried to fund the Black Star Line by selling 'shares' in ships he had not yet bought to disaffected black people all over the USA and Caribbean. He was jailed, later deported to Jamaica, and died in 1940 in obscurity in London. Older black Costa Ricans remember Garvey's visits to the country, and the Black Star Line Club still operates in Limón as a social centre.

Maribel Guardia

Guardia was elected Miss Costa Rica in 1977 at the age of 17, going on to represent her country at the Miss Universe contest, where she was selected as the 'most photogenic' contestant. The contest was held in Acapulco, and she received offers to develop a career there.

She moved to Mexico in 1980 and went on to become a superstar all over Latin America, making multiple telenovelas and releasing a series of CDs in the Nortena music genre. One of her major soap opera hits was *Tú y Yo*, filmed with Joan Sebastián, whom she later married.

Joaquín Gutiérrez

The 'man of the century' in national literature, according to the newspaper *La Nación*, Gutiérrez wrote novels, travel books, and translated both Shakespeare and Mao Tse Tung into Spanish. He wrote his most famous prize-winning novel *Cocorí* in a week, was national chess champion at 25, and twice a vice presidential candidate. A communist like his friends, Calufa and Fabián Dobles, he travelled in the Soviet Union, China and Vietnam. He spent 25 years in Chile, and the Chilean Nobel Prize-winning poet Pablo Neruda was one of his biggest fans. A bronze bust of him can be seen in the Teatro Nacional, along with those of many other great figures from the Costa Rican arts. He is the first Latin American sculptor whose work is included in Saint Peter's Basilica, Rome. He died in 2000.

Bruce Harris

For 15 years, he worked as the Latin America director of the NGO Casa Alianza, based in Costa Rica and working to end child prostitution, exploitation, pornography and the murder of street children. However, he fell from grace in the most dramatic way possible after he was found to have had sex with a 19-year-old Honduran boy in 2003. The organisation had helped tens of thousands of children in the time he was director. Harris lost his job and said he regretted the fact that 15 years invested in the struggle for the rights of children might be wiped away by 'a 15-minute mistake'.

Max Jiménez

Probably Costa Rica's best-known artist. Also a sculptor and writer, Jiménez was strongly influenced by black art in Cuba, and is known for his colourful and monumental paintings of misshapen figures. He died in 1947.

Parmenio Medina

Colombian investigative journalist who lived for almost 30 years in Costa Rica. His irreverent radio show *La Patada* (The Kick) mercilessly sniffed out wrongdoings and dodgy dealings. He was shot in a professional hit-style killing in 2001, which was the first of its kind in the country and left peace-loving Ticos dumbfounded. The murder came after he had spent months lambasting the alleged financial management of the Catholic Church radio station Radio María run by charismatic priest Padre Mínor Calvo, who was later charged with ordering the murder.

Carmen Naranjo

In the vein of many Latin American literary figures, Naranjo has combined her writing work with a career in the civil service. She was the administrative manager of the CCSS, first female Minister of Culture, and ambassador to Israel, as well as a board member of Editorial Costa Rica, a University of Costa Rica professor, director of the National Museum, and an expert advisor for UNICEF and the Organiation of American States. Her works attack the meaninglessness of urban life in abstract, experimental style. She won the Premio Magón, Costa Rica's top culture prize in 1986.

Debbie Nova

One of the hottest new things to arrive on the Costa Rican music scene, Debbie Nova has sung on the Black Eyed Peas album *Elephunk* and is also scheduled to sing on Ricky Martin's new album.

Dr Clodomiro 'Clorito' Picado

Famous scientist who Ticos claim discovered the properties of penicillin before Alexander Fleming. He had published a paper in 1927 on how *penicillium sp* inhibited the growth of streptococus bacteria in his patients. As a young man, he studied zoology and biology at the Sorbonne in Paris, and later became director of the San Juan de Dios Hospital in San José. He published 115 works, studied poisonous snakes (developing many pioneering antivenins), bacterial infections of beans, fermentation of coffee, the benefits of iodine and the morphology of the guava fly before he died in 1944.

Teodórico Quirós

An architect and painter who won the coveted Premio Magón. In his paintings he specialised in Tico themes such as farms, churches and *pulperías*. He died in 1977.

Sor María Romero

Nicaraguan-born nun who was made an honorary Costa Rican citizen and is famous for her work with the poor, apparently miraculous cures and supposed clairvoyance. She died in 1977 and is in the process of beatification by the Vatican.

José León Sánchez

Huetar Indian wrongfully convicted at the age of 20 of stealing religious art from the Basílica of Los Angeles in Cartago and killing a guard. He was sentenced to 45 years on the notorious prison island of San Lucas in the Gulf of Nicoya. Although Costa Rica was the first Latin American country to abolish the death penalty in 1871, life on San Lucas was almost worse than death and few survived more than five years. The prisoners, who wore leg irons and chains, were regularly lashed with steel-tipped bullwhips, caged in inhuman conditions, and drowned if they tried to escape. Sánchez survived being machine-gunned, a suicide attempt and torture by having toothpicks forced into his ears. He spent 20 years on the island, during which time he was known only as number 1713. Sánchez taught himself to read and write on San Lucas and became the jail's letter writer. He is now touted for potential Nobel Prize nomination, having written such books as *La Isla de los Hombres Solos* (The Island of Single Men), which recounts with horrifying clarity conditions of life on the island. Sánchez, who was not declared innocent until 24 July 1998, now lives in Mexico, where he has written several works about the Aztecs. He is a vocal campaigner against miscarriages of justice and the death penalty.

Oscar Arias Sánchez

Hugely popular president in the 1980s who was responsible for drawing up a peace plan for the war-torn neighbouring countries of Central America which, although only partially implemented, won him the Nobel Peace Prize in 1987. The constitution was later changed to allow him to stand for a second term as president in 2006.

Juan Santamaría

A Costa Rican national hero, Santamaría was a young soldier who, despite being shot repeatedly, bravely torched the wooden fort where the US filibuster William Walker and his men were hiding out during their failed invasion of Central America in 1855.

Rigoberto Stewart

Controversial black Costa Rican intellectual and the president of Asociación Limón Real, which claims to create a free and autonomous region in Costa Rica, coupled with absolute economic freedom and other individual liberties. Limón has traditionally been ignored by politicians in San José and is one of Costa Rica's most discriminated against and exploited areas.

Robert Vesco

Disgraced US financier indicted for his involvement in the Watergate scandal, he fled the United States in 1972 after being accused of defrauding US$ 224 million and being linked with the illegal drugs trade. He was offered shelter by President José Figueres Ferrer and lived for several years in Costa Rica (as well as the Bahamas, Antigua and Nicaragua), where his wealth gave him massive power. None of these countries agreed to extradition requests and he continued to increase his huge wealth through arms sales to Libya. In the early 1980s, he was accepted in Cuba for 'humanitarian reasons', but was later condemned there for defrauding investors with his mystery drug TX, a supposed cure for AIDS and cancer. He was finally jailed after being extradited to the United States in 1995.

Chavela Vargas

Born in Costa Rica in 1919, she fled the country at just 14 because of its lack of opportunities for starting a musical career, seeking refuge in a more sophisticated Mexico. For many years she sang on the streets but in her thirties, she became a professional singer of *rancheras*—songs traditionally sung by men about their desire for women, and has since recorded more than 80 albums. She dressed as a man, smoked cigars, drank heavily, carried a gun and was known for her characteristic red poncho. In a Colombian television interview in 2000, she openly admitted she was a lesbian. She was partly retired in the late 1970s but came back in her full glory in 1991, debuting at Carnegie Hall in 2003 aged 83.

Paulo 'Chope' Wanchope
Costa Rica's most famous footballer. He has played in the UK for various teams including Manchester City, but ran into trouble with the British clubs for his temper tantrums and supposed sense of self-importance. At home, Chope is a hero and Costa Rican newspapers chart the fate of whichever club the striker is playing for on an almost daily basis. He played in the Costa Rican team at the 2002 World Cup, scoring twice against Brazil.

Ronnie Zamora
Tico sentenced to a life jail term in the US in 1977 at the age of 15 for shooting an old lady during a robbery. He and his friends sold her belongings and went to Disneyland with the proceeds. Zamora was tried as an adult and, famously, his trial was the first ever to be televised in the US. His lawyer raised an insanity defence, saying he had suffered 'television intoxication' and had been 'brainwashed' by violent TV programmes. The case stunned peaceable Costa Rica, and people continue to be divided over Zamora, who is now trying to secure parole.

Francisco Zúñiga
Famous Tico sculptor who was originally trained by his father, a sculptor of wooden religious images. He moved to Mexico in 1936, saying he felt limited and under-appreciated in his homeland. He continued working even after he became blind

in 1990 and died in 1998 of cancer, aged 86, apparently as a result of prolonged contact with sculpting materials. He won numerous prizes, and his biggest works were the 1954 reliefs on the Secretaría de Comunicaciones y Transportes in Mexico City. He also collaborated on the Monumento de la Revolución. His style was simple and austere, and he specialised in pre-Hispanic and rural themes.

Manuel 'Melico' Salazar Zúñiga

Costa Rican opera singer who came to be known as *El Gran Tenor de América*. At the age of 20, he went to train in Italy and performed there as well as in the United States, Europe, Canada and all over Latin America. At 40, he returned to Costa Rica to set up a national school of song. He was a member of the Metropolitan Opera Company in New York where he was given 'all the Italian roles', and performed his favourite opera, *Aida*, ten times. He died in 1940.

ACRONYMS AND ABBREVIATIONS

Avd	*Avenida* (avenue)
Bo	*Barrio* (neighbourhood)
C	*Calle* (street)
Cía	*Companía* (company)
CCSS	Caja Costarricense de Seguro Social The sprawling, obligatory government social security system, which covers more than 90 per cent of Ticos for medical expenses and personal pensions.
EEUU	Estados Unidos (the United States of America)
INS	Instituto Nacional de Seguros (a government-run insurance monopoly)
OEA	Organización de Estados Americanos (Organisation of American States, which has its headquarters in Costa Rica)
OIJ	Organismo de Investigación Judicial Costa Rica's equivalent of the FBI.
ONU	Organización de las Naciones Unidas (United Nations)

PB (in lifts)	*Planta Baja* (ground floor)
PLN	Partido de Liberación Nacional (the more left wing of Costa Rica's two main political parties)
PUSC	Partido Unidad Social Cristiana (the PLN's conservative rival)
SA	Sociedad Anónima (ltd., plc, corporation)
UE	Unión Europea (European Union)

PLACES OF INTEREST
A Coffee Plantation

During a visit to Café Britt (http://www.cafebritt.com), you will learn more than you ever thought there was to know about coffee! On the tour, you'll see coffee growing—from tiny seeds to fully-grown bushes, learn about its lengthy history, find out the different ways in which it's roasted, how expert tasters grade it, and much, much more. Café Britt is in Heredia. To get here by car, ask directions to Heredia's Universidad Nacional de Costa Rica (National University). Then travel uphill (north) until the road ends and follow the Coffee Tour signs. Many hotels and tour companies also offer day trips to Café Britt.

The National Theatre

San José's beautiful Teatro Nacional, built in 1897, and described soon after by foreign visitors as 'a jewel in a mud hole', was designed and built by French and Italian artists. Every stone, pane of glass and lick of gold paint was brought from Europe too. The stunning baroque design features ample use of 221/2 carat gold overlay and Carrara marble.

An exact small-scale copy of Paris' Opéra Comique, the Teatro Nacional was built with funds raised by the coffee barons through a self-imposed export tax. The tax was implemented after Italian opera singer Adelina Patti, who was touring Central America, refused to sing in Costa Rica as she felt that there was no venue worthy of her.

The National Symphonic Orchestra season runs from March to November with performances on Thursday and Friday evenings and again on Sunday mornings. Periodically, other activities ranging from the Moscow ballet and Chinese acrobats to state dinners and Costa Rican theatrical presentations are also scheduled. The coffee shop next to the main lobby is a wonderful place to sit and watch the world go by. During the day, the building is open to the public for viewing from 9:00 am–5:00 pm, Monday to Saturday [tel: (506) 221-1329].

National Museum

The building that houses the museum was once a fortress—an oddity in itself in military-free Costa Rica! It was converted into the museum following the abolishment of the army in 1948. The most noteworthy exhibits are the pre-Columbian artefacts, but it also has very interesting displays on Costa Rican religious art and the history of the country since the Spanish conquest.

The museum is located on calle 17, between Avenidas central and 2, and is open from 8:30 am–5:00 pm, Tuesday to Sunday [tel: (506) 257-1433].

Gold Museum

The Gold museum, situated under the Plaza de la Cultura and next to the National Theatre, is easily the best museum in the country, with thousands of different examples of pre-Colombian gold artifacts, weighing in at a total of 20,000 total troy ounces. The pieces in the collection date from 500 BCE to 1600 CE and include simple round earrings to intricately worked representations of local animals. Tastefully exhibited with great lighting and clear concise descriptions, the museum opens from 9:00 am to 4:30 pm, Monday to Friday.

Jade Museum

Although the numerous pre-Columbian jade pieces on display are among the most impressive anywhere, the museum also features excellent examples of indigenous craftsmanship in stone, ceramics and gold. The museum is on the 11th floor of the National Insurance Company (INS) building, also offering a stunning view of the city and surrounding mountains. It is on calle 9 and Avenida 7,and is open from, 8:30 am– 3:00 pm, Monday to Friday, [tel. (506) 223-5800].

Corcovado National Park

You will have a better chance of spotting wildlife, including the elusive jaguar, here than probably any other part of Costa Rica and you will leave having experienced a remote side of the country that comparatively few visitors ever see.

The flora is stunning too—with spectacular trees to rival those in the Amazon. In a few days, you should be able to take in everything from the waters where whales come annually to mate to deserted beaches and untouched rainforest.

Unless you are feeling particularly adventurous, though, taking an internal flight to Corcovado is probably the best way to reach it. Driving there in a 4x4 will mean crossing small rivers and many narrow bridges, and this can only be done in the dry season. Otherwise it's a 20-km (12-mile) hike along hot beaches and you'll have to wade through deep river mouths, sometimes full of small sharks and crocodiles!

The Forest by Night

You might think there couldn't possibly be more wildlife in the forest than what you've seen during your daytime hikes. But a whole new cast of characters takes to the stage by night. It's a bizarre experience, walking through the moist, pitch-black undergrowth armed only with a torch—don't hang around too long watching that amazing stick insect—it's a disturbing feeling to be left behind the group! Night excursions are on offer everywhere from Monteverde to Corcovado—and will give you the chance to see creatures difficult to find by daylight, from armadillos and tarantulas to tiny frogs and stick insects—even fungi that glow in the dark.

A Butterfly Farm

A quarter of the world's known butterflies live in Costa Rica and some of them are spectacularly beautiful, such as the stunning electric blue morpho with a huge 15 cm (5.9 inches) wingspan. It can be hard to see some of the rarest species in the wild though—a problem easily solved by a visit to a butterfly garden. There are several in the country, but the one attached to the Nature Farm Private Wildlife Refuge in Manuel Antonio (http://www.butterflygardens.co.cr) is one of the best, with multi-level walkways allowing you to wander or even sit among the beautiful plants that attract some of the country's most spectacular species. Don't plan your visit for a rainy day—butterflies like to stay dry.

Turtle Watching

The sight of a green turtle fatally injured by poachers in 1970 drove the country's then president to launch a campaign for a series of protected national parks.

Today, you can spot these incredible, ancient creatures on well-organised tours, at most times of the year; or even work on a voluntary programme to help tag them or protect hatchlings.

Tortuguero National Park is one of the best places to spot one emerging from the sea at night to lay its eggs. Tours run nightly at 8:00 pm and 10:00 pm from March to May during the leatherback turtle nesting season and from July to October during the green and hawksbill nesting season.

Watching Arenal Volcano Erupting at Night

Arenal volcano is Costa Rica's number one tourist attraction, and for good reason.

Watching brilliant orange lava erupt from its mouth into the night sky is a mesmerising experience. You can even sip a cocktail from the swim-up bar in the Tabacon Hot Springs complex (http://www.tabacon.com) while watching Arenal's nightly display—James Bond, eat your heart out! This hotel and day spa has a series of cleverly designed hot outdoor pools heated by the volcano itself, although it's best to time your trip to coincide with a good forecast—or you may well not see anything but the clouds shrouding the mountain!

CULTURE QUIZ

SITUATION 1 (FOR LADIES ONLY)

During a break at a roadside café during a long bus ride, a friendly older male passenger holds the door open for you, calling you *mi reina* (my queen) and offers to buy you a drink. Do you:

A Snort in disgust at his sexism and walk off.

B Insist on your buying him a drink instead (after all, you probably earn four times more than him).

C Accept and thank him, but say that next time you meet (which you both know will probably be never), you will buy him a drink.

Comments

If you answered **A**, you're going to end up very irritated, very quickly, and possibly rather lonely, in Costa Rica. Try to accept the omnipresent chivalry with a sense of humour—you will get on a lot better, and probably meet a lot of interesting people along the way. **B** would injure your friend's pride and embarrass him in front of anyone watching—a Costa Rican *caballero* NEVER lets a lady buy him a drink, and definitely not a first drink. **❻** is ideal. Everyone is happy and now you can sit back for a chat.

SITUATION 2

You're in a small town and need to catch a bus back to San José. Your taxi to the bus stop has to stop to allow a large herd of cows to pass on the road, and you arrive 20 minutes after the bus has left. Do you:

❹ Sit down with a coffee and wait, fuming with frustration, for the five hours until the next bus leaves.

❺ Hire a taxi to drive you the 150 miles back to San José.

❻ Think laterally. Hail a passing taxi or pick-up and ask the driver to chase down the bus.

Comments

❹ is a possibility if you have time on your hands and a good novel to read, or something else to do in a one-horse town. **❺** is another option if your budget stretches to it, but if you answered **❻**, you're thinking like a Tico. The driver will go like a bat out of hell to run down that bus in record time. When you overtake it, horn honking, both you and the driver should lean out of the windows waving furiously until the bus stops to let you aboard.

SITUATION 3

You meet a Tico at a party, hit it off right away and swap phone numbers. You call your new friend shortly afterwards to ask him to dinner a few days in advance. He gladly accepts—but on the night in question never turns up. Next time you bump into him, he offers no apology or explanation. Do you:

❹ Feel insulted and resolve to reduce your circle of friends to those who take social engagements seriously.

❺ Decide, next time, to only ask him out on the spur of the moment when there's no chance for forgetfulness or mind-changing.

❻ Invite him to dinner again in a week's time.

Comments

If you answered **Ⓐ**, there's no point taking it to heart or feeling paranoid—Ticos are just notoriously *incumplidos*. To you, simply forgetting about an arrangement or turning up two hours late may seem tantamount to rudeness, but if you confine yourself to friends who share your attitudes about time, you will probably find yourself with a rather small social circle. Answer **Ⓒ** will probably see you being stood up again. **Ⓑ** is probably the best answer. Call up one evening and ask what your friend is doing. If he's going out, he'll probably invite you along. If he has no plans, suggest meeting up.

SITUATION 4

It's a rainy afternoon and you go into a clothes store to have a leisurely look around. You're hardly over the threshold when a sales assistant pounces on you asking if you're looking for anything in particular. You say no, but she proceeds to follow you around the store at a distance of approximately six inches. Do you:

Ⓐ Feel horribly intimidated, tense and leave the store in a hurry.
Ⓑ Round on her and ask if she suspects you of shoplifting.
Ⓒ Tell her your size and ask what she has that might look good with your colouring. Oh, and are there any discounted clothes?

Comments

Ⓐ will mean you're going to miss out on some great deals in Tico stores. While it is easy to feel 'oppressed' by the constant shadowing of shop assistants, in Costa Rica this is considered customer attention. **Ⓑ** will shame and baffle the poor girl, who is simply attending to you as she has been taught. Never react in anger in Costa Rica—and especially not in public. **Ⓒ** is the best solution—simply take a leaf out of Tico shoppers' books and bask in the attention. Sit out the rainstorm trying on a whole selection of clothes you might never have thought of, and you may well come away with a whole new outfit.

SITUATION 5

You're taking a crowded bus home after a long day at work when a browbeaten man stands up and starts telling a heart-breaking story about losing his job and having six children to feed. Can any of the passengers please help, he asks. Do you:

ⓐ Shake your head as he approaches you. You've already given to three of these beggars today.

ⓑ Tell him he's just a lazy opportunist. A survey on the TV last night showed that beggars in San José can make US$ 30 a day—much more than a blue collar worker.

ⓒ Meekly give him a few colones. You don't really believe his story, but then again, you can't be sure. Plus you don't want to look stingy in front of your fellow passengers.

Comments

There's nothing wrong with **ⓐ**, but if you were a Tico you would probably find it hard not to fork out a few coins for the *pobrecito* (poor little thing). **ⓑ** will not earn you the round of approving nods it might get in New York or London. Fellow passengers will be deeply unimpressed by your uncultured behaviour towards someone who has fallen on hard times. If you want to blend seamlessly into your environment, **ⓒ** is the right answer. Many Ticos grumble privately about the number of beggars on their streets, but in reality most people give. Ticos are generous, good-hearted people—who are also driven by Catholic guilt and a fear of looking bad in public.

SITUATION 6

You are setting up a new business in Costa Rica. After a few weeks, nothing seems to have gotten done. Calls to potential clients are going unanswered, people turn up for meetings on 'Tico time', and visits to government offices involve interminable queues and confusing bureaucracy. Do you:

ⓐ Try to hurry up potential clients by telling a white lie—you are only in the country for two days before flying off for an important meeting in the United States, you say.

B Ask around and employ a trustworthy *gavilán* to take care of the confusing document-processing in government offices.

C Discreetly offer a bribe, or *mordida*, to the relevant officials in the hope of speeding up the slowly grinding wheels of bureaucracy.

Comments

A is a good answer. People are much more likely to call back promptly if you make it seem that you are an important type who has to jet around to international meetings. **B** is also good—*gavilanes* know all the ins and outs of the local system. Combined with **A**, this will help to free up a lot of time. **C** is definitely illegal. While many people do still pay *mordidas*, and many underpaid civil servants accept them, if you're caught out you could end up being deported.

SITUATION 7

You've only had a Tico acquaintance for a short while when he starts to call you *gordito* (fatty). You've always been rather self-conscious about your size. Do you:

A Feel terribly offended. He seemed to be really nice, so why would he say such a hurtful thing?

B Laugh it off and start calling him *flaquito* (skinny).

C Tell him in no uncertain terms that he is an ignorant, size-ist pig and never see him again.

Comments

There is no point in being offended. Ticos use all kinds of nicknames based on a person's physical weak or strong points, but with no hint of malice. In fact, they are usually a strong form of affection. It's best to develop a thick skin and go for answer **B**. If you really and truly can't do this, there's no point suffering in silence (**A**) or offending his Tico sensitivities by getting angry with him, thus risking wrecking the friendship (**C**). Maybe it's better to ask him to call you by a special pet name which, you say, you only allow close friends to use.

SITUATION 8

An employee is very sweet, but regularly late for work and doesn't seem to get much done while she is there. You often catch her putting on make-up or chatting to friends on the telephone. Do you:

A Grin and bear it. She's really popular with the rest of the staff and could turn them all against you if you say anything.

B Wait until she has made you so angry that you storm up to her in the middle of the office, shouting that she is taking advantage of your good nature and that you will have to sack her if she doesn't pull her socks up.

C Take her aside and explain how much you value her strong points. The organisation is going through a bit of a difficult patch at the moment, and you need her to help you get the whole team pulling together. She would be doing you a real favour if she could get in on time and put 100 per cent effort into the job.

Comments

A will drive you crazy, and you do not want to be metaphorically held hostage by your staff. Offending a Tico in public, **B**, especially if you are commenting on his or her intellect, is the biggest social faux pas you could possibly make. If you sack her or she walks out, remember that Costa Rica's labour laws are also often loaded in favour of the employee and you might find yourself facing litigation. Your actions will probably also lose you the respect of the rest of your staff. **C** is most likely to achieve results. You are not offending the employee's honour, and are also trying to resolve a problem Tico-style through peaceable consensus.

SITUATION 9

You have had a Tico friend for some time when it dawns on you that you have told him or her all of your most intimate secrets, problems and family issues. However, your friend has not revealed any comparable information about him or herself except in the most oblique terms. In fact, you're not even sure where he or she lives! Do you:

A Think nothing of it. Your friend is witty, interesting and great fun to be around, and you realise that it can take some Ticos a long time to wear their hearts on their sleeves about personal stuff.

B Stop seeing your friend so often. To you, opening up emotionally lies at the core of friendship.

C Start probing your friend to open up more, telling him or her it is unhealthy to keep things bottled up.

Comments

A is the best solution. You come from a culture where people may immediately be very open. However, in Costa Rica one must often nurture friendships for some time until a person feels completely confident that he or she can really trust you to be discreet and supportive. It would be a shame to give up on what could become a very solid relationship (**B**), and **C** could make your friend feel embarrassed and awkward, possibly driving him or her away.

DO'S AND DON'TS

DO'S

- Learn to love eating black beans and rice three times a day.
- Expect lots of very upfront interest from the opposite sex if you're single and available (and even if not).
- Think twice about what people mean—Ticos may often not say what they actually mean in order to *quedar bien*, and avoid causing offence or embarrassing people.
- Shout *Upe!* when arriving at someone's house rather than knocking on the door.
- Expect people to be more conservative in both attitudes and dress than in many other Latino countries.
- Sound like a Tico by saying *pura vida* at every opportunity, and *con mucho gusto* every time that someone thanks you for something.
- Read up everything you can in the newspapers about what's going on in the country. This will impress Ticos to no end. They love their country and will immediately draw you into conversation.
- Really make an effort to learn Spanish. Even though most Ticos can speak English, they will greatly appreciate your efforts, and you will have a much fuller experience of the country.
- Ask questions with specific answers. "Where is the soda?" is much better than "Is the soda around the corner?" If Ticos can answer a question with 'yes' or 'no', they may well do so even if they have no idea, simply to avoid looking silly.
- If you're male, you can expect to be gently teased for being insufficiently macho.
- Keep an open mind about traditional remedies and magic. You're bound to encounter at least one of these at some stage and a huge amount of Ticos swear by them.
- Remember that life doesn't begin and end in San José. To really know the country, you must also get to know its 'forgotten' people—the black population of the Caribbean coast and the indigenous peoples.

- Expect to hear *mi amor* (my love), *mi vida* (my life), *mi corazón* (my heart) and *te quiero* or *te amo* (I love you) a lot. Don't get freaked out—people use these terms a lot more glibly than they might where you are from.
- Expect to sit in huge lines in government offices, banks and hospitals.
- Buy your fruit and vegetables at the local weekend *feria* rather than in the supermarket—much more fun!
- Resolve any conflict through consensus rather than confrontation.
- Drive carefully after weekend football matches—Tico driving gets even worse at this time, with plenty of drunks on the roads.
- Try out all of Costa Rica's amazing range of bizarre and delicious fruits, cakes, sweets and home-made drinks.
- Err on the side of formality when meeting people, unless told otherwise. Use *usted* rather than *vos*, and with older people use *Señor*, *Señora*, *don* or *doña*.
- Learn some *Tiquismos* so you can pepper your language with local colour and have a better understanding of your Tico friends and their humour.
- Get to know your cardinal points or even buy a compass so you can easily follow Tico directions.
- Learn to relax—things in Costa Rica can take ages, and raging against 'Tico Time' is pointless—you'll just end up with high blood pressure.

In Business

- Be charming and make friends with everyone. The country is very small and everyone knows everyone else. A bad reputation travels fast and is not easily forgotten.
- Do plenty of market research before starting up any business in Costa Rica. The Tico consumer can be fickle, and a seemingly sure-fire bet may not be such a safe choice as you thought.
- Instead of wasting huge amounts of time and slowly going mad with frustration, pay a *gavilán* to sit in those interminable lines and wade through the seemingly infinite wreaths of red tape.

- Be on the lookout for con men, be aware of the differences between the legal systems of Costa Rica and your own country, and get a good lawyer.

DON'TS

- Don't expect Costa Rica to be as 'First World' as it may appear to be on the surface.
- Don't grumble about the state of the country, even if Ticos do so themselves. They're a very proud and nationalistic people, and may take offence.
- Don't refuse a shot of *guaro* or other hospitality from strangers. Such generosity might seem dubious at home, but it's natural in Costa Rica. Ticos are naturally warm and friendly and may be publicly embarrassed by your refusal.
- Don't get upset if your Tico friends rarely, if ever, invite you to their houses. Ticos are intensely private people at times, and the home is a sacred family haven.
- Don't eat turtle egg *bocas*—these are nearly always illegal, and are helping to drive the country's endangered sea turtles to extinction. The same goes for coral and turtle shell jewelry for sale on beaches, pinned exotic butterflies and any other trinkets or foods made from endangered species.
- Don't shout at people or employees, no matter how frustrated you are, and especially not in public. Ticos take offence easily, and this will cause you more trouble than what the momentary relief was worth.
- Don't block a fan's view at a football match—social suicide in terms of soccer etiquette.
- Don't confuse Costa Rica and San José with Puerto Rico and San Juan—the mark of the most ignorant and unwelcome kind of tourist.
- Don't be flashy and ostentatious—Ticos hate such behaviour, and much prefer people who are *humilde* (humble).
- Don't poke fun at people worse off than you. The concepts of class and snobbery are very understated in egalitarian Costa Rica—people are charitable towards the poor or

those who have fallen on tough times, often calling them *pobrecitos* (poor little things).

- Don't expect to have the kind of 'modern' relationship you might have at home. Men in Costa Rica always pick up the tab, while women generally turn a blind eye to their mates' socially-acceptable infidelity.

- Don't miss out on a football (soccer) match. Following a particular team is a defining feature of many Ticos' lives, regardless of sex.

- Don't get angry when men whisper *piropos* or hiss at you in the street—just ignore it, or try to see it as a compliment.

- Don't expect much of a social life in the countryside. Relaxing with an Imperial in a broken rocking chair at the local *pulpería* may be the sum total of a Saturday night's excitement.

- Don't wear shorts in the city. Away from the coast, such informality, as well as general scruffiness, is definitely looked down upon by the well-groomed Costa Rican fashion police. Forget innovation and wear what those around you are wearing if you want to blend in.

- Don't talk about Costa Rica on the same footing as the rest of Central America. Ticos still see themselves as important players on the world stage and won't thank you for lumping them together with their neighbours—especially Nicaraguans.

- Don't be surprised if Ticos think you strange for reading anything more taxing than beauty magazines. They may be the most literate people in the region, but they're much more interested in soap operas than the written word.

- Don't ive alcohol as a gift when visiting a Tico's home. A family member may be a recovering alcoholic, or the family may be teetotal. Instead give a durable and unique gift, which can be enjoyed and shown-off indefinitely.

- Don't overstay your visa. You could be deported, and the Tico immigration police don't seem to share the famed friendliness of the general public.

- Don't expect any Tico to retain any of their niceties once behind the wheel of a car. A Costa Rican road is one of the most dangerous places you could find yourself this side of a war zone.

In Business

- Don't pay bribes. It may or may not work out—but could easily end with your being deported.
- Don't use an overly-aggressive sales pitch. This will really turn potential Tico buyers off.
- Don't expect to get straight down to business. Personal contact is very important in Costa Rica—expect a fair amount of good-natured banter and chit-chat before the serious business begins.

GLOSSARY

USEFUL BASIC SPANISH PHRASES

Buenos días	Good morning/ good day
Buenas tardes	Good afternoon
Buenas noches	Good evening
Sí	Yes
No	No
Por favor	Please
Gracias	Thank you
Cómo se llama (usted)?	What's your name?
Me llamo Pedro (literally 'I call myself Pedro')	My name is Pedro
Permiso!	Excuse me! (when trying to pass someone)
Disculpe! (Generally, to summon any person under the age of about 35, particularly a waiter or shop assistant, call them *muchacho/a* (boy/girl) or *joven* (youngster). While in many other Latin countries this would sound incredibly rude, and one would use *señor* or *señorita*, Ticos find this form of address endearing.)	Excuse me! (when trying to attract attention/ apologising for standing on someone's foot etc.)
Cómo está (usted)?	How are you?
Estoy bien gracias (y usted?)	I'm fine thank you (and you?)

Quisiera, quería or *me gustaría...* (more polite than *quiero* which is 'I want')	I would like...
Tiene... ?	Do you have... ?
Con mucho gusto.	Not at all/ My pleasure
A qué se dedica?	What do you do?
Cómo se dice...?	How do you say?
Hasta luego.	Goodbye/ see you later
(No) entiendo.	I (don't) understand
Bueno(a)/ malo(a)	Good/ bad
Grande/ pequeño(a)	Big/ small
Viejo(a)/ joven	Old/ young
Gordo(a)/ delgado(a)	Fat/thin
Mucho(a)/poco(a)	A lot/ a little
Feliz/ triste	Happy/ sad
Más/ menos	More/ less
Correcto(a)/ equivocado(a)	Right/ wrong
Abierto(a)/cerrado(a)	Open/ closed
La entrada/la salida	Entrance/ exit
Cuándo?	When?
Cuándo sale el próximo bus para... ?	When does the next bus leave for... ?
Cansado(a)	Tired
Cómo?	How? or Come again?
Por qué?	Why?
Le gusta... ?	Do you like... ?
Me gusta/ me encanta	I like it/ I love it
No me gusta	I don't like it
Me siento mal/estoy enfermo(a)	I feel bad/ I am sick
Dónde está... ?	Where is... ?
...el baño	...the toilet

...el hospital	...the hospital
...el banco	...the bank
...el mercado	...the market
...la policía	...the police station
El médico	Doctor
El correo	Post office
La embajada	Embassy
La iglesia	Church
El aeropuerto	Airport
Norte	North
Sur	South
Este	East
Oeste	West
A la derecha/izquierda	To the right/left
Arriba/abajo	Up/down
Un tíquet (de ida y vuelta)	(Round trip) ticket
Cuánto cuesta/vale?	How much?
Es muy caro	It's too expensive
No tiene algo más barato?	Do you have anything cheaper?
Aceptan tarjetas de crédito?	Do you take credit cards?
Tiene un cuarto libre?	Do you have a free room?
Con cama individual/ matrimonial	With a single/ double bed
El aire acondicionado	Air conditioning
El abanico/ ventilador	Fan
Con baño privado/ colectivo	With a private/ shared bathroom
Agua caliente/fría	Hot/ cold water

Food

Buen provecho!	Bon appetit!
El desayuno	Breakfast

El almuerzo	Lunch
La cena	Dinner
El postre	Dessert
Podría ver la carta, por favor?	Could I see the menu, please?
Soy vegetariano(a)	I'm a vegetarian
La cuenta, por favor	The bill please

Time Phrases

Hoy	Today
Mañana	Tomorrow
Ayer	Yesterday
Esta mañana	This morning
Esta tarde	This afternoon
Esta noche	Tonight
La semana/el mes/el año	Week/month/year
La semana que viene	Next week
El mes pasado	Last month
Temprano/tarde	Early/late
Verano	Summer (dry season)
Invierno/temporada verde	Winter (rainy season)

Telling the Time

Qué hora es?	What time is it?
Es la una	It's one o'clock
Son las dos	It's two o'clock
Son las tres y media (literally three and half)	It's half past three
Son las cuatro y quince	It's 4.15
Son las cinco menos veinte (literally four minus twenty)	It's 4.40

Days of the Week

Lunes	Monday
Martes	Tuesday
Miércoles	Wednesday
Jueves	Thursday
Viernes	Friday
Sábado	Saturday
Domingo	Sunday

Months of the Year

Enero	January
Febrero	February
Marzo	March
Abril	April
Mayo	May
Junio	June
Julio	July
Agosto	August
Septiembre/Setiembre	September
Octubre	October
Noviembre	November
Diciembre	December

Numbers

Uno	One
Dos	Two
Tres	Three
Cuatro	Four
Cinco	Five
Seis	Six
Siete	Seven
Ocho	Eight

Nueve	Nine
Diez	Ten
Once	Eleven
Doce	Twelve
Trece	Thirteen
Catorce	Fourteen
Quince	Fifteen
Dieciséis	Sixteen
Diecisiete	Seventeen
Dieciocho	Eighteen
Diecinueve	Nineteen
Veinte	Twenty
Veintiuno	Twenty-one
Treinta	Thirty
Cuarenta	Forty
Cincuenta	Fifty
Sesenta	Sixty
Setenta	Seventy
Ochenta	Eighty
Noventa	Ninety
Cien	One hundred
Doscientos	Two hundred
Trescientos	Three hundred
Quinientos	Five hundred
Mil	One thousand
Un millón	One million
Mil millones	One billion
Un billón	One trillion

These are some of the non-English words used in this book.

Agua	Water
Amarillo	Yellow
Atún	Tuna

Baldazo	Downpour
Banano	Banana
Blanco	White
Sabaneros	Cowboys
Cacique	Chief
Camarón	Shrimp
Campesinos	Peasants
Caseríos	Hamlets
Cédula	Identity card
Chapulines	Grasshoppers; slang for thieves
Chorizos	Literally 'sausages', meaning kickbacks/bribes
Ciudadanos de oro	Old age pensioners, literally 'golden citizens'
Comehuevos	Literally 'egg eaters'; the Costa Rican equivalent of American 'white trash'
Corrientes	Rip tides
Corvina	Sea bass
Culto	Cultured
Curtido	Pickled vegetables and chilies
Fresa	Strawberry, slang for a rich kid
Fútbol	Football
Gotera	Hangover
Guanábana	Soursop
Hidalgos	Noblemen
Humilde	Humble
Incumplido	Unreliable
Langosta	Lobster
Leche	Milk
Limpiabotas	Shoe shiners

Mal de ojo	Evil eye
Marimba	A giant xylophone with gourd resonators
Mestizos	People of mixed blood
Mora	Blackberry
Mota	Marijuana
Muy caliente	Very passionate
Indígenas	Indigenous people
Pargo	Snapper
Pelo de gato	Drizzle, literally 'cat's fur'
Perico	Cocaine
Piña	Pineapple
Piratas	Illegal taxi cabs
Playos	Homosexuals
Plebeyos	Commoners
Pobrecito	Poor little thing
Pollo	Chicken
Pulperías	Small stores
Pulpo	Octopus
Salsa rosa	Thousand Island dressing
Sandía	Watermelon
Sodas	Cafés
Telenovelas	Soap operas
Temporal	Heavy rain falling without let-up over several days during the rainy season
Tugurio	Shanty town
Vinear	To gossip

RESOURCE GUIDE

THE RESIDENTS' ASSOCIATION

This is the one-stop shop for most people moving to Costa Rica. A non-profit organisation, it can help you with anything from bringing your car or pet into the country to building your own house, sorting out residency applications, or making friends.

- **Association of Residents of Costa Rica**
  Casa Canadá Avd 4 C 40
  PO Box 1191-1007
  Centro Colón, San José
  Tel: (506) 233 8068, 221 2053; fax: (506) 233 1152
  Email: arcr@casacanada.net
  Website: http://www.casacanada.net/arcr

KEY TELEPHONE NUMBERS

- Emergencies 911
  (Includes fire, Organismo de Investigación Judicial (OIJ—the Costa Rican equivalent of the FBI), traffic police etc.).
- International calls through operator 116
- Directory enquiries 113
- International directory enquiries 124
- Speaking clock 112
- Cruz Roja (Red Cross Ambulance) 128
- Fire brigade 118

EMBASSIES

- American tel: (506) 220-3939
- Belgian tel: (506) 225-6633
- Canadian tel: (506) 296-4149
- Dutch tel: (506) 296-1490
- French tel: (506) 234-4167
- German tel: (506) 232-5533
- Israeli tel: (506) 221-6011
- Italian tel: (506) 234-2326
- Nicaraguan tel: (506) 222-2373
- Panamanian tel: (506) 257-3241

- Spanish   tel: (506) 222-2128
- Swiss   tel: (506) 221-4829

HOSPITALS
- Clínica Bíblica (private)
  Tel: (506) 257-5252
- Clínica Católica (private)
  Tel: (506) 225-5055
- Hospital Calderón Guardia
  Tel: (506) 257-7922
- Hospital Cima (private)
  Tel: (506) 231-2781
- Hospital de la Mujer (women's hospital)
  Tel: (506) 257-9111
- Hospital de Niños (children's hospital)
  Tel: (506) 222-0122
- Hospital México
  Tel: (506) 232-6122
- Hospital San Juan de Dios
  Tel: (506) 257-6282

MOVING
Recommended by the Residents' Association, ABC Mudanzas offers a complete delivery, storage, insurance, and customs brokerage package. Tel: (506) 227-2645; fax: (506) 226-8134. Email: movers@sol.racsa.co.cr

NEWSPAPERS ONLINE
- *Tico Times*   http://www.ticotimes.net
- *La Nación*   http://www.nacion.com
- *La República*   http://www.larepublica.com

TELEPHONE AND THE INTERNET
- To have a telephone installed, contact the Instituto Costarricense de Electricidad (ICE) at tel: (506) 220-7720 or 225-0123 (http://www.ice.go.cr)
- For an Internet account, contact Racsa at tel: (506) 287-0508 or at the website, http://www.racsa.co.cr or.

- For Internet provision by cable companies, contact these companies directly, for example Amnet: http://www. amnet.co.cr or tel: (506) 210-2928.

ACCOMMODATION

There is a bewildering array of hotels in San José and around the country to meet the requirements of every pocket. Contact the ICT (see section on Tourism later on), scan the Internet or look in a web directory such as http://www.costaricapages. com for details. (Be warned that the very cheap hotels around San José's Mercado Central can be really scummy, and this is a pretty dodgy area after dark).

A highly recommended alternative is a home stay—staying with handpicked, hospitable Tico families all over the country. This can be part of a language immersion package, or simply for those who want to get closer to the people than staying in a hotel can allow. There are many useful websites on this subject, such as: http://www.transitionsabroad.com

MAIL

Mailboxes Etc. (three offices in San José)
Tel: (506) 229-0282, 224-6317, 204-7441.
Email: mbeetc@racsa.co.cr

CHAMBERS OF COMMERCE/
BUSINESS CONTACTS

- **American Chamber of Commerce (AMCHAM)**
  Also produces the useful magazine Business Costa Rica
  Tel: (506) 220-2200; fax: (506) 220-2300
  Email: chamber@amcham.co.cr,
  Website: http://www.amcham.co.cr
- **CINDE**
  Private, non-profit organisation for assistance in establishing a business in Costa Rica. Highly recommended.
  Tel: (506) 201-2800, 201-2867
  Email: invest@cinde.or.cr
  Website: www.cinde.or.cr
- **PROCOMER**
  Government-funded organisation to assist companies. looking to locate in Costa Rica.

Tel: (506) 299-4700; fax: (506) 233-5755
Email: info@procomer.com
Website: http://www.procomer.com
- **Cámara de Comercio de Costa Rica**
  (Costa Rican Chamber of Commerce)
  Tel: (506) 221-0005; fax: (506) 233-7091
  Website: www.camara-comercio.com
- **Bolsa Nacional de Valores**
  (Costa Rica Stock Exchange)
  Tel: (506) 243-8700
  Website: www.bnv.co.cr
- **Oficina de Simplificación de Trámites**
  Office for Simplification of Procedures
  Tel: (506) 2357855; fax: (506) 236-7192
  Co-ordinator Tatiana Cruz: email: tcruz@meic.go.cr
  Website: http://www.tramites.go.cr

MAPS

Most travel agents and tourist offices give away fairly decent free maps, such as the 1:12,500 Central San José map, the 1:1,000,000 Costa Rica Road Map, and 1:700,000 Costa Rica Tourist Map. If you need maps before you go, a variety of detailed maps are available from publishers in North America and the UK. Write for details to:
- **International Travel Map Productions (ITM)**
  530 West Broadway, Vancouver, British Colombia, V5Z 1E9, Canada
  Tel: (1-604) 879-3621
  Website: http://www.itmb.com
- **Treaty Oak**
  PO Box 50295, Austin, TX 78763-0295, USA.
  Tel: (1-512) 326-4141
  Website: http://www.treatyoak.com
- **Stanfords**
  12-14 Long Acre, London, WC2E 9LP, UK
  Tel: (0044) (0207) 836-0189
  Website: http://www.stanfords.co.uk

CHILDREN'S EDUCATION

In Costa Rica's private schools (including those with education in English or bilingual education—see following listing), some follow the American school year schedule with vacations in June, July and August, while others follow the Latin American calendar, with the school year beginning in February and ending in November or December. Note that fees in some schools can top US$ 3,000 for pre-kindergarten up to more than US$ 5,000 per year for grades nine and above.

Schools which also offer day-care facilities include:
- **Lincoln School**
  Pre-kindergarten to grade 12 with classes in English. Follows the Costa Rican academic year.
  Apdo. 1919, San José
  Tel: (506) 247-0800; fax (506) 247-0900
  Email: director@ns.lincoln.ed.cr
  Website: http://www.lincoln.ed.cr
- **American International School**
  Pre-kindergarten to grade 12. Classes in English, US-style education. Follows the US school year.
  Apdo. 4941-1000, San José.
  Tel: (506) 239-0974; fax: 506-239 0625
  Email: aiscr@cra.ed.cr
  Website: http://www.cra.ed.cr
- **International Christian School**
  Has classes from pre-kindergarten to grade 12.
  Apdo. 3512-1000, San José.
  Tel: (506) 236-7879; fax: (506) 235-1518
  Email: intchris@sol.racsa.co.cr

The following private schools offer bilingual education (cheaper than the above):
- **Anglo American School**
  Tel: (506) 225-1723
- **Canadian International School**
  Tel: (506) 272-7097
- **Colegio Internacional**
  Tel: (506) 224-3136

- **Escuela Británica**
  Tel: (506) 220-0131
- **The European School (Heredia)**
  Tel: (506) 261-0717

Many more can be found at:
  http://www.stayreality.com/dir_education.htm

LANGUAGE SCHOOLS

There are literally scores of language schools in Costa Rica. The best will offer home stay with a Tico family, as well as the chance to take part in field trips, volunteering and cultural activities. One of the top schools is:

- Academia Tica
  Tel: (506) 229-0013
  Email: actica@racsa.co.cr
  Website: http://www.academiatica.com

  A huge range of the country's other language schools can be found at:
  http://www.westnet.com/costarica/education.html

ENGLISH LANGUAGE BOOKSHOPS

Getting hold of English reading material isn't a problem. Even big Tico bookstores such as Lehmann's in San José (Avd 0, Cs 1 and 3) have a large English section. The posher hotels and some bookstores also have foreign language magazines and newspapers.

Some of the best English bookstores are:

- **Seventh Street Books**
  (new, used, English, Spanish, novels, travel, nature, etc.)
  Calle 7 between Avd 1 and 0
  Tel: (506) 256-8251
- **Mora Books**
  (huge selection of second hand books and magazines)
  Omni Centre, Avd 1, Cs 3 and 5
  Tel: (506) 255-4136
- **Librería Internacional**
  Multiplaza Mall (near Sta Ana)
  Tel: (506) 253-9553

VOLUNTEER OPPORTUNITIES

For a full list of the opportunities available in both social and environmental projects, visit:

- http://www.volunteercostarica.com
- http://www.bruncas.com/volunteer.html

Three of the most famous NGOs are:

- **Caribbean Conservation Cooperation**
  (turtle tagging in July and August)
  Tel: (506) 710-0547
  Email: ccc@cccturtle.org
  Website: http://www.cccturtle.org
- **Talamanca Dolphin Foundation**
  (dolphin data collection)
  Tel: (506)750-0093
  Email: info@dolphinlink.org
  Website: http://www.dolphinlink.org
- **Asociacion ANAI**
  (organic farming and sustainable forest management in Talamanca)
  Tel: (506) 224-6090
  Website: http://www.anaicr.org
  To find out about volunteering in a national park, contact:
- Volunteer Association for Service in Protected Areas (ASVO)
  (You must normally be prepared to work at least 30 days.)
  Tel: (506) 224-1331

TOURISM

The Instituto Costarricense de Turismo (ICT) is excellent and staffed by friendly, English-speaking employees who can give you advice on anything from fiestas and the best surfing spots to hotels and where to track down the resplendent quetzal or Baird's tapir. They also give away free maps, and provide publicity material and great assistance to anyone setting up a tourist facility.

- Walk-in office in San José
  Located underground in the Plaza de la Cultura next to the entrance to the pre-Columbian Gold Museum
  Tel: (506) 223-1733, 257-6057
  Website: http://www.tourism-costarica.com

CAR RENTALS

Rates range from around US$ 30–120 per day depending on vehicle size and the season, with most companies offering weekly discounts.

- **Avis**
  Tel: (506) 293-2222
  Website: http://www.avis.co.cr
- **Dollar**
  Tel: (506) 257-1585, 222-8920, 223-9642
  Website: http://www.dollarcostarica.com
- **Hertz**
  Tel: (506) 221-1818
  Website: http://www.costaricarentacar.net
- **Toyota**
  Tel: (506) 258-5797
  Website: http://www.toyotarent.com

DOMESTIC AIRLINES

- **Sansa**
  Tel: (506) 255-2176
  Email: reservations@flysansa.com
- **Travelair**
  Tel: (506) 220-0413
  Email: info@natureair.com

CHARTER AIRLINES AND HELICOPTERS

- **Tobías Bolaños Airport** (for charters)
  Tel: (506) 232-2820
- **Aerolíneas Turísticas de América**
  Tel: (506) 232-1125
- **Paradise Air**
  Tel: (506) 231-0938
- **Helicópteros del Norte**
  Tel: (506) 232-7534
- **Helicópteros Internacionales**
  Tel: (506) 231-6867, 290-1563
- **Helicópteros Turísticos Tropical**
  Tel: (506) 220-3940

FURTHER READING

Many old books and theses about local culture are out of print and only available in libraries, which are always worth a visit. However, remember that in Tico libraries (except some university libraries) you cannot just browse among the shelves—you must look for what you want in the card files, fill out a form and give it to the librarian, who will find the publication. You cannot take books out of the library.

GENERAL

Amcham's Guide to Investing and Doing Business in Costa Rica. San José, Costa Rica: AMCHAM.
- Detailed run-down of the country's business and investment climate.

The New Key to Costa Rica. Beatrice Blake and Anne Becher. Berkeley, CA: Ulysses Press, 2000 (15th edition).
- Great guide to the country, particularly for the eco-minded, with a 'sustainability rating' for resorts and businesses supporting the country's environmental, economic and cultural balance.

The Essential Road Guide for Costa Rica. Bill Blaker. Losa Angeles, CA: International Marketing Partners, Inc.,1995.

Costa Rica: A Kick-Start Guide for Business Travelers. Guy Brooks. Brampton, ON: Self Counsel Press, 1996.

The New Golden Door to Retirement and Living in Costa Rica. Christopher Howard. Costa Rica: Editora de Turismo Nacional, SA, 2000-2001.
- Chockfull of contacts and tips, especially on visas, house-buying, investing and setting up businesses both on and off-shore.

The Hispanic Way: Aspects of Behaviour, Attitudes and Customs in the Spanish-Speaking World. Judith Nobel and Jaime Lacasa. Lincolnwood, IL: Passport Books, 1991.

- Not specific to Costa Rica, but an excellent overview of how to understand and acclimatise to the idiosyncrasies of the Latin world in general.

The Legal Guide to Costa Rica. Roger Peterson. San José, Costa Rica: Centro Legal SA, 2002 (3rd edition).
- Available through http://www.costaricabooks.com.

Driving the Pan-American Highway to Mexico and Central America. Raymond and Audrey Pritchard. Costa Rica Books, 1997 (6th edition).
- Crucial guide if you're planning on driving from the United States to Costa Rica. Also available through http://www.costaricabooks.com

LITERATURE
Antología del Relato Costarricense. Ed. Jézer González Picado. San José, Costa Rica: Editorial de la Universidad de Costa Rica, 2000.
- Good selection of short stories by most of the country's top authors.

When New Flowers Bloomed: Short Stories by Women Writers from Costa Rica and Panama. Ed. Enrique Jaramillo Levi. Pittsburgh, PA: Latin American Literary Review Press, 1991.
- Includes works by Rima de Vallbona, Carmen Naranjo, Carmen Lyra, Yolanda Oreamuno and Emilia Macaya.

Negros y Blancos, Todos Mezclados. Tatiana Lobo. San José, Costa Rica: Editorial de la Universidad de Costa Rica, 1997.
- Chilean writer, long-time Costa Rican resident, focuses on Afro-Caribbean themes.

Costa Rica: A Traveller's Literary Companion. Ed. Barbara Ras. San Francisco, CA: Wehreabout Press, 1994.
- Ideal introduction to Costa Rican literature.

La Loca de Gandoca. Anacristina Rossi. San José, Costa Rica: San José EDUCA, 2001.
- A thinly-veiled fictitious account of real events involving corruption, intrigue and illegal resort-building in the Manzanillo-Gandoca Reserve.

En la Isla: Diario de un Viaje. Yanina Rovinski. San José, Costa Rica: Editorial Universidad Estatal a Distancia.
- An account of a month's stay on the remote Isla del Coco, the island that was the inspiration for Robert Louis Stevenson's *Treasure Island.*

The Old Patagonian Express: By Train through the Americas. Paul Theroux. USA: Houghton Mifflin. UK: Penguin, 1997.
- Includes some amusing descriptions of Costa Rica (circa 1979) by the relentlessly grumbly travel writer.

In the Shadow of the Sphere: A Journey of Heart and Spirit. Thomas Youngholm. San Diego, CA: Creative Imagination Concepts, 1999.
- Echoes of *The Celestine Prophecy* in this spiritual adventure book.

ANTHROPOLOGY

The Ticos: Culture and Social Change in Costa Rica. Mavis Hiltunen Biesanz, Richard Biesanz and Karen Zubris Biesanz. Boulder, CO: Lynne Rienner, 1998.
- Easy to find and very readable anthropological text. The authors have been almost half a century in the country, although many Ticos accuse them of seeing everything through rose-tinted spectacles.

De Que Vuelan, Vuelan!: Un Análisis de la Magia y la Brujería en Costa Rica. May Brenes Marín and Mayra Zapparoli Zecca. San José, Costa Rica: Editorial Costa Rica.
- Interesting account of the witchcraft and superstition that still persist beneath the country's modern skin. (Out of print.)

Santa Cruz Guanacaste: Una aproximación a la historia y la cultura popular. Roberto Cabrera. San José, Costa Rica: Ediciones Guayacán, 1989.
- Anthropological text on the customs of Guanacaste.

In Focus Costa Rica: A Guide to the People, Politics and Culture. Tjabel Daling. USA: Interlink; UK: Latin America Bureau, 2001.
- The most up-to-date book on the subject, well researched and illustrated.

El Negro en Costa Rica. Quince Duncan and Carlos Meléndez. San José, Costa Rica: Editorial Costa Rica, 1989.
- Very interesting historical and current account of the situation and customs of black people in Costa Rica.

The Costa Rica Reader. Ed. Marc Edelman and Joanne Kenen. USA: Grove Atlantic, 1989.
- Essays by Costa Rican historians and sociologists.

Hostile Acts—US Policy in Costa Rica. Martha Honey. University of Florida Press, 1994.
- Minutely-detailed discussion of the US policy of 'dual diplomacy' in Costa Rica during the 1980s as the Nicaraguan civil war raged to the north.

El Costarricense. Constantino Lascaris. San José. Costa Rica: Educa, 1994.
- Though written many moons ago, it is humorous and still holds water. The book that Ticos say best describes them.

The Costa Rican Woman's Movement: A Reader. Ilse Abshagen Leitinger. University of Pittsburgh, USA: Pitt Latin American Series, 1997.
- German feminist asks 41 women about their lives and changing conditions.

What Happen?: A Folk History of Costa Rica's Talamanca Coast.
Paula Palmer. San José, Costa Rica: Publications in English,
1993.
- Memories of older members of the Caribbean coast's
  black community.

Taking Care of Sibö's Gifts. Paula Palmer, Juanita Sánchez and
Gloria Mayorga. San José, Costa Rica: Editorama, 1993.
- Discussion of beliefs and practices of Bribri Indians in
  the KeköLdi indigenous reserve, and their often unhappy
  relationship with their Tico neighbours.

Mo. Lara Ríos. San José, Costa Rica: Farben, 1993.
- Description of the life and customs of Cabécar Indians
  told through the story of a young girl.

Limón Real. Rigoberto Stewart. Alajuela, Costa Rica: Inlap,
1999.
- Controversial black academic's call for economic and
  political autonomy for Limón province.

Atlantis in America: Navigators of the Ancient World. Ivar Zapp
and George Erikson. Kempton, IL: Adventures Unlimited
Press, 1998.
- Esoteric theories about Costa Rica's mysterious stone
  spheres being used as a kind of sea chart for pre-historic
  navigators.

*Leyendas Ticas de la Tierra, los Animales, las Cosas, la Religión
y la Magia.* Elias Zeledón Cartín. Costa Rica: Editorial Costa
Rica, 2000.
- Selection of Tico legends still used to frighten children, such
  as *La Cegua* (a beautiful woman who seduces unsuspecting
  men and then at the last minute develops the head of a
  horse), *La Carreta sin Bueyes* (the cart without oxen) and
  La Llorona (the weeping madwoman, who drowned her
  child in a river).

NATURE AND SPORT

Costa Rica's National Parks. Mario A Boza. San José, Costa Rica: Editorial Heliconia.
- Great introduction to the national parks. Out of print.

The Butterflies of Costa Rica and their Natural History. Philip J De Vries. USA: Princeton University Press, 1997.
- Beautifully illustrated, but quite scientific.

Costa Rican Natural History. Daniel H Janzen. USA: University of Chicago Press, 1983.
- Everything you could need to know about the country's species, natural history and archaeology.

A Neotropical Companion. John Kricher. USA: Princeton University Press, 1997.
- Must-read introduction to the American tropics and its eco-systems, plants, animals and conservation.

The Rivers of Costa Rica: A Canoeing, Kayaking and Rafting Guide. Michael W Mayfield and Raphael E Gallow. USA: Menasha Ridge Press, 1998.

The Surfer's Guide to Costa Rica. Mike Parise. Surf Press Publishing, 1999.
- The definitive guide to the country's top surf spots, with details of more than 70 breaks on both coasts.

Life Above the Jungle Floor. Donald Perry. New York, NY: Simon and Schuster, 1998 reprint.
- Biologist Perry's story of designing and setting up his extraordinary Rainforest Aerial Tram in the Braulio Carrillo National Park.

A Guide to the Birds of Costa Rica. F Gary Stiles and Alexander F Skutch. USA: Cornell University Press; UK: Black Press, 1990.
- Definitive bird guide.

ABOUT THE AUTHOR

Claire Wallerstein's journalism career started 12 years ago in London, although she soon escaped the British climate to work as a freelance foreign correspondent for *The Guardian* and the BBC. Claire loves languages (ss well as English, she speaks Spanish, German and French) and also works as a translator. She has lived and worked in Germany, Spain, the Philippines and Venezuela, and has travelled widely through Europe, East Africa and South-east Asia. During two years spent criss-crossing Latin America, she visited Angel Falls, Machu Picchu and the Panama Canal—but left feeling most impressed by her experiences in tiny Costa Rica. She spent several months living among the Ticos to research this book, doing everything from participating in archaeological expeditions and crossing crocodile-infested rivers to spending time in indigenous communities and hanging out with the country's top surfers.

INDEX

A

accommodation 127–131
 deals 128
 mail 130
 notaries 129
 plumbing 130
 utlities 130–131
activities
 bicycle touring 195–196
 courses 201
 dance 200–201
 golf 194–195
 horse riding 200
 photography 201–202
 rafting 198–199
 scuba diving 197–198
 sport fishing 199–200
 surfing 196
 tree top tour 197
 windsurfing 198
Afro-Caribbean English 220
Afro-Caribbean food 171
agriculture 40–42
alcohol 174–175
arts and culture 178–184
 art 182
 literature 182–183
 music 183–184
 theatre 181–182

B

blacks 68–72
bribing and bargaining 113
business 222–243
 bribery/dodgy dealings 237–239
 business customs 231–232
 business environment 232–236
 employers' rules 230–231
 free trade zones 243
 intellectual property rights 241–242
 NGOs/volunteering 228
 red tape 226–228
 security 241
 setting up 228–230
 shady characters 239–240
 stock exchange 243
 tax incentives 240
 translation 242–243
 unions 241
 workforce 236–237

C

Calvo, Padre Mínor 105, 248, 253
Cañas, Moreno 91
Catholicism 87–88, 90–92
Central American Free Trade Agreement (CAFTA) 28, 32, 127, 223, 224, 226
climate 39
coffee 16–19, 171–173
Columbus, Christopher 9, 12, 43, 73
conversation topics 112–113
Costa Rican Spanish 209–220
 cognates 211–212
 commas and points 212
 gender 212
 grammar 214
 pronunciation guide 213
 stress 211
 Tiquismos 216–220
 voseo 214–215
 vos/usted 215–216
crime 156–158

D

Diquis Delta 10, 11, 11–12, 72
Don Pepe *See* Figueres Ferrer, José
dress sense 121–123
drinks 173–174

E

eco-tourism 2, 56, 59, 62, 79
education 33–35, 37
entertaining etiquette 175–176
environment 56–63
 pollution 60–61

F

fiestas and events 202–207
 calendar 203–207
Figueres Ferrer, José 22, 33, 70, 250, 255

financial matters 151–152
  banks 151
  inflation and currency 152
  tax 152
flirting and romance 113–115
free time 193–194

G
Garvey, Marcus 70, 251
geography 37–40
gestures 110–112
getting around
  bus 140–141
  car 137–139, 142–143
  directions 134–136
  horse 142
  plane 140
  rail 139
  taxi 141–142
gossip 115–116
gringos (North Americans) 84–86
Guanacasteco culture
  bombas 187
  bull riding 184–185
  folkloric dancing 186
  Guaitil pottery 185–186

H
health 143–150
  AIDS 146–147
  alcoholism 148–150
  health insurance 150
  hospitals 150
  natural remedies 145–146
  pharmacies 150
  stomach cancer 147–148
hidalgos 15, 214
history 9–25
homosexuality 104–106

I
indigenous peoples 72–82
  Bribris 74, 75, 76, 77, 79
  Brunjkas/Borucas 77
  Cabécares 76, 77
  Chorotegas 10, 13, 78, 186
  Guanacastecos/Cholos 80, 80–82
  Guaymíes/Ngäbës 74, 76, 78

  Huetares 75, 78
  Malekus/Guatusos 76, 79
  Teribes 77, 78
insults 113

L
literacy 35–37

M
media 159–160
Meseta Central 12, 17, 39, 42, 43, 59, 66, 67, 70, 74, 80, 128, 147, 151, 165, 173, 192, 210
mestizos 15, 66

N
names and surnames 118–119
National Theatre
  See Teatro Nacional
Nicaragua 3, 13, 14, 16, 19, 24, 25, 39, 55, 57, 62, 69, 73, 78, 80, 82, 83, 125, 141, 159, 162, 189, 210, 214, 215, 245, 247, 255
Nicaraguans 82–84
nicknames 119–120
nightlife 194

P
Panama 12, 35, 54, 69, 73, 77, 78, 125, 141, 157, 189, 206, 220, 245
piropos 116–118
politics and government 25–33
  elections 22, 25, 26, 28, 31
protected areas 47–56
provinces and towns
  Alajuela 14, 16, 42, 61, 119, 140, 191, 204, 246
  Cahuita 46, 62
  Cartago 13, 14, 16, 42, 43, 91, 115, 151, 190, 204, 205, 215, 246, 248, 254
  Ciudad Quesada 44
  Escazú 85, 90, 128, 134, 150, 191
  Fortuna 46, 52
  Golfito 13, 45, 54, 199
  Guaitil 10, 45, 78, 155, 185
  Guanacaste 3, 16, 19, 38, 39, 42, 44, 45, 67, 68, 80, 81, 82, 164, 165, 174, 175, 184, 186, 195, 196, 200, 203, 205, 206, 210, 231, 246
  Guápiles 44

Heredia 14,16,42,43,66,80, 128,190,191,246,258

Jacó 46,49,192,196

Liberia 44,45,205

Nicoya 12,44,45,48,53,54,57, 61,78,185,200,207,254

Puerto Jiménez 46

Puerto Limón (Limón) 12,42,43, 44,46,53,67,69,70,72,118, 137,171,182,204,206,246, 251,255

Puerto Viejo 46,70,72,79,116, 119,193,196

Puntarenas 17,42,44,47,102, 137,205,246

Quepos 45,46,50,105

Santa Elena/Monteverde 47,48, 56,57,86,126,166,197,201,260

San José 2,3,5,6,14,16,19,26, 27,37,39,42,42–43,43,44,47, 51,59,60,61,65,66,67,69,70, 71,73,74,75,84,85,90,97, 98,99,100,101,102,105,106, 108,127,128,131,133,134, 137,140,141,150,153,155, 156,158,163,175,179,181, 186,191,193,194,195,196, 201,203,204,207,215,217, 225,229,233,234,235,245, 246,247,248,253,255

San Ramón 47,50,128

Turrialba 45

Zarcero 47

pulpería 76,121,132,254

Q
Quakers 86–87

quedar bien 108–110

R
Romero, Sor María 91,205,254

S
sabaneros 80,81,82,200

Sánchez, Oscar Arias 25,254–255

Santamaría, Juan 19,42,119,140, 204,231,255

shopping 153–156

Sibö 10,75,77

sports
football (soccer) 188–192
surfing 192–193

T
Teatro Nacional 19,43,112,178, 179,183,252,258,259

telecommunications 131–134
Internet 132–133
television and radio 133–134

Tico food 162–168
bocas 166
cakes and desserts 166–167
cheese 86,166
fish and seafood 165
fruits and vegetables 168–170
meat 165
merienda favourites 167
popular dishes 164–165
roadside sweetmeats 168
salad and condiments 166

U
United Fruit Company 20,45,69,74,250

V
values and attitudes
choteo, class and snobbery 100–101
family and privacy 92–95
infidelity and machismo 96–98
lottery 102–103
national pride 99
pobrecito 99–100
Tico time and broken promises 101–102

Vesco, Robert 85,239,255

visas and residency 125–127

volcanoes 37,49,50,52,147,201
Arenal 46,52,200,261

W
'white Ticos' 66–67

Walker, William 19–20,23,49,248,255

witchcraft 88–90

women 103–104

300

Titles in the CULTURESHOCK! series:

Argentina	Hawaii	Pakistan
Australia	Hong Kong	Paris
Austria	Hungary	Philippines
Bahrain	India	Portugal
Barcelona	Indonesia	San Francisco
Beijing	Iran	Saudi Arabia
Belgium	Ireland	Scotland
Bolivia	Israel	Sri Lanka
Borneo	Italy	Shanghai
Brazil	Jakarta	Singapore
Britain	Japan	South Africa
Cambodia	Korea	Spain
Canada	Laos	Sweden
Chicago	London	Switzerland
Chile	Malaysia	Syria
China	Mauritius	Taiwan
Costa Rica	Mexico	Thailand
Cuba	Morocco	Tokyo
Czech Republic	Moscow	Turkey
Denmark	Munich	Ukraine
Ecuador	Myanmar	United Arab
Egypt	Nepal	Emirates
Finland	Netherlands	USA
France	New York	Vancouver
Germany	New Zealand	Venezuela
Greece	Norway	Vietnam

For more information about any of these titles, please contact any of our Marshall Cavendish offices around the world (listed on page ii) or visit our website at:

www.marshallcavendish.com/genref